MOTI-MAPS

The Definitive Guide to Self-Propulsion and Getting Your Dream Life

Copyright © Kava Funding Limited Partnership., 2021
All Rights Reserved

Published by
The International Institute of Trading Mastery Inc.
102a Commonwealth Court
Cary, NC 27511

919-466-0043
www.vantharp.com

No part of this book may be reproduced by any mechanical, photographic, or electronic process, or in the form of photographic recording, scanning nor may it be stored in a retrieval system, transmitted, or otherwise copied for public or private use, except as permitted under section 107 or 108 of the 1976 United States Copyright Act, without either the prior written permission of the Publisher or authorization through payment of the appropriate copyright fee to the publisher.

First Printing, 2021.

Printed in the United States of America

ISBN 978-0-935219-19-7

Trademark Acknowledgments
Many of the designations used by publishers and sellers to distinguish their products are claimed as trademarks. Where those designations appear in this book and the author is aware of a trademark claim, the designations were followed by the symbol—® or ™.

Photo Credits
The picture of Baron Montague Norman and that of Sir Thomas Moor were purchased from Alamy, Inc in Brooklyn, NY. Other photos were either personal photos taken by the author or were purchased through the publisher's account with www.storyblocks.com. The Skycar photo is courtesy of Paul Moller. Fish graphic on front cover purchased through Can Stock Photo Inc.

Dedication

This book is dedicated to She who lights the way for me each day and to all my spiritual teachers. Those teachers include Ammachi, Sri Amma-Bhagavan, Brenda Paraja, Byron Katie, the late Diadra Price, Doug Bentley, Kumar-ji, Dr. Leo Fishbeck, Libby Adams, Marianne Williamson, Rev. Michael Milner, Mother Meera, Neale Donald Walsh, Rev. Dr. Patricia Keele, Dr. Rajinder Loomba, Sheldon Butler, Sri Siva-Premananda-ji, Stuart Mooney, Tajasa-ji, Uma-ji, Uttima-ji, Yuktesh-ji, and probably many others I've forgotten.

Acknowledgments

This book is written with the inspiration of all my clients and my Super Trader students over the years. I appreciate you all for your efforts in self-transformation and the success you have achieved – be it a little or a lot. Every bit helps to transform the world and your lives. Thank you all.

I would like to give special thanks to those who have inspired this book. Those people include Connierae Andreas, Richard Bandler, Robert Dilts, the late Todd Epstein, Steven Gilligan, John Grinder, Michael Hall, Tad James, Anthony Robbins, and Wyatt Woodsmall. I'd also like to thank my clients who inspired me in various ways, including 1) my clients who never sent me a progress report and 2) those who were extremely motivated and sailed through the program. All of you taught me something useful for this book.

I am extremely grateful to my staff members who helped me edit and publish this volume. These include Cathy Hasty, R.J. Hixson, Sarah Koch, Jaime Lewek, Chantal Noreika, Christine Parker, and Revathi Ramaswami.

I would also like to thank some of my Super Traders who contributed their purpose to this volume, including Kim Andersson, Brandon Evans, Nick Falla, Michael Grossbard, R.J. Hixson, Sam Jackson, Maria Kravtsova, Albert Lau, Chunglong-Li, Remus Miclea, Alastair Morrison, Surya Murthy, Jack Smith, and Dave Walton.

Don Sabo, Eugene Crofut, Edwin Mercado, Bob Doig, Rui Luo, Lisa Majors, and Tom Osborne all helped with the book proofing.

The cover was designed and created by Cathy Hasty and Laxmi Narumanchi. The final proofreading was done by Abhilasha Mantri and Karoline Kristen. And the book was typeset by Laxmi Narumanchi and her team in Chennai. Thank you all for your heroic efforts.

And lastly, I'd like to thank my family members who are both wonderful to be around and who, from time to time, have acted as Karma teachers – Kalavathi Tharp, Robert Tharp, and Nanthini Arumugam Green. I love you all very much.

Table Contents

Acknowledgements v
Preface xi

Chapter 1: THE BIG WHY: "WHAT THE HECK AM I DOING IN INDIA FOR SO LONG?"...1
    Values 2
    Empowering Question Exercise...

Chapter 2: UNDERSTANDING PROPULSION SYSTEMS: WHAT ARE THE ROOTS?....15
    System 1: The Qualities of Your Representation 17
    System 2: Your Motivation Strategy 17
    System 3: Metaprograms 18
    System 4: Your Mental States (both positive and negative) 21
    System 5: Metaframes, Metastates, and the Meaning You Give to Things 25
    System 6: Your Values 29
    System 7: Your Perception of Reality and Your Self-Definition 29
    System 8: Your Purpose and Your Mission 32
    System 9: Procrastination – All the Things that Block You 33
    System 10: Moti-MAPS: Motivation, Organization, and Time Management 34

Chapter 3: PROPULSION BASED UPON SENSORY QUALITIES...................39
    The Effectiveness Of Just Using Metamodalties 48
    Exercise: "True For Me" Versus "No Longer Me." 49
    Exercise: The Swish Pattern..59

Chapter 4: PROPULSION AS A STRATEGY..63
    Strategy 1: Eating Food I Don't Like..64
    Strategy 2: Moving Away From A Food Addiction...67
    Postscript..68
    Exercise: Motivational Pattern..69
    Van's Example 72

Chapter 5: STATES, METASTATES, MEANING, AND YOUR SELF-DEFINITION......75
    Exercise: Becoming Bold And Ferocious 79
    Van's Example 82
    Exercise: Giving Yourself A Super Power Pleasure 84
    Van's Example...88

Summary 91
What's Left To Learn 92

Chapter 6: METAPROGRAMS AND PROPULSIONS 95
Are You A Stick Or Carrot Person 96
Evaluate All The Other Metaprograms Related To Propulsion 99
Black-and-white or "either/or" thinking 99
Solid, Impermeable versus changing or permeable Metaprogram. 100
Others reference thinking 101
Pessimism 103
Necessity and Impossibility 105
Perfectionism in Achieving Goals 106
Low Self-Esteem 108
Self-Monitoring Is Low and Externally Based 108
What We Deem to be Important (Values) 110
Conclusion 111

Chapter 7: VALUES AND YOUR PROPULSION SYSTEM 113
Value Elicitation Exercise 113
Move Toward 114
Move Away From 117
Mixed 118
Van's Example Of Value Elicitation 119
How Do You Spend Your Time 136
Time Awareness Exercise 137

Chapter 8: USEFUL MODELS FOR VALUES 145
Key Models For How Values Are Organized 145
Maslow's Needs Hierarchy 145
Clare Graves' ECLET 147
Why Use the Graves Model? 156
David Hawkins Levels of Consciousness Model 157
What is the Value of Hawkins' Model in our Discussion of Propulsion Systems .. 160
The Van Tharp Institute (VTI) Model of Consciousness 160
The Ten stages of Consciousness of the VTI Model 162
Victim Stages of Consciousness 162
Personal Power Level of Consciousness 163
Awakened Leveles of Consciousness 163
Enlightened Levels of Consciousness 164

Chapter 9: PURPOSE AND YOUR INNER GUIDANCE 169
Some Examples Of Purpose 169
How I Found My Purpose Rm 172
Discovering My Purpose Mg 173
The Power Of Knowing My Purpose In Life: Be 175

Conclusions for You to Consider 177
How To Connect To Your Purpose 177
The Why Are You Here Café Method 177
Durga's Method 177

Chapter 10: WHAT'S LEFT TO STOP YOU: FOCUSING ON SOMETHING OTHER THAN ONE'S PURPOSE 181
Why Can't You Get Things Done 181
Focus 1: What is Your Purpose 182
Focus 2: What You Don't Want 182
Focus 3 Lack of Energy 184
Focus 4 Compulsions and Distractions/Wanting to Feel Good Now 184
Compulsion Pattern 185
Vans Example Of The Compulsive Pattern.. 187
Focus 5 Immediate Accomplishments or Creative Procrastination 188
Focus 6: Less Significant Obligations or the Demands of Others 189
Focus 7: This is More Urgent; I'll Do it Later 190
Focus 8: Perfectionism 191
Focus 9: Overwhelm: It's Too Much Work. 192
Focus 10: Not Enough Juice to Do it 193
Focus 11: Lack of Know-How 194
Focus 12: Secrets and Hidden Agendas 196
Three Exercises to Overcome What Stops You 196
Exercise 1: Getting Rid of Addictions 196
Van's Example: 200
Exercise 2: Exploring the Higher Level Meanings of Procrastination 202
Van's Example: 205
Exercise 3: Demolish Excuses. 207
Van's Example 210

Chapter 11: SECRETS AND HIDDEN AGENDAS: THE ULTIMATE KILLER OF SELF-MOTIVATION.. 215
Types Of Secrets 217
How To Determine Your Secrets... 220

Chapter 12: THE MOTI-MAP PROCESS: MAKING A MAP TO ACHIEVE YOUR DREAMS.. 225
Develop Your Moti-map... 238
Working with Your Moti-map 238

Chapter 13: YOUR PROPULSION SYSTEM TEMPLATE.. 243
Exercise Determining How You Motivate Yourself. 243
Van's Example of Doing the Exercise 245
Motivational Reasons To Do Massive Self Work 248
Desired/New Propulsion System, Part II 250

    Van's Example: Desired/New Propulsion System Part II 254
    Exercise Pattern to Clean Your Mind 257
    Van's Example 264

Chapter 14: POSTSCRIPT: HOW DID INDIA TURN OUT? 271

REFERENCE NOTES 279

INDEX OF PROPULSION RELATED TOPICS 281

Preface

Perhaps you are wondering what a Moti-Map is? Why is this book called Moti Maps? "Moti" is short for motivation and this book is all about self-motivation or self-propulsion. In addition, the primary way that we motivate ourselves is through our internal maps of the world. Hence, the word "Map" and the first part of the title Moti-Maps.

I also like to emphasize Alfred Korzybski's famous quote from his book *Science and Sanity*[1] that "the map is not the territory." Your internal map of the world is basically a fiction that you've made up and then project onto the world, thinking it is real. This is important because you are in charge of your own motivation. You only have to change your internal map of the world to motivate yourself. It has nothing to do with the world itself, because you can only experience your internal map of the world.

Lastly, when I was almost finished with the book, I learned that Anthony Robbins has used the anacronym MAP – standing for Massive Action Plan – as a means of self-motivation. And while that had little influence on the concepts above, it was a good reinforcer for the title chosen.

Why This Book?

When I was in India in 2015, I swore I would never go back. I don't like Indian food, and generally, my experience of the country is one of organized chaos. Today is February 5, 2019, and I'm going to be in India for the next seven weeks at an Ayurvedic Hospital undergoing treatments and eating food that I (so far) don't like. Seven weeks is a long time. For example, one of the foods I like the least is eggplant, another is ivy gourd and the worst is bitter gourd. Every meal I had here today featured one or more of those dishes. And what's interesting to me is that I ate it all.

I'm in a 10-foot by 14-foot room for about 22 hours each day. The chairs here are not comfortable and have little back support. My bed is made of wood and has a two-inch-thick mattress on top of it …I have a bucket and available water to take a sponge bath. I'm here six weeks at the clinic plus another week after that in India.

As a result, it's the perfect time to write *The Moti-Maps Book* since it is about motivation. I need to motivate myself to get through this experience, so part of this book will be based upon my own experiences. For example, can I eat eggplant seven days a week for the next six weeks? What about three times a day for seven days a week? If that were required, would I 1) eat it and say nothing; 2) stubbornly stop eating it (there still is enough to eat without consuming the eggplant); 3) complain loud enough that I get something else to eat; or 4) decide to leave before the end of the six weeks?

When it comes to self-work, many people find it way too painful and run away from negative feelings and pain. But that doesn't solve anything. It just delays the process and doesn't fix problems. If you have negative feelings that you constantly avoid, then you will continue to have them for the rest of your life and perhaps many more lifetimes.

For example, when people go through my **Peak Performance Course for Traders and Investors** (on their own), I've noticed that the first time they go through it, they skip everything that is important to them. If they do it a second time, then they might do some of the essential exercises, but they still skip a lot. And perhaps if they work through the course a third time, they will begin to get whatever it is that they really need to make significant changes.

The first part of the Van Tharp Institute Super Trader Program is all about self-discipline. I've designed a series of lessons that require people to really look at themselves and get the maximum amount out of the first time through the home study course. What happens is that they have to send each lesson to me and my job is to make sure they get as much as they can through doing each lesson. I won't pass them on the lesson unless I'm certain that they've gotten out of it what's important for them. The lessons include a lot more than you will find in the home study course alone. For example, lesson 3 of the Super Trader program was all about propulsion systems. It was designed to give people the motivation to get through the course. It also includes about 50 pages of instructions about propulsion systems. Much of the material in those 50 pages will now be part of this book to give everyone valuable information about self-propulsion.

As examples of motivation, I'm going to give you my own examples of how I plan to get through these seven weeks in India. Thus, the timing is excellent.

In addition, we will be reviewing a few other ideas and concepts that are important to understanding your own motivation. These include such topics as:

- How beliefs are filters to reality.

- How beliefs are useful in a context, but not universally true. However, the wider the context the more useful they are and the more likely they are to be held onto as facts.

- How "who we are" is shaped by our values and how to determine your values.

- In other words, if you make it all up, then why not make up something that is useful and helps you with your motivation?

Let's review them briefly now.

Beliefs are Filters to Reality

One of my favorite quotes is by Harry Palmer, the Founder of *Avatar*. It goes as follows:

> *You experience what you believe, unless you believe you won't, in which case you don't, which means you did.*
>
> *Harry Palmer – Founder of Avatar*

Preface

When I received my undergraduate degree in psychology, it always struck me how valuable it would be if they taught this sort of concept to undergraduate psychology majors. In fact, everyone should be taught how you create your reality with your beliefs at an early age, but psychology didn't teach this in the 1960s. Several years ago, and more than 40 years past my educational experience in psychology, I went to a graduation party for a recent college graduate who majored in psychology. I wanted to see how much psychology had changed so I asked her, "Did they teach you that you create your reality through your beliefs?" Her response was, "Oh, I don't believe that." That's all I needed to hear. Nothing had really changed.

Harry Palmer is not the only one to teach the importance of beliefs.

- "What the mind can conceive and believe, and the heart desire, you can achieve." — **Norman Vincent Peale**

- "There are those who say that seeing is believing. I am telling you that believing is seeing." — **Neale Donald Walsch, *Home with God: In a Life That Never Ends***

- "It is impossible not to believe what you see, but it is equally impossible to see what you do not believe. Perceptions are built up on the basis of experience, and experience leads to beliefs. It is not until beliefs are fixed that perceptions stabilize. In effect, then, what you believe you *do* see." *A Course in Miracles*, **T-11.VI.1-4.**

- "I confused things with their names: that is belief." — **Jean-Paul Sartre, *The Words***

- "Nonsense is that which does not fit into the prearranged patterns which we have superimposed on reality ...Nonsense is nonsense only when we have not yet found that point of view from which it makes sense." — **Gary Zukav, *The Dancing Wu Li Masters***

- "The highest court is in the end one's own conscience and conviction—that goes for you and for Einstein and every other physicist—and before any science there is first of all belief." — **Max Planck, *The Dilemmas of an Upright Man: Max Planck and the Fortunes of German Science, with a New Afterword***

- "WE BELIEVE in the unity of all life, and that the highest God and the innermost God is one God. We believe that God is personal to all who feel this indwelling presence. — **Ernest Holmes, *Science of Mind Magazine*, "*What We Believe*" 1927**

My point is that our beliefs shape our reality and that's what shapes your experience of life. For example, Neil deGrasse Tyson stated:

"The good thing about science is that it's true whether or not you believe in it."

Basically, he is stating a belief that, in his opinion, dominates his idea about the power of beliefs without realizing 1) how often science changes its theories about what is true and 2) that underlying presuppositions such as his statement about science are also beliefs.

But what if no beliefs are true, just useful within a particular context or perspective?

The Size of the Context for Which a Belief Seems Useful Determines Whether Something Seems to be a Fact

Most of you think that a "fact" is reality whereas a belief may not be. However, a "fact" is just a belief that is useful in a wide context. For example, most of you probably believe that if you fell off a 20-story building you would probably go "splat" on the pavement below. You might believe that's a proven fact. However, it's just a belief that's useful in a wide context, namely, for those living on planet Earth. If you live on planet Earth, it's generally true but even then, I've heard of one case of a person who fell from more than 30 stories and survived. So even in the context of this planet, it is not universally true.

Now imagine you live on a smaller planet with less gravity (such as the moon). Here you could easily fall 20 stories and you would be significantly less likely to get hurt. In space, if you jumped off a 20-story space station you might go up, not down. So, this is just one of many examples that show that a fact is just a belief that's useful to many people in a broad context.

Who You Seem to Be Is Shaped by Your Values

I call values high-level beliefs that determine what's important for us. For example, if you value money above all else, you will probably have a lot of money. John Rockefeller, when his net worth was about 20% of the US GDP, was once asked, "You are the richest man in the world, what do you want now?" His response was: "More!"

Now you might think that money is very important for you. But you don't have a lot of money, so you doubt the statement that your life is determined by your values. However, you might have hidden values that keep you from it. Such values might include beliefs such as "People who are close to God don't value money" – plus a value that it's important to be close to God. Or you might have a belief that says "Having fun is more important than hard work" – plus a belief that money only comes from hard work. Or how about this one: "My friends are important to me and if I had a lot of money, I'd lose them." Or "Our relationship would change in ways that I wouldn't like."

This book has a complete value elicitation exercise. It takes about three days to complete and you'll be able to do it just by reading and doing the exercises. Tony Robbins has a $10,000 workshop called *Date with Destiny* that is all about values. It's about discovering what your values are and making sure they are right for you to give you the future you want. But you already have the exercise with this book. It's one of the most common exercises that people skip the first time they go through the book. Don't be one of those people. It's too valuable.

Now, let me tell you my primary values to illustrate how they shape me. My *top value* is **self-transformation**. I used to think it was helping others transform, but then it dawned on me that it would be hard for me to take other people to levels that I have not achieved myself.

My *second value* is **helping others transform themselves.** Our company mission is **self-transformation through a trading metaphor.** It's important to me because I think good trading requires that you raise your consciousness so that you stay away from states like fear and greed and move into more advanced states such as acceptance. However, it's also important because everyone in our company is super motivated when we hear people talk about "how you and your company changed my life." And that impacts not only the person who made a major change but everyone around them.

My *fourth most important value* is **health**. I've done a Vedic Astrology reading (and these can be very accurate when done by someone competent) that says I'll live to be over 100 years old. That gives me another quarter of a century. I will greatly enjoy that if I can continue to enjoy my top values.[2] But if I become senile, or an invalid, or very sickly, I won't enjoy it at all. I do not believe in taking drugs to control symptoms (especially since many of them produce side effects that can be worse than the symptoms). Instead, I believe in determining how my body is out of balance and undergoing treatments to rebalance the body. That's the primary reason that I'm writing this book from an Ayurvedic Hospital in India.

My *third value* is **my family**. This might be higher for me if I had a larger family, but I don't. My father's parents were both born in 1865. My mother's parents were born in 1883 and 1884. Consequently, even the children of my aunts and uncles were older than I am and are now mostly dead. I had a sister who was 15 years older than me, but she died when she was 57. So, I primarily have my wife (who is a very special woman), my son, and my niece from Malaysia (who lived with us for about 16 years and is like my daughter).

However, because I don't know much about my family, my family value also comes out in research through www.ancestry.com. I have at least 50 ancestors who were in the United States before the Revolutionary War. Two of them came over on the second sailing of the Mayflower in 1630 –Thomas Blossom and his daughter Elizabeth Blossom. And Elizabeth (my eighth great grandmother) married Edward Fitz Randolph, who was from English royalty and is said to have been related to both William the Conqueror and Charlemagne. This lineage comes through my great grandfather, Timothy Tharp. I also learned that when there was some question about President Obama's legitimacy as a president, his mother's lineage was also traced to the same Edward Fitz Randolph. If this is true, then I'm also related to President Obama, but we'd probably be 14th cousins 10 times removed or something of that nature.

From Timothy Tharp's wife, my great grandmother, Amanda Jane Hull, I am directly related to Daniel Boone (first cousin seven times removed). George Boone III, his grandfather, was my seventh great grandfather who arrived in America in 1721.

My other famous relative through Amanda Jane Hull is Abraham Lincoln (third cousin five times removed) and his second great grandfather (Mordechai Lincoln II) is also my seventh great grandfather. He was born in America in 1686. My guess is that anyone who has roots going back a long-ways in the US could find these sorts of famous ancestors, but I'm just mentioning them to illustrate my "family" value.

My *fifth most important value* is **creativity**. I love to create new things and I'm endlessly doing creative things. These include:

- Modeling successful traders and developing models, which often have emerging properties, to help others.

- Writing new creative ideas down. For example, I'm excited to be writing this book. And I have several other books waiting to percolate once this one is finished.

- Developing new workshops. I love that and often I will look back at a workshop and realize that it was a co-creation with my Inner Guidance because there is no way my ego could have created that material – it's usually so good.

And the list could go on and on.

My wife is also like that. She is an artist and she has to be doing something creative to feel meaning in her life. It might be painting, but it could also be remodeling and decorating a house, gardening, or creating a landscape in the yard.

And my *sixth top value* is **financial freedom.** I was going to put down my business, but that's one aspect of financial freedom and my business tends to incorporate the other key values as well, so it's not listed as a separate value. I need about $6K per month for financial freedom and I have that from quite a few different sources – so this is an example of how this value includes other things that might also be of value. Thus, can you see how my values shape who I am? If you want to know your values, then skip ahead to Chapter 7 and do the values elicitation exercise now.

People Motivate Themselves to Do Strange Things

I remember when I was watching the fourth season of the hit television series *Outlander*. In the second to last episode of that season, I found a classic example of motivation that I had trouble understanding. Here is the setting.

A priest around the year 1770 is working with the Mohawk Indians, converting them to Christianity. He falls for a female member of the tribe, makes love to her and they have a child. The Indians accept the situation; in fact, they welcome it. But they have one request. They have now become Christians and the new child, the priest's son, should be baptized by the priest. But suddenly the priest is full of conflict.

He has the following beliefs. First, he believes that he has sinned against God by having sex and producing a child and that he is now condemned to Hell. As a result, he believes that he is not a legitimate priest and he cannot baptize the baby or he will also go to Hell (another not-so-useful belief). And in case it's not obvious to you, these two beliefs put him in "Hell on Earth." These are great examples of non-useful beliefs that could ruin someone's life.

The Indians are very upset with him. They cut his ear off and tell him that if he doesn't baptize the baby in the next 24 hours, he'll die an excruciating, slow death. He has witnessed this death before. The Indians tie the person to a stake, and they build a fire around his feet and lower his legs. The fire does not burn the whole body, but it will burn his feet off and eventually, more and more of his legs. The last person who died this way, according to the priest, first endured three full days screaming in agony.

The priest, who is already in immense pain from having his ear cut off, has to either baptize the baby or face a prolonged, painful death. Apparently, he doesn't have a strong motivation to move away from pain. The other person in the tent, where he is held prisoner, says to him, "The Indians don't know anything. Just say the Lord's Prayer over the baby in Latin and they won't know the difference." He also says, "For God's sake, be reasonable, man, and have some common sense."

Our priest has an easy way out. He can baptize the baby (or even carry out a false baptism). If he does so, he gets to be with the woman he loves and raise his new child and live out what some might call a happy ending to life. Or, he can elect to die a very slow and painful death by slowly having his lower extremities burnt off. This seems like an obvious choice to me, and probably to you. But what does he choose? He chooses the slow death.

Why? I can't imagine making that choice, but I also understand that beliefs are filters to reality – not reality itself. Given that as an understanding, you might as well have useful beliefs (those that bring value to yourself and others).

What are the priest's beliefs?

- First, he has sinned and is already condemned to Hell. This is a ridiculously non-useful belief. And what it does, is produce the Hell he is condemned to – torment over decisions, having his ear cut off, and a very painful and slow death, while leaving the woman he loves and his child to an unknown future.

- His second non-useful belief is that if he performs the baptism, he will be condemning his son to Hell as well. How does he know this? I guess he knows it on faith. Is it useful? No, it basically leaves his child without a father. But he believes it to be true and that's what's important.

- His third belief is that Jesus' main contribution to humanity was to die on the cross to save us from our sins. Many Christians believe this. And, that death was a slow, painful death. So, if Jesus could save humanity, the least the priest could do is save his son from Hell.

- Finally, he probably also has a belief that dying is what God wants him to do and, if he does so, he will be rewarded in Heaven.

Our priest is also unaware that his beliefs shape his experience of reality, and has not examined his beliefs to see if they are even useful.

Would these three beliefs be enough for you to give up a life with someone you love and the chance to raise your son? They wouldn't for me. But then again, I know that beliefs are not true – they are just filters to reality. And that puts me in a different perspective from someone who is already believing that he is condemned to Hell and is actually experiencing that Hell he is creating. Beliefs are just useful in a context and if that context is narrow, then they are not very useful. I personally think (if I were in the priest's situation) that I would be more useful taking care of the woman I love and raising my son. I'd probably be happy doing so. And I would probably do whatever was necessary to avoid a slow and painful death. A quick death is okay but I don't like the idea of a slow and painful death.

You might be wondering that if he is already condemned to Hell, what difference would a little lie make. Why not just fake the baptism? Well, he doesn't want to condemn his son to Hell. And saving others (like Jesus did) is important to him. As a result, he chooses to be a martyr.

But there is more to this story. The other man in the teepee escapes and is on his way to freedom. But he hears the cries of the priest being burnt and decides to return. He throws gunpowder on the fire which totally consumes the priest in flames – so it is still a painful death, but it is over quite quickly.

Suddenly, we have a second act of strange motivation. The second man is on his way to freedom (also to find the woman he loves), but instead elects to go back and end the torture of the priest. He knows that by doing so he is 1) giving up his freedom, and 2) he is risking the possibility that the Indians might decide to give him the same type of death for his deed. Why would he do something so stupid? What are his beliefs?

- Don't let another human being suffer, even if it means giving up your own life and freedom.[3] Is this a useful belief? Well, it certainly has value to others, although within the context of life on earth, it doesn't have much value to one who holds it.

- He also might have a belief that he is somehow protected by God and if he does what he is called to do, he will somehow be protected (and while he is recaptured, he doesn't get tortured and he is instead freed within a week or so of that time). Thus, perhaps that was a useful belief.

- And he also might have a belief that if he sacrifices himself, he will somehow be rewarded by God.

Notice how many of these strongly motivating beliefs are spiritual beliefs of the highest level. Many of them are not necessarily useful spiritual beliefs, but people kill each other because of strongly-held spiritual beliefs.

In the *Outlander* episode, there is a third interesting motivational act that occurs at the end of this ordeal. The priest's Indian woman is watching all of this with her baby. When the priest is suddenly consumed with flames because of the gunpowder, she puts the baby down and steps into the fire with him.

Now, what possessed her to do such a thing? She loved her man and wanted to join him even in death. She probably had different beliefs about life after death. She might have just thought, "I can't live without him."

Obviously, her man was more important to her than her baby who was now left with no parents. But she probably had some sort of faith that the baby would be taken care of by the other Indians in the tribe. Or perhaps she just did it on impulse without thinking about the baby. And we never know what happens to the baby.

These values, of course, come from a made-up story, but there are real examples from history that are a similar. One example is King Henry VIII versus one of his closest advisors, Sir Thomas More. Henry VIII decided to divorce his first wife, Catherine of Aragon,[4] and set up a decree to that extent, thus defying the Catholic Church. The Act of Succession was to be signed by all nobles. Thomas More resigned from Parliament rather than sign because he was loyal to the Catholic Church and to God.

Later, Henry formed the Church of England with himself as the head and demanded everyone sign an oath of allegiance. More refused to sign and was sent to prison. At first, it was a house confinement, but then Henry got more serious about getting his old advisor, More, to support him. The King took away all of More's properties, thus also hurting his family. But More refused to sign anything, despite visits from his family and others to encourage him to do so. Eventually, he was tried for treason and sentenced to be hanged, drawn and quartered[5] as a traitor to his King. Thomas More would rather have this horrible death than sign. In More's own words (preserved from the 16th century at the British Library in London),

"The King's good servant by Gods first." Based on his values and beliefs, he elected to save his soul rather than his body.

More's death in 1535 was simple and quick, because the King probably remembered that they used to be friends. They took him out and beheaded him, but he didn't know that would be his fate until it happened. He was willing to face a much more painful and gruesome death rather than give up his principles.

Sir Thomas More was canonized by the Catholic Church in 1935 and he is always portrayed in films and television shows as being a very saintly person. However, people forget that for a while he was the High Chancellor of England under Henry the VIII. In that role, he had six protestant men burned alive at the stake for saying things that he didn't like and for refusing to recant their statements. Perhaps there was some karma to his death.

Let's look at the values here for Thomas More. First, he believed, like a good Christian, that the Bible is the word of God. Now the sixth commandment given to Moses says "Thou shalt not kill." If the Bible is thought to be the word of God, shouldn't everyone have the right to read it? Protestants also believe that everyone should have access to God – not just those in the priesthood. Well, that's what protestants believed, and apparently Sir Thomas More did not believe they had such rights. Thus, he was willing to break what he must have believed was a firm law of God (the sixth commandment) to prevent others from saying that the average person should be able to read the Bible. He basically died over another strange belief. He wasn't willing to sign a statement that his friend, King Henry the VIII, was the supreme head of the Church of England. Instead, he believed that the Pope has authority delegated from Jesus to rule over the entire Church – but that was not believed by Christians until the writings of Pope Innocent I in 416 AD.

Beliefs and values, when unexamined, can really cause people to do some strange things. What conclusions can we make from this?

We live in a made-up world of beliefs and values and those seem to determine who we are and our motivation. But no belief is 100% true; they are just useful within a wide or very narrow context. And many beliefs, taken from another's viewpoint, are not true at all. For example, if you think there is such a thing as a true belief, then you are right from your perspective and that will shape your life.

When we understand that all this is made up, it gives us powerful tools for shaping our destiny. Hence the name of Tony Robbins workshop, *Date with Destiny,* which deals with values.

Some people do strange things that are difficult for others to fathom. However, if you examine their beliefs, then you can begin to understand their motivation and how it works. And if you can do that, then you can be in control of your own motivation.

And beliefs don't have to make sense or be logical. You can believe that the Bible is the word of God, and yet believe that others should be killed (which violates the sixth commandment) if they advocate that everyone has the right to read the Bible in their own common tongue.

This means that:

- You can motivate yourself to achieve your goals.

- You can avoid procrastination.

- You can motivate yourself to overcome addictions and all sorts of undesirable habits that you currently struggle with.

- And you can believe anything you want, making it seem real, even if it conflicts with other beliefs. Thus, why not do this in a useful way that helps you.

These things will be the topic of this book, with the hope that it motivates you toward incredible self-transformation that will make you happy without reason and capable of achieving your dream life.

CONTENTS

In the coming chapters, you will learn all of the known ingredients of self-motivation. This will include: 1) how sensory details (or meta-modalities) are the basis for our judgments; 2) how we have motivation strategies which are the sequencing of our thoughts to produce such a meta-modality change; 3) how our unconscious programs, called metaprograms, result in automatic behavior; 4) how values dominate motivation along with some models for values that could provide a structure for motivation (if you believe them to be true); 5) your purpose in life which tends to change everything when you find it; 6) what stops you from motivating yourself; and 7) Moti-Maps, the key to achieving your dreams. We will also help you develop a complete guide for your propulsion systems, show you how to manage your time to accomplish what you deem to be important, and show you how to deal with the personal demons of compulsions and procrastination.

How to Use This Book

This book was meant to be a *Definitive Guide for Propulsion Systems*. For example, if you are reading it as part of the Super Trader program to learn about propulsion in general, then I'd recommend 1) that you read the entire book to get an overview of the material and then do the exercises. We plan to develop a supplemental exercise book, to be published later in 2021, so you might read the entire book and then do the exercise book once it is published.

Some of you might be reading this book to solve a particular motivational problem. For example, you seem to procrastinate doing important projects and you don't know what to do about it. If you have that sort of problem or another specific motivational problem, then we recommend that you first read the summary chapters and then do the essential exercises that are specific to your problem. There is an index of various motivational issues at the end of the book to help you find the relevant material that you need.

Eight of the fourteen chapters in this book might be considered summary chapters and should be read if you wish to determine what your motivational problem might be. Those chapters include:

- Chapter 1 *The Big Why:* Contains good introductory material.

- Chapter 2 *Understanding the Roots of Propulsion Systems:* Includes 10 subsystems involved in propulsion. Finding what pertains to you will save you needing to read the other chapters that are not pertinent.

- Chapter 6 *Metaprograms*: If you have a driver metaprogram (i.e., meaning that you have no choice in that pattern), then that metaprogram would limit your ability to control your own motivation. As a result, you will not know about it unless you read this chapter and determine where you stand with each metaprogram.

- Chapter 7 *Values*: Values are key to your motivation so unless you've determined your values elsewhere, then I'd recommend you read this chapter and do the exercises.

- Chapter 8 *Models of Values*: This is a good summary chapter that you should read as an overview.

- Chapter 9 *Purpose*: If you know your life purpose, it will change everything in your life, so I'd recommend that you read this chapter and use one of the methods given to determine your purpose in life.

- Chapter 10 *Focusing on things other than what you want to do will kill propulsion*: If you are good with the material up to Chapter 10, then there are 12 areas that you might be focusing on that contribute to your self-propulsion issues. Thus, reading this chapter is a must.

- Chapter 11 *Secrets and Hidden Agendas*: If you have something that you want to keep hidden, it is because you have some very non-useful beliefs. Those non-useful beliefs might undermine your ability to motivate yourself. We've determined that there are 16 different types of secrets that might undermine your motivation.

Finally, one of my beginning Super Trader candidates said that he didn't have any problems with motivation and that he thought that this book might be implying he was broken. However, that is not the case at all. If you are perfectly happy with your life, then you do not need this book. On the other hand, if you have problems with addiction, compulsion, distraction, procrastination, or perfectionism, then this book should enable you to solve these issues. Furthermore, if you have a dream life that you cannot seem to achieve, then this book could easily be your roadmap to getting that dream life.

If you purchased an electronic version of this book, then you'll need the *MotiMap Workbook* to do the exercises.

Notes

[1] Korzybski, Alfred. *Science and Sanity: An Introduction to Non-Aristotelian Systems and General Semantics.* 5th ed. Fort Worth, Texas: Institute of General Semantics, 1994.

[2] My wife got a Vedic astrology reading when she was about 12 years old. She was living in Ipoh, Malaysia, but she was told she would marry a man with the highest education, live overseas, and travel a lot. She didn't believe any of it, but it came true.

[3] Today in India when I started my morning massage treatment, I heard what sounded like a man screaming. I was told it wasn't a man but a pregnant sheep in pain. But it sounded like a man. And there is a natural (I think) motivation when you hear that to want to do something to help – at least there was for me.

[4] The story of Catherine of Aragon is being told in the series on Starz entitled the *Spanish Princess*. Sir Thomas More's story is featured in the *Tudors* television show and in the academy award winning movie, *A Man for All Seasons*.

[5] **Don't read if you are squeamish**. In the 1500s the world was led by feudal noblemen who were tyrants (Level 3 on the Graves value scale, tyrants, as discussed in the values chapter) who needed to get others to do their bidding. If you defiled the king (for example, the king requests something and you say "no"), it was called high treason and each culture devised a nasty death for such people. For the English, they would drag the person by horse through the town which would probably rip off much of the skin. They would hang him by the neck on a ladder, so he was choked but not enough to kill him. They would then cut off his private parts and burn them in front of him. Next, they would then make an X in his chest which meant cutting through the breast bone and remove the entrails while the person was still alive. They would stretch his body between four horses and quarter him, and then they would chop the head off of what was left. It must have been brutally painful, and the time to die probably depended upon how fast you were taken through these procedures – probably not three days as in the Outlander episode, but it could take hours. **You have to have pretty strong values to subject yourself to that possibility when you could avoid it.** And, by the way, many of the religious wars of the time had to do with whether the Pope was God's representative on earth versus the divine right of Kings. Both were power struggles that have nothing to do with spirituality (which is my belief).

CHAPTER 1

The Big Why: "What the Heck Am I Doing in India for So Long?"

Last time I was in India I swore I'd never come back. I was at Oneness University and, in my opinion, they were extremely disorganized. Being there pressed every button I had about how to run an educational program. I was asking myself, "Should I be working on my issues that produce this experience so I no longer have these buttons? Or is this just a signal telling me that am I supposed to do something else?" It turned out to be the latter and I swore I would never go to India again. But before we get into why I'm here, let's explore the why of motivation just a little bit. There really is no motivation without a "Big Why."

First, there are two types of motivation. One is called **"carrot motivation"** or **move-toward motivation**. For example, everything changes when you find your purpose in life and we'll help you work on that in this book. But when you are really motivated to do something it's because you have a strong why behind it. It's a big carrot.

Let's take the strange example of the priest from the *Outlander* episode who allowed himself to be burnt slowly starting with his feet. His "Big Why" was to save his son from Hell and to be a martyr like he thought Jesus was. He was willing to die to save his son from what he perceived to be his sins. And that's a "Big Why" – at least for him. And the other man who saved him from a slow agonizing death (and gave him a quick one) was motivated to help someone else and had the faith that if he did so everything would turn out okay. Those are both strong move-toward motivations.

However, in both examples we also have the other type of motivation. It's called **"stick motivation"** because the donkey might be more likely to pull the cart if you hit him with a stick. It's also called **move-away motivation**. If you don't want to be hit with the stick again (make sure it doesn't happen!), then pull the cart.

An example of a big stick is being slowly burnt to death starting with the feet or having your ear cut off or thinking that if you help your friend, you might suffer from the same fate that you saved him from. Those are all big sticks. And you must be strongly motivated by a carrot to overcome such big sticks.

So that brings back the question, "What the heck am I doing in India again?" First, there are plenty of sticks to push me away. For example:

- I don't like Indian food. I like the western style of Ayurvedic food, but the food being served here tastes like the Indian food I don't like. In fact, one of my least favorite foods is eggplant and the first day I was here I got a main dish with each meal that had eggplant in it. And I'm here for six weeks!

- I'm spending 22.5 hours a day in a 10-foot by 14-foot room. I get about 1.5 hours of treatment each day, but the rest of the time, I'm in my room. And I'm here for six weeks.

- My bed is made out of wood with a 2.5-inch mattress on top of it. It's the hardest bed I've ever slept on, and I'm here for six weeks.

- The bathroom is primitive. You are supposed to fill a pail with water, wet yourself, scrub down, and then use the water to wash off the soap.

Those are a lot of sticks, and I must admit I didn't know about some of them before I came here. Again, what the heck am I doing here?

Values

Now let's look at my values. And each value means something unique to me. If you had described your values using the same words, your experience of those values might be quite different from mine because the meaning you give to the words is different. And by the way, if you don't share my beliefs and values, then what I'm doing may make absolutely no sense to you. And thus, it would not be a big enough WHY for you to do what I'm currently doing in India.

First, my fourth value was to avoid poor health. I believe I could live to be over 100 and I want the next 30 years (if it happens) to be healthy productive years. I don't believe in allopathic medicine, which prescribes expensive drugs. These drugs ameliorate the symptoms you might have, but do nothing to fix the cause. At the same time, allopathic drugs have many potential side effects that could impact your health (in the long run?).[1] Here are some examples.

When I was in my mid 30s, I had a kidney stone. The doctor said my uric acid was high. He wrote me a prescription for something to control my uric acid levels – even though the kidney stone had nothing to do with uric acid. I asked, "How long am I supposed to take this?" He said, "For the rest of your life." He also said that if I didn't take it I'd suffer from gout. I never filled the prescription and it was about 20 years before I had my first gout symptoms and they are still rare almost 40 years later.

When I was around 60 to 65, I was told I had high blood pressure and put on some medication I was supposed to take for the rest of my life. I did take that for a year or so. However, in March 2017 (after I stopped taking it), I went to the Whitaker Wellness, an alternative medicine clinic in Newport Beach, California. They took my blood pressure upon admission to the clinic and it was a little high. But they took my blood pressure before each treatment as well. And often those readings were normal to low. It turns out I have high blood pressure at the doctor's office when they first take my BP. I get my blood pressure taken 1 to 2 times a day here at the Ayurvedic Hospital – and it's always normal with a range of 140/80 to 100/60. A majority of the readings were 110/70, which is very good for someone my age.

At about the same time I had an A1C reading at the doctor's office of about 6.5. Suddenly I was labeled as a diabetic and told to take Metformin. It's interesting because one used to have to have a reading of 7.0 before they gave you that label. I've never had an A1C reading above 6.7. Anyway, I took the prescribed medication for a year or two. But several years later, I was complaining of diarrhea. The doctor thought it might be the Metformin, so he changed my prescription. When I filled the new prescription, I was told that I had to wear a medical warning label because of the new drug I was taking. I never took the drug and I've never taken any medication for high blood sugar since that time. I still have never had an A1C reading above 6.7. And I'm doing other things to balance the body and essentially "cure" my high blood sugar issue. By the way, I've never had any experience with low blood sugar, but my wife's friend (who believes everything her doctors tell her) has been on diabetic medications for years. She is about my age, and she controls her diet much better than I do, but she frequently has issues with low blood sugar and must now take insulin. I think that's the effect of taking all those diabetic medicines over the years. We now have the advantage of hearing all the side effects of the drugs advertised on television. I think some of the diabetic medicines are the worst.

Lastly, I know people who work for drug companies. First, they cannot patent anything that is found in a living organism (animal or plant). They can synthesize something they find and patent that. If the drug you take is not found in any living organism, how healthy do you think it is? And for drug companies, it's not profitable to find a cure. Take this pill and you'll be fixed within a few days – no, no, no. Instead, they treat symptoms (as if those are the problem) and they can charge you high prices for a lifetime. Did you know that 25% of people over 65 in the United States take 12 or more different prescription drugs at the same time?

Ayurveda is an ancient and very effective healing technique that rebalances the body. Rebalancing the body is a cure for symptoms that is much more effective than any prescription drug. That's why I'm here. I'm starting to feel run down and don't have enough energy. I expect that that problem will be gone by the time I return to the US. Do you understand why that's a "Big Why" for me?

But I have a lot more "Big Whys" for being here.

Let's look at my top value, transforming myself, which to me means obtaining more and more awareness to the point of perhaps becoming a Siddha yogi. A Siddha yogi is someone who has reached an advanced spiritual state and can do many magical things by tapping into Source. But the Siddha yogi, unlike someone who lives in a cave all day long, brings this state back into everyday life where they can influence the consciousness of others and help reshape the world. Doing something like that is the symbol I have for my top value.

How does this relate to health? My friend, Bruce Du Ve, who in my opinion is one of the best healers in the world, takes people through various cleanses and eventually through a Ketogenic diet (when they are ready) to get them down to their ideal body weight – before their metabolism went out of whack. When they reach that ideal body weight, which means they stop losing weight, they will have cleared out most of the toxins in their body as well. At that point, he requires them to go through a 70-day fast – yes, just water for 70 days.[2] What this does is cause the body to eat up all the excess in the body such as the excess blood vessels (i.e., you double the size of your circulatory system for every extra five kilograms of body fat you have). It also cleans out the plaque and non-useful material in the blood vessels. And during this time, you totally replace your liver with a new and largely healthy one.

I'm bringing this up because Bruce reports that when people are fasting, they go through immense spiritual transformations. First, their senses sharpen immensely, and they become much more aware. Second, they often report sensing God to be everywhere around them and within them. And these states occur without meditation or any sort of spiritual practice. They occur with fasting and they seem to remain if one keeps one's body healthy.[3]

I've tried Bruce's ketogenic diet. It took five days for my fasting blood sugar to drop from about 130 to below 100 – meaning that I suddenly wasn't diabetic. I'm not ready right now to do that for several months. However, I believe that after my six weeks of Panchakarma in India, I will be ready to do so again. So now my top value comes into play.

Another thing related to my first value is that I'm determining what it is that makes me hate particular foods. I'm mostly eating food I previously said "I don't like" but now I get to determine how I decide that. I usually would not get that opportunity. In the past, if I started to eat something and didn't like it, I would immediately reject it and that's it. But here almost everything falls under that label. So, part of what I plan to do is discover the qualities of the tastes that I don't like and see what beliefs might be behind my not liking them.

I also made a decision to attempt to change not liking a food into liking it, and then a part of me said, "But then you'd be eating something you don't like," which gave me a horrible feeling in my gut. So clearly there is a sense of identity in not liking it. That was a real insight. The rest involves the details of the taste, and I'll talk about that in Chapter 3. After all, isn't that motivation? What if you could change things you don't like into liking them? Some people jump out of airplanes where others would say, "I'm afraid of heights and I'd never do that." If you could like jumping out of airplanes (i.e., you would decide it is exciting rather than scary), then you would be more motivated to do so, right? Thus, by exploring how I decide I don't like something, I will be transforming myself and using my creativity (another strong value of mine).

There is one more way in which I am satisfying my top value. I have a very strong Internal Guidance. See Chapter 10 of my book *Trading Beyond the Matrix*. I'm working very hard on surrendering to Her (Divine Mother). I had no intention of coming to India again, but suddenly here I am. I don't completely remember the exact steps involved in getting here. But I think it went something like this.

- I tried to do a Ketogenic diet under Bruce Du Ve's guidance and found that I couldn't run my business and do that diet. It was a full-time commitment. Plus, I was getting all sorts of secondary health crises as I was healing, and those become strong motivators to stop the diet.

- I stopped Bruce's diet and 15 months later, gained back the 25 lbs. I had lost. Yet I knew I needed to do something about my health.

- Last March, I went to Ecuador to attend a five-day Vedic Astrology workshop. We were fed Ayurvedic food, and I loved it. As a result, I said to myself that I should find an Ayurvedic doctor and try Panchakarma (the treatment I'm doing here).

- I began to think I should do this quickly and that I don't want to be in India in the summertime when temperatures can skyrocket into the 100s for most of the day. Kochi, where I am, is very close to the equator. It's February and high temperatures here are around 98 degrees Fahrenheit each day.

- We had workshops scheduled in January and I thought I should go in February after the workshops. Bruce Du Ve said I needed to do six weeks rather than the three weeks that most tourists do.

- I was scheduled to do several workshops in Australia in late March through early April. And suddenly international business class flights were on sale to both India and Australia. If I came back to Cary, NC directly from India, I'd only be home a few days before I had to leave again, so the next thing I knew, I had an around the world trip scheduled going from February 2 through April 16. This was the longest I'd been out of the country since I was in the US Army from 1969 through 1970.

- Suddenly I had to cancel my trip to Australia, and I was only going to India.

All of this happened so fast that I had forgotten that I had said I'd never go to India again. This sort of thing happens when my Divine wants me to do something. Following my Inner Guidance is part of my spiritual transformation. And it had all happened so fast that I did not realize it until it suddenly dawned on me – "I'm going to India again. How did that happen?"

There have also been some special benefits to coming here. I had a hair transplant about 18 months ago. My hair looks much better, but it would look almost normal if I had a second one. However, these are quite expensive in the United States. As a result, I had decided I was fine with my new hair as it was. I didn't need a second operation. However, once the trip was booked, I discovered that Kochi was a center for hair transplants in India. My Ayurvedic doctor has agreed to let me do one about two weeks before I am due to leave. The net result is that I will get my second hair transplant and save enough money to pay for the entire trip (over what it would cost me in the US).

A second unexpected benefit is that I have one of my Super Trader students living in India, near Delhi. He's offered to take me to the Taj Mahal (which I've never seen) while I'm here. And I'm also visiting some people I'm close to in Hyderabad. Getting to Hyderabad from Kochi required a stop and took at least seven hours of travel going business class. There was a non-stop economy flight, but the excess baggage charges would make it the same price as a business class flight. But then, after my Super Trader student invited me to Delhi, I found that there was a direct business class flight from Kochi to Delhi and another direct business class flight from Delhi to Hyderabad. Transportation problem solved. Plus, I get to see the Taj Mahal on this trip. The picture shows the Taj Mahal reflected in my sunglasses.

Next, I also found an inexpensive business class flight from Hyderabad to home via Hong Kong on Cathay Pacific. I elected to take that rather than try to come back the same way even though I could have done it a little cheaper by changing a round trip ticket that was booked as part of my round the world business class trip (to save money). And then it turns out that the American Airlines agent who checked me in canceled the flight that I need to get home and had elected not to use. So, everything worked out well the way it happened. That's the magic that seems to unfold when your Inner Guidance wants you to do something and you do it.

My second highest value is helping others transform themselves. To me this means getting them to a high enough consciousness level so that they are permanently happy for no reason. We measure happiness in all our Super Trader students and in people who come to our workshops. My Super Trader students, by the time they finish Super Trader (ST) 1, usually move up 30 points in happiness to a level of about 65 or higher, and that level seems to last – at least it lasts while they remain in the Super Trader program through graduation. After that I have no information to monitor them.

Thus, being here in India satisfies my desire to transform others in two ways. First, I'm transforming my own consciousness and, second, I believe the higher it goes the more I can help others transform themselves. But there is another way that I'm helping others while I'm here. I knew motivation could be tough for me while I was here. As a result, I'm now writing this book on Self-Propulsion Systems – using myself as a guinea pig. And I think this book, when it is finished, will help a lot of people. This is my fourth day here, and despite the jet lag, I will finish this chapter today and thus will have written two chapters in four days. I should have no trouble finishing this book, or at least the first draft, while I'm here at this Ayurvedic Hospital.[4]

My fifth most important value is creativity. Creativity to me means learning new things and getting new ideas as a result of those learnings. It also means putting that knowledge down in a form that can be used by others. I'm writing this book while I'm here. That's creative. I'm studying my own propulsion systems with the hope of learning new things for the book and that's creative. For example, I seem to be eating food that I very much dislike. And I've already talked about my plan to discover what it is about the taste qualities (covered in Chapter 3) that makes me hate certain food. And perhaps I can change those in such a way that I love the food. That would certainly be an interesting gift to myself while I'm here.

In addition, I also bought about five books as potential source material for this book I'm writing. I plan to read all of them to see what new insights emerge.

And lastly, I have probably purchased about 30% of the Great Courses available from *The Teaching Company*. I've probably only watched/listened to 10-20% of the ones I own, but I plan to get through at least three of them during the six weeks that I'm here. I'm currently listening to *The History of India* and that's probably appropriate given where I am.

As a result, I might be spending 22.5 hours each day in a 10 by 14-foot room, but I'm spending the time doing things I love. I enjoy being by myself, so that part of it doesn't bother me at all. However, an extreme extrovert might find the isolation to be a real challenge. I basically see my doctor (and about three doctors under her) once or twice each day. I have two men who administer my treatments, whom I see twice each day. Someone cleans my room daily. Someone takes my blood pressure and temperature each day. And meals are brought to me, as well as the medications I'm to take. So, I probably have about 15 interactions each day. Except for the therapists, they usually last only a few minutes (at most) each. Can you see now how I'm fulfilling my top four values by being here and the negatives don't seem too bad at all within that context?

Myfamily and creativity only partially come into play being here. My wife will be delighted if I dramatically improve my health. As a result, I'm partially fulfilling a family obligation. In addition, my business will probably be much better off if I'm healthy and productive for the next 25 years, so again I'm partially helping with my business value. Plus, writing this book will help the business. It's what I consider a creative obligation.

As I said, my "Big Whys" for being here might not resonate with you. For example, you might have health as a top value, but you might believe that a western medical doctor is all-knowing, and you believe it's necessary to turn your health around under that sort of care. As a result, you'd share my value of health for being here, but because it has a totally different meaning for you, you would not share the primary "Big Why" that I happen to have.

You might even share my transformation value. You'd like to transform yourself into a very good trader. But that's a totally different meaning for transformation than I have. Consequently, if such a person were in my place, they'd probably be thinking, "What does all of this have to do with trading success?"

Perhaps my "Big Whys" don't empower you at all, and that might be true for most people. But if you ask the right questions, you might find that it makes a big difference in your life. Here are some empowering questions that could immediately change your life. Think about the idea of making super transformations, looking at all your beliefs (useful and non-useful, charged and not-charged). Think about uncovering everything that ever happened in your life, including all the unpleasant events you would rather never visit again, but this time with the idea of discovering how they shaped and influenced you. And think about doing all of this with the idea of changing your level of conscious by clearing out all the negative stuff. How do you react to that? As you think about that, read over each question, and then write a possible answer in the box below it. At the end of this chapter I've included my answers to each of these questions.

What issues can I uncover? And how can I clear them out?
How can I use this to create a better life for myself and others?
How can I make my life even more productive?
What resourceful states would enable me to function best in conflict?
How can I access such states with greater ease?
What empowering questions can I ask myself in my goal to make huge transformations?
For people I resist, what can this person teach me?
What expressions of excellence can I discover and replicate today?
How can I turn things around?
What would give me more passion for life? Ideas? Experiences?
How can I become more playful and curious about things?
What else can I use this for?

What can I do today to gather in more resources?
What have I added to the quality of life today?
What do I have to be grateful for today?
What can this person teach me?
What would happen if?
How can I become even more productive? Or make my life even more productive?
Where else can I apply this?
How can I go outside my comfort zone today to really expand myself and learn new things?

Now let's conclude this chapter with an exercise. In your opinion, why am I here in India? Write down as much as you can grasp of it in the space below.

_____

_____

_____

_____

_____

_____

Do you honestly get why I'm here doing what I'm doing – eating food I don't like, confined to a 10 by 14-foot room (I can leave but there is no place to go), and sleeping on a very hard bed? So now let's see how much you really understand. What would it take for you to spend six weeks here doing what I'm doing? What would you have to believe? What "Big Whys" would be necessary for you to do it?

_____

_____

_____

_____

_____

_____

_____

_____

Here are my answers to the questions asked above.

What issues can I uncover? And how can I clear them out?
There might be something about my motivation that I don't know and writing this book will help me uncover it. I find that really exciting.
How can I use this to create a better life for myself and others?
When people understand how they motivate themselves and they are aware, then they can basically do anything – and this includes me.
How can I make my life even more productive?
I already know I can make this book more productive and useful for others by doing the exercises myself as an example.
What resourceful states would enable me to function best in conflict?
Well, the doctors have been on what one might call India time. I ask for something, they say "yes" and then nothing happens. That could produce a conflict. But I just go with the flow and everything has worked out. Trusting in my Personal Divine is a huge resource.
How can I access such states with greater ease?
I know at least 20 methods to change my state, which are given in this course and in the Peak 101 workshop. As a result, state change is easy. I have control over my state.
What empowering questions can I ask myself in my goal to make huge self-transformations?
How did I do that? How did she do that? Can I duplicate it?
For people I resist, what can this person teach me?
I used to have an issue with criticism and give those who gave it too much attention. Now I listen to what they say and ask, "Is this true? Or Is this useful?" If it is, I learn from it. If it is not, then I just move on.

What expressions of excellence can I discover and replicate today?
What are ten different ways that people can motivate themselves and how can I explain it and make it useful when I'm writing this book?
How can I turn things around?
What do I believe about this that makes me feel the need to turn it around? Am I trying to control something? What is the perfection in this just as it is?
What would give me more passion for life? Ideas? Experiences?
I think I will have a lot more energy and passion after completing the six week program here.
How can I become more playful and curious about things?
I know how to laugh at almost anything. I'm a laughter yoga instructor. And laughing at things really makes it fun.
What else can I use this for?
I'm going to interpret "this" as being my experience in Kochi. And I'm going to do my best to make the day of each of the attendants who are here.
What can I do today to gather in more resources?
I'm reading and doing the Great Courses. While doing so I will continually look for new ideas or reframes that will give me new maps of the world. And new and useful maps are huge resources.
What have I added to the quality of life today?
I have trouble remembering Indian names. One of my therapists is named Jomah. The first time I met him today I got his name wrong, but the second time (because I'd written it down) I got it right and his face really brightened as a result.
What do I have to be grateful for today?
So many things! I'm on a spiritual journey. I have an Inner Guidance that is speeding things up. I'm in Kerala because of Her and I expect an immense transformation out of my experience here. And I will finish this chapter soon.
What can this person teach me?
Most people react on automatic pilot. I do as well sometimes. When someone acts from a deep state of love, then I can learn to be like them. When someone reacts on automatic pilot, I can learn to see God in them and if I react, then they are teaching me about my map of the world that still requires such an action.
What would happen if?
If the clinic I'm planning on using for a hair transplant cannot fit me in when it needs to be done, then I will find another one. There are many here and I just picked the only one that actually posted its prices on the Internet. (Later, it was a huge hospital, which meant extra red tape, but it is scheduled).
How can I become even more productive? Or make my life even more productive?
I can become more productive by 1) becoming even more aware than I already am and by 2) making sure I do my meditation practice each day.
Where else can I apply this?
Becoming more aware applies to everything in my life.

How can I go outside my comfort zone today to really expand myself and learn new things?
The young female doctors here (those under my doctor) are quite attractive. I'm not likely to tell them I think they are attractive, so I will do that one by one over the next week. That will really put me out of my comfort zone. I want to do so in such a way that each one of them feels good about herself. (After I told the first one, I said my wife is Indian and I like Indian women and showed her my wife's picture. Doing so stimulated a lot of conversation.)

Notes

[1] This is not meant to influence your beliefs about medicine but simply to give you mine. If you find it useful to believe in allocpathic medicine and the need to get rid of symptoms, then by all means believe in it.

[2] For someone who hasn't done the prior stages of Bruce's program, a 70-day fast would probably be fatal, so this is not a recommendation to try it from Bruce or anyone else.

[3] Only do something like this under the supervision of a health professional.

[4] I finished the first draft of the entire book on Feb 25. About three weeks later, and before I'd left the clinic, I'd finished a second draft.

CHAPTER 2

Understanding Propulsion Systems: What are the Roots?

How excited are you to discover how you work and what runs your brain? How excited are you to be able to raise your consciousness to be happy for no reason, even if it means looking at a lot of negative experiences in your past and clearing them out? How excited are you to face that negativity? This is a personal journey that you must take at some point in your existence – now or perhaps 1,000 years from now.

There are several problems that people have in motivating themselves, which include:

- Living a life filled with poorly defined and inadequate goals, rather than living a purposeful life.
- Inadequate and dis-empowering decisions you have made.
- You are caught up in what might be called stick motivation where you move away from being hit with the stick. And notice that you don't control the stick – other people have the stick.
- Too little propulsion (you don't do Super Trader lessons, or you buy The Peak Performance Course and you just put it on the shelf).
- Too much propulsion (you get so caught up in something that you can't do anything else). Compulsions might be an example of this; namely, where you feel compelled to do something that is not important to you.

- Intolerance of pain so that if there is ever any pain at all, you stop moving forward.
- Old traumas, which tend to store feelings in the body, and you tend to resist those feelings and, as a result, they seem to dominate your life. What you resist persists.
- Part of you wants one thing while another part of you wants another thing, which means you are incongruent.
- Distractions or procrastination.
- Others control your propulsion (from your boss to spouse, media, government, or religion).
- Being fearful of using away or stick motivation on yourself.
- Taboos against motivation such as being too excited or too attracted to something because you feel it is sinful.

Take a look at the following checklist and note where you are with respect to the questions given above and with respect to some of the problems that people have with respect to propulsion systems. Choose those that apply to you.

1. _____ I have the same beliefs as Van about self transformation and I'm excited to look at my beliefs and past trauma in order to clear them out. The pain of looking at them is nothing compared with the joy of having them cleared out.

2. _____ I know my purpose and in order to fulfill it, I must work on myself and become more self-aware.

3. _____ I just want to be a better trader and I'd rather not look at all the negativity in my life.

4. _____ There are certain things in my past that are best left buried. Perhaps one day I'll get to them but not right now.

5. _____ I really want to do this, but I just keep procrastinating.

6. _____ It's probably better not to look at what runs me; who knows what I might discover.

7. _____ I want to do this, but I seem compelled to do other things that are a waste of time.

8. _____ There are a lot of other things in my life that are much more important to me than working on myself.

9. _____ I'm not very organized and I just don't know what to do next.

Which items did you check? The first two indicate a strong motivation to work on yourself, but if it's combined with other checked items such as procrastination (#5), compulsions (#7), or lack of organization (#9), then you probably won't do the work. However, there are exercises to help you with all of those things in this book.

Other items that you might have checked indicate that you clearly are not motivated to do the work (#8), or that you have stick-type motivation (move away from) that will prevent you from doing this work (#3, #4, or #6). If this is you, then you need to build BIGGER WHYs to do it or you need some stick motivation that is strong enough to make you do it. Again, there are exercises in this book to help you with those.

And what about all the misdirected forms of propulsion listed above? Do you have any of those that might prevent you from getting the most out of this book and in the process change your life for the better and perhaps even become happy for no reason for the rest of your life.

In this chapter, I intend to go over at least ten different systems that you can use to motivate yourself and, in the process, give you an overview about how propulsion systems work.

System 1: The Qualities of Your Representation

The first, and perhaps most important aspect of propulsion systems, is given in the qualities of how you represent something to yourself. Richard Bandler and Neurolinguistic Programming (NLP), in general, call these submodalities because they are the details of the five sensory modalities whereby you represent things to yourself. Dr. Michael Hall, the developer of Neurosemantics, calls them metamodalities, because he says they are more important than the modality by which you represent things. Metamodalities drive you.

For example, how do you know if something is good or bad, positive or negative? Most people are not that aware so they might say "I don't know" or give a very abstract reason for such judgments. The real answer is the metamodalities. I had cataract surgery about two years ago. One eye was so bad that when I covered the better eye, all I saw were wiggly lines. I had cataracts in both eyes, so surgery was performed on the bad eye first. Suddenly, after the surgery, when I looked out of that eye with a new artificial lens, what I saw was very clear. Words like "clear" or "bright" are the qualities of the visual modality. I liked clear. Clear was good.

The other eye, however, which I could still see out of, produced an "orange-like" visual image. That's also a metamodality – although not a normal one. But what was apparent to me was that I didn't like "orange-like" nearly as much as I liked clear. Thus, I was showing a preference for one metamodality over another. However, there is nothing inherently bad or good about clear and/or orange-like, except that normal vision is usually clear so naturally we might prefer that.

Let's look at another example. When I say that I like some foods over others, the reason I like some foods more than others are the taste metamodalities. What qualities of taste do I like? Well, I like sweet, slightly salty, and crunchy. And while I'm here getting treatment and eating food I normally would reject, I'm going to explore the metamodalities of what I don't like. We will talk about that extensively in Chapter 3.

System 2: Your Motivation Strategy

A strategy is how you sequence your thinking. For example, when you open a position in the market, all the work should have been done when you developed your system. Consequently, what remains should be the following strategy or sequence of steps in how you represent things to take action in the market:

- You see the signal. This is a signal on your computer or in a chart that you have predetermined is your signal to act. This is a visual external signal.

- Next, inside your brain you need to recognize the signal as the one you should take. This is now an internal visual remembered stimulus.

- Most people act from feelings, so the next step is to feel good about it. This is now an internal feeling that has the metamodalities you might label "good." But perhaps it's just a warm feeling that fills your chest that you label "good."

- And lastly, you press a button on your computer to open the position.

This is a typical example of a mental strategy and it's all going on inside your brain. For example, imagine what would happen if you added one more step. Let's suppose that after you saw the signal, you suddenly had an internal voice (this is the auditory dialogue modality) that asks, "What could go wrong?" Suddenly, you don't feel good about the signal. Instead, you are imagining scenarios of events going wrong, so your action strategy is now much more complex. It might take lots of manipulations in your head to get back to feeling good so you can take the signal. The net result is that you miss the trade.

You also have a motivation strategy that you employ when you are not motivated to do something. In essence, it is a series of steps that you take to produce the critical metamodality (which you already determined) that will get you to be motived to act. See chapter 4.

System 3: Metaprograms

Metaprograms are largely unconscious ways of behaving that become automatic for you. Dr. Michael Hall, in his book *Figuring Out People,*[1] identifies 60 such metaprograms. When you become aware of these programs, you suddenly have more choices simply because you are aware of your programming. However, some of them can be so strong that they are called driver metaprograms. This means that you don't have any choice over what you do within the realm. Your largely unconscious metaprogram drives you to behave in a certain way.

Dr. Hall has identified 24 metaprograms that could be related to propulsion systems. But let's talk about the most important one here – do you tend to move towards things (carrot motivation) or do you tend to move away from things (stick motivation).

We talked about this topic in the last chapter. And in some cases, there are many conflicting move-toward and move-away motivations. Remember the case of the priest from the TV series, *Outlander?* The priest had such a strong drive to 1) be like Jesus and 2) to save humanity (in this case his son) and that was his move-toward motivation. And that motivation predominated over his desire to avoid pain and death (in his case a very slow and painful death). And it certainly predominated over a move-toward motivation of being with the woman he loved and raising his son. (It's a different move-toward motivation that he probably didn't even consider as an option). Had I been trying to motivate him, I would have asked him to picture a life with his Mohawk Indian woman and raising his son and perhaps making sure that his son eventually gets baptized properly. I'm sure this didn't really cross his mind.

Next, there was the case of the man that saved him from a slow death by giving him a quick death. He had the following options to consider:

- Saving someone from agony – perhaps with a faith that everything would work out if he did so. Perhaps that was a strong move-toward motivation for him.

- And that motivation predominated over 1) losing his freedom again and 2) the possibility that he would be killed the same way as the man he was trying to save. These would have been move-away motivations.

- But he had another move-toward motivation that wasn't as strong: to find the woman he loved. But he wasn't sure whether that would happen or not, so perhaps it wasn't that strong for him. He had also been thwarted twice in his attempt to be with her so perhaps he was thinking about the pain of being thwarted again.

Both examples are where carrot motivation, or move-toward motivation, predominates. But sometimes move toward and move away from are simply derived from the meaning you give to things. Here are numerous examples:

Push/Pull is all in "the meaning you give it." Notice how the same thing can be something you avoid or something you are attracted towards.	
What do you avoid?	**What attracts you?**
Failure/what doesn't work.	Finding out what doesn't work/learning/ feedback.
Drinking beer – tastes awful and I can't imagine how anyone enjoys it.	Drinking beer – it's great to do with my buddies and I do so each day. I feel good drinking beer. I love beer.
Fear of heights. Looking over a cliff 3000 feet up terrifies me.	I love to ride roller coasters.
Eating Indian food which for some reason I find quite revolting.	Eating Indian food because I really enjoy the spices and unusual tastes.
Being famous – everyone watching, wanting my commentary, and I find it hard to get privacy	Being famous – it's what I want most in the whole world. I want to be known and be the center of attention.
Solitude, being lonely with no one else around.	Solitude – meditation/personal development
Spending several days watching a cricket match (to someone who doesn't know cricket).	Spending several days watching a cricket match (to a cricket fan).
Challenge – feeling put upon.	Challenge – excitement of adventure
Scary movies in which many people are killed and tortured – it horrifies me.	Scary movies in which numerous people are killed and tortured – it turns me on.

Climbing a 15,000 ft. mountain – dangerous and scary.	Climbing a 15,000-foot mountain – a challenge and very exciting.
Spending money – using up resources.	Spending money – getting things of value, bargain hunting.
Poisonous snakes – avoid at all costs.	Poisonous snakes – collect as a hobby.
Looking stupid, standing out.	Looking stupid, being the center of attention.
Drinking wine – why would anyone drink anything that tastes like that?	Drinking wine – very enjoyable, especially a very fine wine.
Speaking in front of crowds – fear of making a fool of myself.	Speaking in front of crowds – the thrill of adoration.
Change – being out of my comfort zone.	Change – improvement, exciting new things.
Drinking an expensive bottle of bourbon – it tastes awful.	Drinking an expensive bottle of bourbon – it's easy to tell it's the best and worth its high price.
Getting drunk – feeling out of control	Getting drunk – feeling high.
Discovering my personal buttons – avoiding any possible pain.	Discovering my personal buttons – a new issue to work.
Driving fast – very dangerous.	Driving fast – very exciting.
Spending five weeks at basecamp to prepare to finish climbing Mount Everest – cold, boring, little oxygen.	Spending five weeks at basecamp to finish climbing Mount Everest – beautiful, prelude to a challenge, and a peak experience.
Exercising – a pain and the last thing I want to do.	Exercising – necessary to get in shape and doing so gives me an endorphin high.
Smoking cigars – smelly, filthy habit which makes me feel awful and will shorten my lifespan.	Smoking cigars – makes me feel special and important.

While the stick and carrot motivations may be the most important metaprogram in terms of propulsion systems, it is not the only one. Here are 23 other metaprograms that could influence your motivation:

1. Black-and-white, or "either/or" thinking
2. Emphasis on procedures (versus options)
3. Others reference thinking
4. Scenario thinking: pessimism
5. Nature as static
6. Durability: mental constructs are impermeable, solid
7. Causation: linear-external
8. Convention: conformist
9. Exuberance: desurgency (cling to certainty and predictability)
10. Work style: dependent
11. Change adapter: closed to change; late adaptor
12. Modal operators: necessity and impossibility

13. Goal striving: Perfectionism
14. Risk taking: avoid risk
15. Self-instruction: compliant
16. Self-confidence: low
17. Self-esteem: low
18. Self-integrity: low
19. Responsibility: extreme in either direction
20. Ego Strength: unstable
21. Self-Monitoring: low/external
22. Time Zone: living in the past
23. Quality of Life: having

In Chapter 4, you'll be doing some exercises to determine whether you tend to be a move-toward or a move-away person. In addition, I think all of the metaprograms could in some way influence your motivation and we'll be discussing the ten that I think are most important in Chapter 6.

System 4: Your Mental States (Both Positive and Negative)

A state refers to the mental or physical processes that we experience at any moment. States tend to filter our interpretations of our experiences. If we are worn out, tired, hungry, and exhausted, then we are likely to be less tolerant of changes and not motivated at all. If we are excited and energized, then we are highly motivated and it would be difficult to stop us from whatever we want to do.

What's more important – your mental strategy or your mental state? You could probably put up a good argument for either one being important. In fact, I remember attending an early workshop taught by Robert Dilts and John Grinder on *State versus Strategy*. John Grinder argued that the state was most important while Robert Dilts argued that the strategy was most important. It didn't matter who won because the fact that they could do such a workshop implies that both are equally important. However, different NLP trainers seem to take a stance on this issue. Dr. Michael Hall, for example, seems to emphasize "states" while Robert Dilts seems to emphasize "strategies" more.

Our mental state can change due to chemical processes going on in the body. Food, water, oxygen, blood sugar, and circadian rhythms all change regularly and influence our state. And at the same time, there are many ways that you can change your own state. One simple example is to "Remember a time when you felt [fill in the blank]." So, remember a time when you felt motivated!

Since mental states involve bodily changes, they are noticeable on both the inside and the outside. Inside, when you are aware, you can notice changes in your breathing, your posture, your heart rate. And a well-trained NLP practitioner can notice such changes in other people, even subtle changes such as voice tone or facial expression. For example, do you think you can tell the difference in facial expression betweem someone who is motivated and someone who is bored? What would you say about the man in the picture to the right?

What is his state? Why do you say that?

_____

_____

_____

_____

What is most important about mental states is having the right state for the situation you wish to be in or for the task you want to perform. In other words, given the context you are in (i.e., for example, I need to do this task of writing well right now), what is the best state for me to be in to do it. Chances are, it has something to do with motivation.

A relaxed state is not useful in an emergency. An active state is not useful when patience is required. If you are in an unsuitable state for the task you are trying to do, then anything you do will be more difficult. You must match the appropriate state and task.

Imagine doing any of the following things. All of them might make you much more motivated. For many of you, if you want to work on yourself, do any of the things below and see what happens.

- Dream vividly and wildly. Allow it to just happen and notice what that does to your motivation. Dream about making the changes necessary to take total charge of your life and your trading.

- You learned some powerful questions to ask yourself for motivation in the last chapter. Now, put yourself in a state of intense questioning. Imagine that those questions, the right questions, will empower you. So, elicit a ferocious questioning state. Interesting questions to consider have been added to the end of this section of the book.

- Now imagine yourself completely clear of much (if not all) of the baggage you carry around with you. In order to do that, ask yourself, "What states do you want to evoke?" And then ask, "What experiences do you want to make possible for yourself?"

- Now remember a time when you were full of wonder and amazement at something. What was that experience like? What does that experience do for you in terms of motivation?

- Elicit the state of "Yes" inside of you. Think of something you really want and say yes to it with excitement and passion. What does that do for your motivation?

- Now imagine that you have a ferocious fetish. If you don't drool over it or have smoke coming out of your ears, then increase the metamodalities which drive the fetish. Determine what they are and make them stronger, more dominant.

- Go back in time until you access yourself as a child. Imagine having childlike wonder and fascination. What does that do for your motivation?

- Now imagine that you are in a situation in which you really want to go for something. It might involve risk, but you are fully committed and willing to go all-out to get it. What does full commitment do for the task?

- What is something that you really love to do ...that turns you on, that you'd pay to experience again? Find the metamodality drivers that really lock it in place. Make those even stronger.

- Now imagine yourself full of energy. You have so much energy that you can't contain yourself. So, fill yourself up with energy? What does that do for your motivation.

Now let's also look at states that you might want to move away from (stick states) and let's elicit some of those. Imagine that if you don't do what you want to do, then this is the state you'll have.

First think of at least five aversions that you will no longer tolerate. Make a list and then imagine that they are what you will experience if you don't do what you want to be motivated to do.

_____

_____

_____

_____

_____

- What's a fear or phobia that you'd like to avoid? The motivation that we are trying to instill is self-improvement and self-awareness that will raise your consciousness. Now imagine that state of not changing and having to deal with the same problems repeatedly. Fear that.

- Think of something that you'd absolutely say "No" to experiencing. Imagine that this is what could happen if you don't open yourself up for improvement. Notice the qualities of saying no and make them stronger. Now associate that state with staying stagnant and not raising your level of consciousness.

- There are several other ways to develop an aversion to something, but I'm just going to give them to you as information. Use the top three if you really want to build an aversion state to move away from.

- The fourth method would be to think of terrible, terrible things and step into that state. What's a terrible state for you? Imagine that this is what you'll have if you don't do what you want to motivate yourself to do?

- And the fifth one would be to think of a lot of limiting and self-sabotaging beliefs. Again, there is no sense in trying on such beliefs as they could limit you in many ways.

Questions, as mentioned above, can be very powerful in changing your state. However, there are empowering questions and there are questions that have very little impact. Asking "why?" is a useless question because you can just invent a reason that has no impact on you. Consequently, avoid such questions. In contrast, here is a list of questions that can have an enormous impact upon you. Ask them and see what they do for your motivation.

Awareness Questions	Impact on You	Advanced Questions	Impact on You
Strategy question: In what way have I sabotaged myself?		As I appreciate these insights, how can I use them to totally transform the old pattern?	
What would help me succeed?		How is this useful?	
What is my perspective on this and what would another perspective do for me?		The "what is" is perfect, and how can I see this for myself?	
What can I learn from this?		How did I make this up from my perspective	
What resources do I need?		What's fun about it?	
How would acceptance help?		How can I contribute to make this more ecological (useful for the whole system)?	
What would help me to succeed?		How can I totally define success so I can experience success every day?	
What if I didn't fail?		What if I go for it and enjoy the process?	
What if I don't make a fool of myself?		How can I enjoy foolishness as part of an adventure?	
What questions can I ask myself to make this more motivating?		How can I relate this to my purpose and my life's mission?	
What new ideas and concepts do I get to learn?		How can I enhance my life by learning new words and concepts?	

Awareness Questions	Impact on You	Advanced Questions	Impact on You
What resources, relationships, ideas will help me be more likeable?		How can I create even more value in life for others?	
What resources will increase my own likeability?		How can I pace (model their physiology through matching and mirroring), support, and validate this person?	
What's great, valuable and positive about my life now?		How can I increase my gratitude even more?	
What positive intention drove this undesirable behavior?		What different response would make that response unnecessary?	
Did I make this up and is it useful?		What can I make up that would be most useful in this sort of situation?	

Hopefully, you now understand the pull of motivating states and the push away from aversive states. Write down what you learned in the space below.

_____

_____

_____

_____

_____

System 5: Metaframes/Metastates and the Meaning You Give to Things

One of our primary qualities as human beings is that we are meaning-makers. We are constantly giving meaning to things, which basically determines our experience. Dr. Michael Hall, for example, has developed a different type of NLP that he calls *Neurosemantics*.[2] And the key difference here is that the emphasis in Neurosemantics is the meaning.

Dr. Carol Dweck, a rather famous psychologist, has written two books based upon a core assumption that we as human beings are meaning-makers. The first book is called *Self-Theories* and this book is a summary of much of her research. The second book is called *Mindset: The Psychology of Success*. It is interesting to see a research psychologist take this stance and even more exciting to see all the useful material that has come from her taking such a stance. When I was studying psychology as an undergraduate and as a graduate student, a concept like meaning-making was not observable so you could not study it. It was taboo based upon the culture of behaviorism that dominated psychology in those days.

Someone on the **Quora** website once asked the question: **"*Life is meaningless, so what's the point? And don't give me some religious answer to the question because that's just a cop out.*"** I decide to answer the question, and this is roughly what I said:[3]

> You are a meaning-maker. That is your essence and you've illustrated that in your question. You have given a meaning to life; namely, that it is meaningless. Now, that's not a very useful meaning. It doesn't inspire you. It doesn't give you joy. Instead it leads you to a conclusion like "so what is the point?" But the point is really to give life a meaning that will allow enrichment and happiness to flow to you.
>
> You have also given meaning to any sort of answer involving God or a higher level being – saying that it's a cop-out. That's another example of you giving meaning to it. So, if you want some meaning to your life, then give life a meaningful answer.

As an illustration of what you could do, my life's meaning is all about my purpose in life and that purpose is to transform myself to higher and higher levels of awareness, which equates to being happy for no reason at the very least. And, I believe, that to the extent that I've transformed myself, I can also help others transform themselves and that's my purpose in life. Don't you think that my meaning to life is probably a little more useful than to just say "life is meaningless?"

What ultimately motivates you is the meaning you give to things. We feel motivated when something makes a lot of sense and is full of meaning for our life. For example, how motivated is the person who says, "Life is meaningless so what's the point?" He/She isn't motivated at all – except perhaps to end his/her life. Compare that with my meaning to transform myself and others. I'm sitting in a 10-foot by 14-foot room, with little human contact for 22.5 hours each day, and I'm having a blast. I'm writing this book on motivation, and I expect to finish it before I leave here – at least a first draft.

It's also critical to note that there are layers to your frames and to your states. These are called metaframes and metastates, respectively. We are talking about layered levels of meaning and states. And we must understand these many layers to really get at the basis of how all this works.

First, we represent the world in terms of the various sense modalities – seeing things, hearing things, feeling things, as well as tasting and smelling them. On top of that we have the details or the sub- or metamodalities. These are what drive you and that might be enough to get propulsion going forward.

Next, language takes over and we develop beliefs about our various representations. And we might give those beliefs some overall meaning. At this point, one might say that we've gone up four levels, which are 1) sensation; 2) details of the sensation; 3) using language to name the sensation; and 4) developing a belief about the representations.

Now, step back and look at what just happened and you'll move up to the fifth level. You might look at it all and say, "Wow, that's interesting!" Interesting is a useful metaframe. It elicits wonder and a desire to explore. You could also step back and say, "Boy, it's scary that I can do all of that. I really shouldn't mess with it." Notice how that frame has an entirely different reaction. Notice that we are now on the fifth level and that this frame or meaning or state seems to predominate.

We can keep going up higher and higher. The highest frame or state always seems to predominate and control things. Dr. Michael Hall has come up with some metastate principles that seem to govern how such metastates work. And I've taken the liberty to add a few more of my own to Dr. Hall's list, given below.

Higher levels tend to organize the lower levels. The highest frame will tend to dominate the lower levels. Notice things changed in the examples above from "Isn't that interesting?" versus "Boy, it's scary that I can do all of that?" One almost forgets about the lower levels and thus focuses on interesting or scary. So, ask yourself the question: "How can I make use of this principle in motivating myself?" Going to a useful metaframe becomes all-important when you understand this key principle.

Someone (or something) will always set that higher frame of reference for you if you don't do so yourself. Sometimes the frame just occurs through the way we live our life. It just happens. But it can also be controlled by you (hopefully in an empowering way) or by someone else. It's probably more useful if you retain that control. For example, fast forward about a year and we're about to go to a Safari in Africa and there is a coronavirus scare in the world. However, there are no cases in southern Africa where we are going. Nevertheless, my wife said to me, "I just heard that United Airlines cancelled all of their flights, including domestic ones." She then said, "You better figure out how we can make alternative arrangements to do our trip later." She knew that we'd already paid for the trip and those fees were non-refundable. Now that statement was her trying to set the frame (or at least, allowing something she heard to set the frame). I promptly went to the *United* website and found that only flights to areas with a lot of deaths had been cancelled – mostly because no one was flying there. Thus, I controlled the higher frame, and not my wife.

These metaframes tend to be outside of our awareness. Thus, developing awareness of them could result in a huge increase in consciousness and a huge increase in personal power and self-motivation. What is the highest metaframe that governs you right now at this moment? Are you aware of it now? Were you aware of it before I asked the question?[4]

So much derives from the highest frame – solutions to problems, ideas, beliefs, emotions, and your very experience. Thus, whoever sets that highest frame is in control. If you want to motivate yourself, then that frame should be set by you.

In a sense we are doing systems thinking. All these principles are a system and they influence each other. There are a lot of parts but there is a whole that emerges from the parts and that whole will contain emergent properties that didn't exist before. For example, I've been developing models of top trading for many years and have developed many such models. As a result of that work, we now have a whole that's emerged to train people to become Super Traders and there are properties that have emerged from that whole. For example, I coined the term "Position Sizing" in the mid-1990s and was the first to use it in my book, *Trade Your Way to Financial Freedom*. But many other concepts have also emerged including R-multiples, the impact of market type and how to measure it, System Quality Number®, a concept of Infinite Wealth, and the Tharp Think belief set that now totals over 100 beliefs. When you develop a higher level metaframe, it is composed of the parts below it, but the new frame metaframe controls your thinking and that metaframe might include a number of emergent properties.

Each level of thinking or framing seems to produce a different reality. It's all made up, of course, but each frame is totally different from what was below it. As a result, it transforms everything.

We can step back from any frame, disassociate so to speak, and create a new frame. For example, what's your reaction to these metaframe principles? Look at that and you'll notice that you are setting up a new frame. When you do that, you can establish new meanings for everything below it. And if you do so deliberately, the result can be very interesting. You are creating a new level of reality.

Understanding all of this, and the hierarchy, allows us to reflect back on the different levels. This gives you systemic processes and control mechanisms. This essentially means that we can set up feed-forward and feedback loops. What happens when you step back and say, "That's interesting?" And what if, knowing what the levels are, you suddenly asked, "What would happen if I did it this way?" Do it, feed forward the results, evaluate what happens, and then feedback what happened and try some other modification.

All of this can be very useful, or it can be a living hell. Imagine the following scenario. You have a startle response to a loud noise. You give meaning to that and say, "I'm afraid." Then you give more meaning to that and say, "I'm afraid of being afraid." And then you add another level and decide, "I'm really upset that I did that." And you can keep layering negative frames upon negative frames until you become psychotic and you find that some doctor is now giving you drugs to help you with those symptoms of perpetually layering negative frames. So, be aware of your frames.

And, when you get yourself into negative states, especially layered negativity, the only way to get out of it is to feel the feelings and appreciate it. You might want to resist it with all of your might, but resistance is futile. Instead, you must accept and appreciate and welcome and feel the feelings – which is the last thing you want to do. I'm not sure how much this is a principle of metastates and metaframes as it is of dealing with negativity in general. But let's just say that it applies to layered states and frames as well.

How can you use this material to increase your motivation to work on yourself? Write down as many ideas as you can think of in the space below.

_____

_____

_____

_____

System 6: Your Values

Your values shape who you are. It's possible that different parts of you have different values and thus can lead to inner conflict. But what are your values? I already described my values earlier and how they motivate me to go through my current experience of spending 22.5 hours per day in a 10-foot by 14-foot room.

There are various models for how values are organized. For example, values might be considered needs and Abraham Maslow has developed a hierarchy of needs. He believes that higher-level needs only arise once lower-level needs are met. Maslow is now famous for his hierarchy, but he also received a lot of personal criticism for developing it.

Clare Graves was a professor of Industrial Psychology at SUNY SCC in Schenectady, New York. He developed a model of eight different value levels that people must evolve through, alternating between internal levels (levels 1, 3, 5, 7) and external levels (levels 2, 4, 6, 8). He was a contemporary of Maslow and he saw how much trouble Maslow got into, so he never published his complete theory in a book. Instead, he published articles in psychological magazines. And before he died, he burnt everything.[5] This alone suggests that his ideas had very little utility to him personally. However, his model is at least interesting and there are now many books written about his theories.

I consider values to be high-level beliefs that shape our behavior. Chapter 8 of this book will discuss Maslow's and Graves' models in more detail, plus give you some exercises related to values to help you with your own propulsion template.

System 7: Your Perception of Reality and Your Self-Definition

Reality and your self-definition are very much related to some of the other topics given here.

First, "Who are you?" Any of the definitions below might be used to answer that question (plus there are probably many more useful models). For example, you might say:

- I am a unique person (you are unaware and controlled by unconscious urges and desires).

- I am a collection of parts in conflict, each with its own unique motivations or intentions.

Every time you resist something, you create a part. You don't want to feel fear, so you create a part to not feel fear. Thus, you have lots of emotional parts whose intention is to avoid that feeling. You must deal with other people in your life, especially those who are close to you. Those people can often be difficult, so you resist them and create an internal part that represents the other person. Thus, you might have a part representing your mother, your father, your sister, your brother, and your spouse. And the result is that you never really know the other person, just the part of you that represents that person. Therefore, some people who may have had a difficult relationship with a parent, who is now dead, still cannot hug their internal image of that parent. It's because the only person you really know is your internal part that represents them – you never really knew them.

You also have parts that represent the roles you play in life. These might include trader, excitement part, researcher part, perfectionist part, conservative part, etc. When you think of it, when you say the word "I," you are just talking about some part of you.

Now imagine that each part was created with a positive intention (i.e., to avoid fear; to deal with my father). Each part has its own beliefs about the world and itself, and it wants you to think that it (the part) is you. Some of those beliefs are not useful and have strong negative emotions (charges) attached to them. And this is what you are dealing with every day.

- I am a collection of parts that surround my Higher Self. This definition is probably the most useful for working on yourself. Your goal is to get your parts to join together or to merge with your Higher Self. The fewer parts you have, the higher your consciousness becomes. And if you follow this model to its logical conclusion, believe it or not, in the end when you are totally clear, all that remains is God/Higher Self/infinite potential.

Why is this important? How does it impact propulsion systems? Those are easy questions. Propulsion comes out of who you think you are based upon how you organize yourself. Essentially, it means that the more you work on yourself, which relates to the intention of this book, the easier self-propulsion becomes.

Dr. Michael Hall describes the Self as a giant metaframe that controls us. Remember that I decided that I might want to change my strategy of disliking certain foods because of the metamodalities of how I represent them to one of liking that same food because of those same metamodalities. I wasn't sure how easy it would be to do that. But suddenly, when I made that decision, something happened. It was really disturbing my sense of self. It was like, "I'm not someone who likes those types of food." It was as if there was a giant metaframe about who I was that couldn't make that sort of change. And that's how important metaframes can be to your motivation. However, I was immediately aware of that "sense of self" metaframe objecting and I thought to myself, "That's interesting, how did that happen?"

- The final definition you might have is that "I am the unchanging witness" of the experiences that a body known as (your name) has. If you are at this level in your experience, then you probably don't need this book.

It's also important to understand that your reality is all made up. What's out there in the universe might be called electromagnetic vibrations (and perhaps other sorts of vibrations). We never experience those. Instead, they are impinging upon our senses that those senses translate them into electrochemical sensations.

Here is an example. First, each of your eyes sees a very small, upside down picture of the world out there. Color and detail occupy a very small section (about 2 mm) of the picture and there is a hole in the middle of the picture where the optic nerve joins the eye. These two small images transfer information to about 30 different areas of the brain and what you see appears to be in full color, three-dimensional, and very detailed. But this is just a representation of what is actually there. It's not the same as what is actually there.

Wait, there is still more. For example, 650 nanometer light waves hit the R-cones at the back of the retina and are translated into a sensation. You then use language to label the sensation and call it red. But really understand this: There is no correspondence between the word red and a 650 nanometer wave length – none. Most human beings just label the experience that such a wavelength has on the visual sense mechanism as the color red.

Language also shapes how your brain works. Because of language you divide the world into subjects and objects and the verbs by which they interact. Most languages also give tenses to the verbs you use, thus creating a past, present and future.[6] You see separate things out there. You then develop beliefs which might be useful but are not necessarily true. You add meanings to your beliefs. You make judgements (based upon metamodalities) about those beliefs. You name things and think you know them. And this list can go on and on. But the bottom line is that your internal representation is not the same as what is going on out there in the world. *The map is not the territory*. But what people do is project their maps onto the world and think it's real.

For example, take a walk through the forest and then someone asks you about your experience of the walk. You might respond, "I saw a lot of trees." When you have a label for something you see, you think you know it. Yes, I know, it is a tree. But go stand in the forest and really experience each tree. Notice how different every tree is from every other tree. How could you just call it a tree? You are not getting it. Now take your energy and encompass the tree – be the tree. It's a totally different experience. What's it like being the tree? Chances are that if you do this, you'll understand how labeling helps you avoid an experience of that thing. But that's what language does – make you think you know something through naming it. You need to suspend your sense of self and really become something else to know it.

You also generalize things. It might go something like this.

Billy insulted me by saying that. (By the way, notice that the statement here is a personal interpretation of what Billy said and not necessarily true, and it does not necessarily reflect Billy's intention.) Billy could say the same thing to ten people and perhaps only one of those people might find it insulting.

Next our judger might decide Billy is a bad person who cannot be trusted. Okay, so on Tuesday, May 20, 2019 at 4:17 pm Billy said something you interpreted as insulting and now from that one statement, you decide that you cannot trust him and he's a bad person. That's really generalizing. What you just did is to take an action, nominalize it to become a thing, and then judge the thing (that you made up) to be bad.

Billy is from an island in the Pacific. You suddenly decide that you cannot trust people from that island. (Here we have even more generalization.) We should bomb that island and wipe all those people out. And that last conclusion comes from a judgement of a single action done by one person and interpreted as bad by another.

Notice what has happened here from a single statement Billy made, that one person interpreted to be insulting. Suddenly, he wants to kill everyone on the island that Billy is from because of that one statement. That's what some people will do with generalizations. By the way, this is also a good example of what's called black-and-white thinking – it's either good or bad and there is no in-between.

My goal is not to convince you that this is true – that it is all made up. After all, its just my map (which is not the territory) that says that to me. **But just consider that it might be useful to believe that it is all made up. And if it's all made up, it means that you have total control over how you interpret things, what you give meaning to, what you value, and so much more. It basically means that you make it all up and, when you realize this, you can be in control.** You control what's important. You control what you are motived to do. Thus, I recommend that you take charge and that you head into useful areas.

System 8: Your Purpose and Your Mission

Most people don't have a purpose in life. If you ask them what they want, they might say something like, "I want to make a million dollars so that I have more freedom and don't have to work." However, that desire doesn't reflect a purpose. Your purpose is the ultimate "Big Why" behind everything you do. And your "Big Why" is the essence of self-motivation.

When your consciousness seems to grow, however, you do find yourself with a purpose. It's like – "What is the reason that you are here on this planet?"

When the students in my Super Trader program finish the first phase of their program and list their self-transformations, many of them include finding their purpose as one of their major transformations. Here are some examples, and one of them is mine:

- To brighten the lights around me (meaning he sees others as a light, and he wants to make them all shine brighter).
- To attain a higher level of consciousness and spread that to the rest of the world.
- To channel love by bringing "wealth" inside and out to my family, to myself, and to others.
- To create joy, calm, peace of mind, love, and freedom for myself, and to spread that to the world.
- To live a life of joy and love, and demonstrate that to the world.
- To live life to my full potential: a joyous expression of peace, love, truth, and awareness.
- To make a difference and help millions of people improve their lives.
- To be a guiding light for myself and others toward our higher purpose and enlightenment.
- To become One with my Higher Self and surrender.

When people discover their purpose, and it's usually done in concert with finding their Inner Guidance, it seems to change everything. Suddenly, one's purpose is everything. When people have a task to do, they simply ask, "Is this in alignment with my higher purpose or not?" If it's in alignment, it becomes very easy to do. It's rather like one's purpose becomes one's highest value.

Here is how it worked for me.

I noticed that I started doing *A Course in Miracles* in 1982 and that was the same year that I started my business, which in those days was a sole proprietorship.

By the time I finished doing *A Course in Miracles* in 1986, I had a full-time business. And my mission was clear to me: Self-Transformation Through a Trading Metaphor.

I had an eight-year relationship with a client who was a major source of income. He ran a $50 million hedge fund and was my best client, probably spending well over $100,000 with us. But in

February 2000, the headline in *Barron's* magazine was about the Ponzi scheme he was running. I had no idea what he was doing but when I look back at the mistakes I made, if I could have corrected any of them, it would have been that I got "off purpose." I'd say that my business was all about helping others transform their lives. My con-artist client would say, "We change people's lives by making them a lot of money." And after a while I began to buy into his way of thinking. That got me off purpose.

I used to think that my mission was to help transform others, but one day I realized that there was a limit on what I could do to help others and that limit was my own level of consciousness. At that point, my top value (and to some extent, my purpose) became transforming myself to raise the level at which I could help others.

Finally, as my connection to my Inner Guidance grew stronger and stronger through my daily dialogues, my purpose became to become one with my Higher Self – to merge with my Higher Self so that was all that was left.

My Inner Guidance doesn't predict the future[7] but She occasionally gives me an idea of what direction She wants me to move. I enjoy being famous anonymously – a lot of people know about me, but people seldom walk up to me and say, "Oh, you are Van Tharp." In fact, in Cary, NC where I live, I'm probably known more as Kala Tharp's husband than anything else. However, my Inner Guidance says that one day I'm going to be famous for helping others awaken (think "become more aware"). She says I'll write a book that will make me famous, and from that point on I'll be recognized a lot. I already know what that book is about, and I'll probably finish it by the end of 2022. I don't really want to be famous, famous, but I seem very motivated to take the steps that will get me there – that is, write the book.

I now understand that in order to become one with my Inner Guidance, my sense of self will no longer exist. The Divine will be running the show and there will be no sense of me left that wants to avoid being famous. And basically, that's how my purpose developed and how it currently dictates my life.

System 9: Procrastination – All the Things that Block You

There are a huge number of things that can block you from being motivated. These include:

- Fear – This could include all sorts of fears such as fear of success, fear of failure, fear of looking bad, fear of change.
- Lack of Energy – If you don't have a certain amount of passion that you can channel into doing what you want and following your dreams, then they will never happen.
- Compulsions and Addictions – These are things you are compelled to do but that have little value. For example, your goal might be to lose 40 pounds. but you feel compelled to eat certain foods that will stop the weight loss.
- Perfectionism – Your need for something to be perfect because you are too concerned about what others will say.
- Creative Procrastination – You have all sorts of small, easy-to-do tasks that you decide to tackle before you do something big. But the problem is you never run out of the small tasks.

- Less Significant Obligations – You have a number of obligations that fill your day. There might be one or two key ones, but activities from the less significant ones continually jump up and distract you.
- Urgent Not-Important Tasks – While this may resemble Items 5 and 6, this can be as simple as needing to answer the phone when it rings. It's like you are compelled to answer it, even though you might end up talking to a salesman, or to a friend who suddenly distracts you with all the drama they are going through.
- It's too much work. Whatever it is you need to do, say a major project like the Super Trader Program, just seems like too much work. It's 20 hours of your time every week for a year and that just seems far too demanding.
- Not enough juice to do it. This is related to lack of energy, but number one is about passion and this is about everything that could be draining energy such as stress in your life.
- Not Enough Know-How. If you have a major task in front of you and you have no idea how to do it, that could stop you cold.

All these topics are covered in Chapter 10: What Could Stop You. However, there is one last area that most people don't think about and that could be the biggest block to it all – your *secrets and hidden agendas*. These are things you have buried in your subconscious and thus don't want to face. However, if these secrets become threatened by whatever task you are attempting to undertake, they will stop you in your tracks. They are so important that I've devoted a separate chapter to them, Chapter 11: Secrets and Hidden Agendas.

System 10: Moti-Maps: Motivation, Organization, and Time Management

As I have shown in the prior steps leading from simple metamodality changes to finding your purpose, what you are doing is determining your motivation. What is it you want to do? What is your focus. When you change your focus, you change your life. What is your thinking like? How are you feeling about it? And what are you doing about it. When you take control of those things, you take control of your life.

If you understand what we've been doing in this chapter, you'll understand that it's necessary to step backward and become aware of what you've been thinking. You need to know that the map is not the territory. However, useful maps can be the steps to genius. What are the maps you use? How are you running your life? And can you adopt more useful ones? You might notice here that what we are doing is simply asking powerful questions that can change everything.

The next step involved is to really know what you want and the "Big Why" behind it, your purpose. Remember that you are just playing a game. You are making it all up in your head through your beliefs and values. As a result, there is no reason to limit yourself in any way, really go for it.

Ask yourself, "What do you want?" What's the "Big Why" behind it? And how will you get there? I'd like to think that at this point in your development you already understand that the more aware you are of how you run your brain and the clearer you are of impediments to running it efficiently, the easier it will be to get what you want.

And now that you have these key principles let's look at 11 steps toward effectively managing your time. Chapter 12 will specifically help you to apply these steps to one of the important areas for trading success 1) raising your level of consciousness and clearing out blocks (i.e., for example, going through the Peak Performance course or going through the Super Trader awakening lessons; 2) developing a business handbook to guide your trading success; and/or 3) developing three non-correlated systems that work in different market types and trading them at an efficiency level of at least 95%.

The 11 steps are outlined below. Chapter 12 will show you how to apply them.

Step 1: **What is it I'm trying to accomplish?** It could be one of the three things just listed, but these steps could apply to any goal you might have. Turn your goal into a vision and the only standard for that vision is to be outstanding. For example, what are your criteria for knowing you've done a good job. How can you change those criteria to be outstanding?

Step 2: **What is the "Big Why" (purpose) behind the goal.** You want to always keep this in mind. And if someone else is going to approve what you are doing (i.e., such as Van approving a Super Trader lesson), then you need to know the intentions that person has for you in doing the lesson. That's why I state my objectives for you in each lesson.

Step 3: **List the action steps that might be necessary to what you are going to accomplish.** This probably means that you need to become familiar with what you are trying to do. For example, if you want to complete the Super Trader program you will need to at least skim each Super Trader lesson and the related chapters in the Peak Performance course.

Step 3: **Become familiar with Steven Covey's dimensions of importance and urgency.**[8] Too often people become distracted by what they think is important (i.e., a phone call you seem compelled to answer) but has nothing to do with the task at hand. Allowing something that trivial become urgent is a great way to get little accomplished.

Step 4: **Find useful maps.** We have been talking about useful maps. You make up those maps and thus you have total control over them. Ask yourself, what useful maps can I develop to make this fulfillment easy, fun, and quick? These are the things you can control. There might be other things in your map that seem out of control or that it only seems possible to change slightly and thus influence. What are those things? Concentrate on what you can control.

Step 5: **What areas of concentration within your vision will make the biggest difference?** List several areas that will make the biggest difference and make those your primary focus

Step 6: **Divide your vision into steps and set time goals.**

Step 7: **Determine what seems totally out of your control.** Remember in some way it is always in your control because you only experience your map, not the territory. So, if it seems out of control, notice what meaning you are giving it to make it seem important. How can you change that meaning so that it is no longer important?

Step 8: **What's the Outcome?** Anthony Robbins has a procedure that he formerly called OPA for Outcome, Purpose, Action. The key part of this is the outcome. For example, you might have a to-do list for the day. But when you focus on the outcome and the purpose, you might find a better way to accomplish everything without all the "to-dos."

Step 9: **Work on Your Plan Daily**.

Step 10: **Do a Weekly Planning Process.**

Step 11: **Deal with Anything that Might Cause Overwhelm.** Now let's move on to understanding the role of sensory detail in your motivation that is covered in the next chapter.

Notes

[1] L. Michael Hall, and Bobby G. Bodenhamer *Figuring Out People: Reading People Using Metaprograms*, 2nd ed. Neurosemantic Publications, Clifton, CO; 2009.

[2] See www.neurosemantics.com for more information.

[3] I don't know the exact words about what I said because my answer is no longer on Quora under "my content." Quora is a useful site, but it also has many limitations because they limit questions you can ask to one or two sentences. If you ask a longer question, they edit it down to one sentence, basically changing the question. I think at one point someone strongly rebutted my answer (although I didn't bother to read what they said), and now it seems to be gone. As a result, the answer given is how I would answer the question now.

[4] Scientists, for example, tend to be governed by a largely unconscious metaframe called philosophical materialism. It basically is the assumption that matter and energy form the basis of the universe. There is assumed hierarchy of physicality going from energy/matter (Physics) to Chemistry to Biology. Something like consciousness is assumed just to be a byproduct of the brain. A lot of the problems physics faces could be solved by assuming that consciousness is the basis for everything. But for most scientists, especially those who have the authority to say who gets grant money or who gets published, you had better adopt a stance behind philosophical materialism. You tend not to believe something when you get paid for not believing it. And that is a perfect illustration of the unconscious power of a high level metastate.

[5] This is one version of what happened. Another version says he was working on publishing it.

[6] Chinese dialects only express time through adverbs and time phrases, but have no tense to the verbs. Vietnamese, Indonesian, and some Native American languages also don't have tenses to their verbs.

[7] My Inner Guidance won't predict the future because She says the future is a set of probabilities. What looks likely now might change.

[8] Stephen Covey and Jim Collins. *Seven Habits of Highly Effective People: 30th Anniversary Edition.*, 1989, 2004, 2020.

CHAPTER 3

Propulsion Based Upon Sensory Qualities

We will begin this discussion of propulsion systems by looking at sensory qualities (submodalities/metamodalities[1]) because they are the basic drivers of judgment and of propulsion. They exist as survival mechanisms.

- Something big moving toward you (and looking very close) is a sign of danger.
- A loud, sudden noise will produce a startle response.
- A bitter taste could mean that a certain food is not healthy for you.
- A rancid smell is something you want to avoid.

We have all of these responses to sensory qualities wired into our neurology, so that even in a different context we still have a reaction to them that one might move toward or away from.

Most of the NLP change techniques involving metamodalities make use of this tendency to like some things and not like others. For example, here is a basic like/dislike pattern:

1. Think of something that you like, but you wish you did not like it? (Determine what it is and how its represented. Usually it is a picture.)
2. Now elicit the metamodalities (there is a table following this description to do that).
3. Now, think of something similar that you absolutely dislike. For example, you might love ice cream but dislike frozen yogurt.
4. Now elicit the submodalities of what you dislike and do this in a different spatial location. For example, one might be to the right and the other to the left.

5. Now change the submodalities of the second item into those of the first item. Now you could also do the reverse if it were something you don't like that you want to like.
6. And now test it, how is the item you changed different?

The table below is a basic table for comparing submodalities or metamodalities.

Meta Modalities Checklist

What do you see?

Visual Qualities	Example 1	Example 2	Distinction
Movie or still			
Panoramic or framed			
Color vs. black-and-white			
Brightness (1-10)			
Location (up-down-left-right)			
Associated/dissociated			
Distance of picture from self			
Color Intensity (1-10)			
Contrast (1-10)			
Movement (tempo)			
Angle viewed from			

What do you hear?

Auditory Qualities	Example 1	Example 2	Distinction
Volume			
Location of source			
Uniqueness of sound			
Voices? Whose?			
Speed			
Intensity			
Other			

What do you feel?

Kinesthetic Qualities	Example 1	Example 2	Distinction
Hot/cold (1-10)			
Movement			
Vibration			
Pressure (sharp, dull)			
Intensity			
Weight			
Size of feeling			
Other quality			

What do you taste?

Qualities	Example 1	Example 2	Distinction
Sour			
Sweet			
Salty			
Bitter			
Umami (savory/spicy)			
Strong/weak			
Warm/cold			
Crunchy			
Stringy			
Mushy			
Rubbery			
Slimy			

What do you smell?

Qualities	Example 1	Example 2	Distinction
Ashy			
Animal-like /musky			
Burnt/smoke			
Chemical/medicinal			
Chocolate			
Caramel			
Toast-like/cereal			

Qualities	Example 1	Example 2	Distinction
Earthy			
Floral			
Fruity/citrus			
Grassy/herbal			
Nutty			
Rancid/rotten			
Spicy			
Tobacco			
Woody			

You might notice that this chart is more extensive than the ones I use in our courses because I've expanded the taste/smell section for my own use to determine why I like or dislike certain foods. At the same time, we have a much better idea about what's important in terms of metamodalities in the three primary modalities, but we know very little about taste and smell.

Most of my life (perhaps even my entire life) I have been very particular about what foods I eat. I usually go to a restaurant and eat the same thing at that restaurant – because I know I like that dish and I also know that there are many foods there that I won't like. Now I'm here in India and I can say definitively that I don't like most Indian foods. But that's what I will get for at least two meals each day. In the morning I get fruit which I like.

Thus, I have something that fits perfectly into this scenario. I also expanded the smell submodality section because smell is strongly related to taste.

So, what did I notice? Well, first, I'd have an immediate reaction of, "Yuck, I don't like it." But then I'd say to myself, "Well, eat it anyway so you can notice the metamodalities." You don't like this, so what are the taste metamodalities? I don't like eggplant and the first day I was here I had three eggplant dishes. I had brought some honey and oat granola bars and I liked those, so those are what I compared.

The eggplant dish was strong and spicy. It was also somewhat rubbery, stringy, and slimy. The bar was crunchy and sweet.

The absolute worst was a combination of bitter and hot/spicy. Bitter gourd was probably the best/worst example of this taste. It was awful. However, if it was sour tasting, then I didn't like it, but there wasn't much of that.

What do you taste?

Qualities	Eggplant Dish	Granola Bar	Distinction
Sour			
Sweet		Yes	
Salty			

Bitter			
Umami (savory/spicy)	Spicy		
Strong/weak	Strong		
Warm/cold			
Crunchy		Very	
Stringy	Somewhat		
Mushy			
Rubbery	Somewhat		

What do you taste?

Qualities	Bitter Gourd	Fruit - Papaya	Distinction
Sour			
Sweet		Yes	
Salty			
Bitter	Very		
Umami (savorysSpicy)	Spicy		
Strong/weak	Strong		
Warm/cold		Cold	
Crunchy		A little	
Stringy			
Mushy	Somewhat		
Rubbery			
Slimy			

It became clear to me what the results were

Sour – I don't like
Sweet – I like
Salty – I like if not too much salt.
Bitter – I don't like at all.
Spicy – I don't really like as there are all sorts of spices in Indian food, perhaps these should all be metamodalities.
Crunchy – I like.
Stringy – I generally don't like.
Mushy – depends upon the context.
Rubbery – I generally don't like.
Slimy – I generally don't like.

When NLP does a metamodality comparison, it's usually on an imaginary representation and not the actual experience. For example, it could be on a memory. And it's often visual memory.

Now, I'm sure in my imagination I could take a bitter and very spicy dish that's somewhat slimy (the ultimate combination that I don't like) and make it sweet and crunchy. And then in my head I could say, "Sure I like that.'

But that doesn't change the fact that some dish might stimulate my taste buds for bitter, spicy, and slimy and then I would not like it.

But is there a way that I could learn to like those tastes? There is some precedence for it in things that people naturally don't like and are probably not that good for you, but people learn to love them. They become connoisseurs. What comes to mind is bourbon, scotch, wine, beer, and cigars.

For example, when I married my wife Kala, she didn't know much about wines, so I introduced her to sweet wines such as Riesling and Gewürztraminer. She liked those. I seldom drink wine, and I mostly drink sweet white wines. But in our 28 years of marriage, my wife has become somewhat of a wine connoisseur. She loves certain wines and sweet wines are seldom part of the equation for her.

I looked up some wine tasting descriptions and got something like:

- With aromas of grass and green pepper along with red fruit and dirt, this wine actually seems more like a Cabernet Sauvignon than a Merlot. That said, it's both boozy and thin at the same time.
- Deep ruby red, with delicious vanilla overtones backed up by juicy soft strawberry and morello cherry flavors.
- Expect plenty of fresh citrus, lime, and tropical flavors.
- This wine is a classic example of a clean modern cool-climate Sauvignon Blanc. It displays aromas of gooseberries and guava on the nose and is dry yet fruity on the palate.

I don't know what kind of training it takes to make those distinctions, but it seems over-the-top to me. I actually don't have representations for what most of what they are saying. Boozy? Thin? Morello Cherry flavor in wine? Citrus flavor? Aromas of gooseberries and guava? Dry, yet fruity?

How about cigars?

It's a medium-full bodied cigar, with a fairly heavy taste in the mouth. The clarity of its flavors are pronounced, somewhat like a mesquite wood flavor.

Okay, and I don't get that at all. I don't smoke but I've tried a strong cigar and a couple of puffs would probably make me sick.

And how about bourbon whiskey?

It has a big carmel note, but it is also spicy.

My lack of discrimination here isn't the point. The point is that people can take something that really isn't good for the body (anything with alcohol or nicotine), that tastes bad to a novice, and with a lot of experience, produce connoisseur descriptions similar to this. In other words, it's possible to take something that tastes bad and learn to really like it. But to be fair, alcohol and nicotine stimulate the pleasure centers of the brain and that might be why it happens. My experience is that eggplant and ivy gourd do not stimulate the pleasure centers of my brain. There is nothing pleasurable about them.

Right now, I can take bitter and make it sweet in my imagination and then like it. But I cannot convince myself (YET) to like something that's bitter, sour, or spicy when I put it in my mouth and it tastes that way.

Also no one really knows the key metamodalities of taste. For example, one visual metamodality is color versus black and white. However, the cones in the eye are red, blue, and green. But those are not submodalities. Thus, why should taste metamodalities correspond to the taste buds as most online sources seem to suggest? My guess is that it's because few people have played around with it and perhaps we don't actually know the submodalities of taste.

There are definitely some foods that I don't like where I can trace that I dislike to an experience. For example, I generally don't like fish. About 15 years ago, I was in Alaska and I watched someone catch a salmon in the river. I watched as he immediately killed it and cut off the head. I felt bad and then suddenly had a flashback to when I was five. I went fishing with my grandfather and I caught a little sunfish. When we returned from fishing my grandfather wanted me to prepare it for eating. I watched him cut off the head and then he wanted me to gut it and take off the scales. I felt revolted, and I don't remember whether I did it or not. That evening we had the fish for dinner, and I was supposed to eat it. I don't know if I even tasted it, but from that time forward I associated fish with that experience of gutting and scaling a fish even though I don't remember doing it. I haven't liked fish since then.

In addition, I don't like shrimp and there is a reason for that. I don't remember exactly why I picked shrimp, but I remember being told that one might get out of military service with a strong allergy – I didn't ask what kind, but I think I immediately formed an allergy to shrimp. It didn't get me out of military service. I was the company clerk of an Infantry Battalion during the Vietnam War (fortunately, in the Canal Zone), but the allergy I formed was real. For example, I remember being at my sister's house and eating something. About four hours later I was vomiting, and the vomit tasted like shrimp. Unknown to me, my sister had served shrimp in one of the dishes I'd eaten. That experience told me I'd developed a real allergy, which I now associate with my experience throwing up. I've never eaten shrimp since that time, yet I know how that dislike happened. I deliberately created it, although I'm not sure how (I sort of willed it), but I don't think I liked shrimp before that time anyway. I also tend to dislike shellfish because it reminds me of shrimp.

I also remember that I spent two years in Japan from the time I was two until I was almost five. But I don't like Japanese food. When I asked my former Japanese nanny why I didn't like Japanese food, she said, "Your mother was a great cook and you only ate her food." That didn't tell me why I didn't like it (except for my narrow taste range). It just told me that I never tried to develop a taste for it.

Okay, so I have all this conditioning in addition to a probably natural aversion to bitter and sour and probably an acquired dislike of spicy (hot spicy is okay, but other versions are not, and I don't know how to describe the distinction). Let's see if I can learn to like some of those foods.

Let's now look at "boring." To do that, let's do another metamodalities comparison related to motivation. Think of a task that you love to do. Here a memory of doing "it" is fine. Compare that with something you might do (that's similar) but that you would find very boring. Also, don't pick something that doesn't have clear metamodalities distinctions for you. In fact, you might pick several tasks you find are "fun" to do and several you find boring so that you clearly get the distinctions.

Meta Modalities Checklist

What do you see?

Visual Qualities	Boring Situation	Motivated	Distinction
Movie or still			
Panoramic or framed			
Color vs. black and white			
Brightness (1-10)			
Location (up-down-left-right)			
Associated/dissociated			
Distance of picture from self			
Color intensity (1-10)			
Contrast (1-10)			
Movement (tempo)			
Angle viewed from			

What do you hear?

Auditory Qualities	Boring	Motivated	Distinction
Volume			
Location of source			
Uniqueness of sound			
Voices? Whose?			
Speed			
Intensity			
Other			

What do you feel?

Kinesthetic Qualities	Boring	Motivated	Distinction
Hot/cold (1-10)			
Movement			
Vibration			
Pressure (sharp, dull)			
Intensity			
Weight			
Size of feeling			
Other quality			

As an example, I'll do this exercise for you. In this case, I'm giving a lecture. I'm really good at talking about position sizing and risk control and I'm really good at helping others apply various transformation techniques. But I don't like talking about position sizing (I've done that and it doesn't excite me), but I love helping people work through a major transformation.

Meta Modalities Checklist
What do you see?

Visual Qualities	Teaching trans-formation	Math related teaching like position sizing	Distinction
Movie or still	Movie	Still	Strong
Panoramic or framed	Panoramic	Panoramic	
Color vs. black and white	Color	Black and white	Strong
Brightness (1-10)	7	3	
Location (up-down-left-right)	Straight ahead	Straight ahead	
Associated/dissociated	Associate	Dissociated	Strong
Distance of picture from self	N/A	2 feet	
Color Intensity (1-10)	7	N/A	
Contrast (1-10)	5	5	
Movement (tempo)	Slight	None	
Angle viewed from	Straight ahead	Behind me	Face audience vs Face math

What do you hear?

Auditory Qualities	Transformational	Math Related	Distinction
Volume		Light	
Location of source		Behind me as I look at problem.	
Uniqueness of sound			
Voices? Whose?		Someone in audience	
Speed			
Intensity			
Other		I don't get it	

What do you feel?

Kinesthetic Qualities	Transformational	Math Related	Distinction
Hot/cold (1-10)	5	4	
Movement	2		
Vibration	0	0	
Pressure (sharp, dull)	None	None	
Intensity	None	None	
Weight	Light	Heavy	Strong
Size of feeling	Fills chest	Stomach	Strong
Other quality	Expansive	Contracting	Strong

In doing transformation, I'm interacting with the audience and I can see the changes happening. In the position sizing one, someone doesn't get how I got a particular answer and that gives me two jobs (explaining how I got my answer) and finding where the other person made an error – and that's the part I really dislike.

I can change the metamodalities to teaching position sizing to one in which I see a movie in color. That gives might a light, expansive feeling that fills my chest. And then I can see transformation happening and them really getting it. However, what I can't stop is a voice that might come up from someone in the audience that says, "I don't get it. My answer is different."

The Effectiveness of Just Using Metamodalities

Richard Bandler used to believe (and may still) that if you determine the metamodalities of something and transfer that to something else, you can produce the same effect in the second thing that you had in the first. For example, if you have a compulsion to do something can you simply just apply that to something useful such as making money. Can you compel yourself to spend your time doing money making activities?

Richard Bandler would say find the metamodalities of some other compulsion and transfer it to making money. But the problem is that it doesn't always work. Why? It doesn't always work because there are often higher frames that drive it.

What could those be? Some examples might be:

- You have a sense that it's not me.
- It's not a "must have" thing for you or you don't believe you can have it or that you don't even deserve it.
- It conflicts with what you believe to be in your control, for example, you might believe that everything is outside of you and in the power of others.

We'll explore these a lot more in subsequent chapters. But, for now, let's look at one of those. It's an exercise on what you define as "me" and "not me."

Metamodalities Versus Self-Image

What's the status of me having to eat foods I don't like right now? The most important thing is that I'm eating them and that's a function of motivation. My health is important to me and part of my Ayurvedic Therapy is to eat this particular food. And I'm doing it. They are giving me small proportions (about a third of the original size) and I'm eating it. And rather than just saying that I don't like it, I'm exploring the specific tastes of each food – which makes it more interesting.

However, when I proposed the idea of making the disliked food become something I like (such as a Bourbon connoisseur or a cigar connoisseur might do), I found myself revolted at the thought. There was a clear – THAT'S NOT ME. I'm not someone who likes those sorts of food.

Thus, if I want further change, then I have to change the essence of who I am. And that's possible with another pattern that we'll explore now. There are seven steps to this pattern.

Exercise: "True for Me" Versus "No Longer Me"

The following pattern is one that I have adopted from Dr. Hall's Cleaning House Pattern.[2]

Step 1: Make an extensive list of qualities that you want, and don't want, about yourself.

What qualities, behaviors, and traits do you have that you no longer want? These could be ways of thinking, ways of being, and emotions that don't work for you in your present context. What qualities and highly-desired traits do you want to include? This step is designed to help you make some major changes in yourself. However, you can simply pick one that you want to change such as my desire to make foods I don't like to become ones that I will at least tolerate. And I'd like to also have a more exploring/open nature about foods.

	Non-Desired Qualities	**Desired Qualities**
1		
2		
3		
4		
5		
6		
7		
8		
9		
10		

Step 2: Determine how you represent the idea that something is no longer you.

Think of something that is true about yourself that you absolutely love, appreciate and value. Pick something that you feel great about. What quality do you really adore about yourself?

_____

_____

_____

_____

In my case I'm going to pick my ability to teach something that helps others transform. It's fascinating how I can take something that I might not have talked about for three to six months, glance down at my workshop notes and perhaps write down a few keywords, and then it suddenly flows out of me, often with new insights. And I especially love the new insights that might result in me changing workshop notes a little bit.

How do you represent the experience (visually, auditorily, kinesthetically metamodalities)?

_____

_____

_____

_____

In my case, it's a process. So, let me talk about how I organized this book. First, I already had written a lesson on propulsion systems. I don't remember how I did that, but I could describe the process of getting there just as I'm describing the process of organizing this book.

- I would probably get several books on the process or concept that I'm going to be studying, as well as Google it.
- I would probably Photoread[3] the books to get the essence of them. And if I found one or two particularly valuable, I'd read them in more detail and highlight them.
- I'd transcribe my notes into my computer.

- I'd probably sit on it for a while and then I'd have a conversation with my Inner Guidance about the topic. A 30-minute conversation with Her can save me hours, even though she often makes me answer my own questions to Her. Here is an example this morning of her comments after I wrote a summary on an essay by Aldous Huxley entitled *Beliefs*.
    - Van: So, what do you think of this article?

- Durga: **What do you think of it?**
- Van: Well, let me list the main points I got out of it and then let's talk about them.
- Durga: **Okay**.
- Van: Here is what I remember:
  - The article is about beliefs, but the word "belief" is not mentioned anywhere in the article. That's strange.
  - He talks about how science only looks at what can be measured or in some way measured by mathematics. And he talks about how limiting that is.
  - He also quotes David Hume saying, "That which is not subject to measurement or mathematic modeling or abstract reasoning is illusory and should be put into flames."
  - And then he says that would apply to Shakespeare, a symphony, or something like Michelangelo's David.
- Durga: **And is that useful to you?**
- Van: Not really except some of the quotes were interesting. I now know that I would probably avoid David Hume.
- Durga: **Then why don't you do what you are trained to do. PhotoRead the article. Decide from that if it's worthwhile. If it is, then activate it and we can discuss it. If it's not, then just move on to something else. That would have saved you an hour today.**
- Van: Thank you.

- As a result of this process, I'd probably have about ten points that I'd want to cover. In this book, for example, I wrote down all of the propulsion systems that we cover and decided that each would be a chapter if I had enough material.

- I would then review whatever I had about a particular topic and list that out, and that would be the basis for a chapter. And at that time, I'd just let the material flow. Right now, as I write this, the process of organizing this material is just flowing out of me.

- Once the book is written, I'd then read it to see how well if flows and if it makes sense. If it doesn't make sense, I'd determine what needed to be changed by asking 1) what doesn't flow?, 2) what needs more explanation? and 3) will people get it?

- And then I'd redo sections I didn't like, using much the same process.

After that, it's just editing and correcting; getting other people to review it and then responding to what they say. I find this process much less exciting and I wish it were not part of the book process. With a book going to a publisher, this process could take a year. This book I expect to write during the six weeks I'm in India and then I'll turn it over to my staff for edits and then to my Super Trader students for comments.

Dr. Michael Hall would next suggest that you run this through his Matrix Model, His eight matrices are listed in the table below and I've added a ninth – God. Dr. Hall, who has been trained as a minister, puts God in the Meaning Matrix.

Meaning	
State	
Intention	
God	
Self	
Other	
Power	
Time	
World	

Here are my comments about this process within the Matrix Model.

Meaning	Some people need to be motivated and if I can provide that, I will increase the amount of self-transformation we can help others make.
State	Creativity, flow state.
Intention	I want to motivate people to get as much out of the Peak Performance course/Super Trader program as I can. So, this book is essential to help them become motivated.
God	My Divine wants me to do this and is inspiring it.
Self	It's not me doing it. I just have to get out of the way and let it flow.
Other	I want to help people who really want to work on themselves and I want to give them as much as I can to aid them in their transformations.
Power	I want to inspire others. I can do that. They can transform.
Time	This book needs to be written now within the next five weeks. It will be finalized when it's time and I have no idea about that.
World	This encompasses my business, my spiritual growth, my family, my customers – almost everybody.

What makes these representations stable?

_____

_____

_____

_____

This is coming out of my highest values. It's who I am.

Step 3: Elicit a self-image representation of what's "No Longer Me"

Think of something that was true of you once but is no longer fits you. What fits into this category for you? For example, was something true of you as a teenager that is no longer true for you as an adult? Is there something that fit you as a child but is totally alien to you now? Did you once hold a limiting belief that you now think is no longer useful or even perhaps stupid?

_____
_____
_____
_____

I once was a research psychologist doing government contract work. I had no freedom of direction. I was told what I could and could not do. My creativity was stifled. I wanted to study success, but instead, I was doing government contract work. My boss on each project was usually some government employee in Washington, D.C.

How do you represent "Not True of Me" and/or "No Longer True of Me?"

_____
_____
_____
_____

The "true of me" was a process that flowed out of me. This (what's not true for me) is a still, black-and-white image. It's in the past (behind me). I made it big to look at it, but it's not useful and I could shrink it down, so it is very small. Over time, I've destroyed or let go of all the details related to that "no longer me." That was sometimes difficult to do because I'd ask, will I ever need this again. Can I go back? But I'm over 70 years old now. There's no chance I'll ever go back to working for the government, and I love what I do now, helping others increase their awareness.

Meaning	
State	
Intention	
God	
Self	
Other	
Power	

Time	
World	

Meaning	It is the past, and it is no longer me. And when it was me, I disliked it intensely.
State	Boring, loathing.
Intention	Move away from and get rid of this.
God	It was useful in my development, but no longer part of my destiny. I now follow my Inner Guidance.
Self	It's not me.
Other	I don't think it really helped anyone either except perhaps for government officials who paid for the research and could say they accomplished something.
Power	Not mine.
Time	All in the past.
World	It reminds me of the models of science and how to get things done that are not useful.

Step 4: Contrast the two representations from Step 2 and Step 3.

Visual	True of Me	Not True of Me
Associated/dissociated		
Location of picture		
Color/Black and White		
Movie or still		
Framed or panoramic		
Contrast (1-10)		
Color Intensity		
Brightness (1-10)		
Focus (fuzzy/clear)		
Horizontal or vertical		
Number of pictures		
How far away?		
Distance to central object		
Other visual differences		
Auditory	**True of Me**	**Not True of Me**
Voice? Whose?		
Other sounds?		
Location of voice		

Visual	True of Me	Not True of Me
Pitch		
Volume		
Intensity		
Speed		
Tonality		
Inflection		
Rhythm		
Clarity		
Duration		
Music? What music?		

Kinesthetic	True of Me	Not True of Me
Location		
Intensity		
Size		
Sharpness		
Pressure		
Duration		
Rhythm		
Vibration		
Movement		
Warm/cold		
Heavy/light		
Other kinesthetic		

Van's Example: *I'm basically comparing a very dynamic process (true of me) with a still image in the past and those are a very, very different. I don't need to fill this out, but I'll complete it as an example. However, you probably cannot have a much greater difference than a still image versus a dynamic process.*

Visual	True of Me	Not True of Me
Associated/dissociated	Associated	Dissociated
Location of picture	Unfolding in front	Small behind (in past)
Color/Black and white	Color	Black and white
Movie or still	Movie	Still
Framed or panoramic	N/A	Framed
Contrast (1-10)	N/A	2
Color Intensity	N/A	
Brightness (1-10)	N/A	3

Focus (Fuzzy/Clear)	N/A	Fuzzy
Horizontal or vertical	N/A	
Number of pictures	Many	1
How far away?		20 feet plus behind me
Distance to central object	N/A	N/A
Other visual differences	Moving organization process.	
Auditory	**True of Me**	**Not True of Me**
Voice? Whose?	Mine	None
Other sounds?		
Location of voice		
Pitch		
Volume		
Intensity		
Speed		
Tonality		
Inflection		
Rhythm		
Clarity		
Duration		
Music? What music?		
Kinesthetic	**True of Me**	**Not True of Me**
Location	Vibration in the chest that is expansive.	No feeling unless I try to bring it closer and associate with it. Then it is a sick feeling in the stomach.
Kinesthetic	**True of Me**	**Not True of Me**
Intensity		
Size		
Sharpness		
Pressure		
Duration		
Rhythm		
Vibration		
Movement		
Warm/Cold		
Heavy/Light		
Other Kinesthetic		

Step 5: Identify the meta-levels in the structures of the two self-representations of "True of Me" or a "No Longer Me."

Identify the meta-levels/meta-states within these experiences.

Matrix	True of Me	No Longer Me
Meaning		
State		
Intention		
God		
Self		
Other		
Power		
Time		
World		

Here are my comparisons.

Matrix	True of Me	No Longer Me
Meaning	Help other with transformation	Stay away, it's not me
State	Excitement	Boring
Intention	Motivate People/ My purpose	Get rid of this/move away from it
God	God inspired	Necessary in past
Self	Let it flow through self	It's not me
Other	Help others	Government bureaucrats
Power	I can do this	Not me
Time	Now	Past
World	Help as many people as I can. Now willing to be famous.	I wish they didn't exist. They are a pain.

How do you represent them?

_____

_____

_____

_____

"True for me" is a visual process that's very organized and unfolds. I can see it happening and describe it easily although it's done unconsciously. "Not true for me" is a distant image in the past that's a long way away.

How do they differ?

_____
_____
_____
_____

Dramatically, as described in the last paragraph, "Unfolding process versus distant image in the past."

What do you say "yes" to versus "no" to?

_____
_____
_____
_____
_____

I say "yes" to my purpose. I say "no" to lack of freedom and lack of creativity and to government restraints and to working for someone else.

What historical representations do you use that "makes sense" of them?

_____
_____
_____
_____
_____

True for Me: *Active unfolding process. It's like a book creating itself.*

Not True for Me: *Small dark picture that I can hardly see a long way behind me.*

Step 6: Look at your lists developed so far and do the following steps:

- What are the differences between "true for me" and "not true for me?"
- Sort them out.
- Step into the differences. Do this for each one until you are fully aware of the two formats.

I have described them in some detail above. And this is a very powerful process for me.

What I need to decide is do I develop a" not me" image of liking certain foods and then use it to become like me.

The "not me" liking certain foods is a small dark image but it is in the future. The image of me liking foods is an unfolding process, I learn to appreciate, and I learn to experiment. And it is part of me transforming myself and getting rid of an old image.

At a restaurant, what's something I haven't tried that I might like but never would have tried?. What are others loving that I'm not trying?

See myself ordering it.

Savor it and notice the metamodalities of the food. Ask, "What do I really like about this?" "How can I feel good about myself for eating this?" "How is this a new, transformed me?"

How am I demonstrating transformation through this?

Ask is there a way I can become a connoisseur of this?

It's part of my purpose. It's a transformation.

Step 7: Build a procedure to automatically delete and install in your mind

With an awareness of "not me" put what you do not want into that format.

Set up a "true for me" image for each "not me" that you wish to change. Put the true image behind and then "swish" it into the true image. The description of the swish pattern is given below. I'd also recommend that you go to YouTube and watch several examples of the pattern before you do it.

This is a little difficult because I'm putting the distant small image in front of the bigger image that gets swished into it.

Do these seven times for each pair and then break your state and move on to the next one when it seems to be in place.

Exercise: The Swish Pattern

One of the most commonly taught NLP patterns is called the Swish Pattern. In it you need to use the images you have already developed above. You should have a "true for me" (desired) image. Put that particular image behind an image that is "no longer me," or the unwanted, image. In other words, start with the "not true for me" image in front and the "no longer me" image behind.

Check the ecology (future impact) of the new self-image and the behavior that might be associated with it. What will you have to give up/take on to install this new "true for me" image? How will it impact others? Is it okay to do this process?

Identify at least two metamodalities that reduce the "not me" image and increase the "true for me" image. These should be metamodalities that vary over a range (i.e., brightness from 1 to 10).

Make sure that increasing it in the "not me," makes it more "like me." And check the reverse, make sure that decreasing it in the "like me" makes it more like the "not me."

Now put the "not me" in front and the new "like me" image behind.

You should be associated in the "not me" picture and disassociated in the "like me" picture so that you don't have the feeling of already making the change.

When you are ready, swish the "like me" through the "not me" as quickly as possible, changing those two critical metamodalities. And you should end up associated with the new "like me" pattern. Do this at least seven times and the last one should take about a second to do.

When you are finished, test it. Imagine yourself in a situation with the new me and notice what that is like.

If you are doing a number of these process, rather than just one, then stand up and move around to break the state between each process.

Van's experience: *I'm going to use the speed of movement of the unfolding together with the expansion in my chest as the primary drivers. I'm associated with the "not me" feeling of liking it (which doesn't feel like me). And I'm moving the new "true for me" image through this one until I'm associated with it and the motion and feeling is quite fast.*

I could only do it about five times, and it became harder and harder to maintain the "not me" image. The swish would take about a second, but the expansion and unfolding would take as much as 30 seconds after that,

It feels as if I will do the unfolding process in a restaurant, but I won't really know until I do it. However, I can test it a little bit on tonight's dinner.

Later comment: It worked well because I actively think about it when I'm with my wife ordering something at a restaurant.

Notes

[1] Dr. Michael Hall says that these are not part of the major sense modalities, but higher levels of organization, so he calls them metamodalities.

[2] Adapted from Chapter 3 of the training manual entitled, *Propulsion Systems: NLP and Nuero-Semantics Propulsion Systems* by Dr. L. Michael Hall, Neurosemantics Publications, Clifton, CO., 2002.

[3] Photoreading is a technique developed by Paul Scheele of Learning Strategies Corporation to read to get information directly into your unconscious mind.

CHAPTER 4

Propulsion as a Strategy

We have talked about motivation as a metamodality change. Now let's look at motivation as a strategy. You find yourself in a situation in which you would like more motivation, and then you employ a mental strategy to get yourself motivated. In other words, you go through a sequence of representations and the last one triggers a specific modality change (probably to your feelings) that gets you motivated.

We discussed such mental strategies in volume 5 of the Peak Performance Course, but here we will focus solely on motivation strategies. Motivation typically comes into play when you want to get yourself to do something that you are not particularly interested in doing. Typical examples might include:

- Getting yourself out of bed in the morning
- Exercising
- Cleaning up
- Doing routine maintenance
- Studying
- Organizing things
- Exercising
- Losing Weight
- Working on Issues Exploring Yourself

The question becomes, "What sequences of steps do you go through to get enough impetus to do it?" Translated in a different way, it might be, "What do you need to do to ratchet up some particular metamodality to the point where you actually do it?"

If you are a move-toward person, the question might be, "How do you get yourself to move toward something positive when you aren't excited about doing it?" If you are a move away from person, the question might be, "How do you get yourself motivated enough to move away from something negative?"

What's important to note is that you must go through some sort of metamodality change to be motivated. But you probably have a strategy (you might call it a context) through which you take yourself in order to get that metamodality change. It's your way of doing it. Our goal here is to make that process conscious for you.

Strategy 1: Eating Food I Don't Like

I'm in an Ayurvedic clinic in India. I don't like the food, but I eat it. How do I motivate myself to eat it? I'm quite surprised that I am eating it. The picture below is an example of what I got on the first or second day here.

First, I have no idea what I was eating. It wasn't like I had a choice. The food for each meal would show up in my room. In this picture, the green slices looked like slices of chili, but they were not hot. It was sort of rubbery and quite spicy. It was ivy gourd. The largest helping was a mix of quinoa with different vegetables nothing particularly bad about it but nothing delightful. The two tangerines were pretty good.

At first, the portions were huge – not only was the food something I didn't like; it was also more than I could eat. But I'd eat it until I couldn't anymore (which is somewhat less than if I'd liked it).

The thought process was:

- I'm here for my health.
- I'm here to learn about myself (like learning the metamodalities of taste).
- So, eat it. And I'd save what I thought I might like (e.g., the tangerines) for the end.
- After each bite I'd notice the metamodalities and the different tastes. And I'd say to myself, "So it has this sort of taste, what's causing you to not like it?"
- That question would often be hard to answer. It might be sour or spicy, or have a very unusual taste. It generally didn't fall into the category of something I liked, but I couldn't answer why I didn't like it. My label for it was "I don't like it." And sometimes I'd feel like gagging after eating it.
- I had a choice. I could eat more. I could just leave it. Or, I could throw it down the toilet. The third choice was tempting but I never did that – at least not for the first two weeks.
- Seeking to answer the question would be enough to get me to take another bite or take a bite of one of the other foods.
- Eventually, I'd feel satiated and a little like, "If I eat any more, then I might throw it up." And so I'd stop.

What's happening here? Two of my top values are immediately coming into play. Health and learning about myself. When I elicit those, there is a lightness in my head that I'd probably label curiosity. And there is a warmth in my chest and gut that seems to be enough to take the first bite. If those two feelings are there, I will continue to eat.

I go onto the next bite, because I cannot figure out what is causing me to have the reaction, "I don't like it." Thus, the lightness in my head (curiosity) continues. I seem to have a rule that says if you cannot tell exactly why you don't like it, keep eating. I never really figure it out. A cop-out, such as it tastes awful, is not allowed. I must decide what specific taste is awful.

Eventually, a new feeling comes up. It's either a feeling in my gut that says, "You are full," or a feeling in my throat that says, "If you eat any more, you'll be sick." Fortunately, I get the full feeling quite quickly these days.

Now there was one exception and that is the dish shown at the bottom of the next picture. Take one bite of it and you get a very strong bitter taste plus a very hot spicy taste. I'm willing to say that those two taste combinations equate to "I don't like it at all." It was bitter gourd.

In this picture you can see rice. I usually love rice, but their rice was very bland (no butter, no salt) which makes it just okay. The small dish (bitter gourd) is what's very, very bitter and hot. Those little black balls are pepper which is also quite hot, but not as hot as something else in the dish.

One of my strategies for getting through my meals is that I asked the staff here to cut the portions down to a third of the initial size. That meant I could pretty much eat everything without feeling full. What you are seeing in the picture is the amount they gave me to eat, minus one small bite.

In this case, I clearly identified the metamodalities of "I don't like." Now what? I went through the following strategy in my head.

One of the beliefs of Ayurveda is that you need to eat foods of all different sorts of tastes. My wife had also said to me, "That's bitter gourd – it's very good for you."

Consequently, I ate about three bites as quickly as I could. I didn't want to explore the taste at all.

It's clear to me what my strategy is for eating this food. First, I immediately bring in two of my highest values as reasons for eating it. Without those I wouldn't touch it.

Those values evoke two feelings that seem to be the metamodalities for motivation. The curiosity feeling (lightness in the head and a push forward) and a lightness in my chest (do it for your health).

That's enough to motivate me.

However, a sub-strategy goes off with each bite. I'm asking the question, "What is the metamodality of "I don't like?" Answering that question drives me to take the next bite. I usually can't answer the why part of the question. I can easily say I don't like it, but not why, so I keep eating. That continues until the other feelings come up (gag reflex in throat or satiation feeling in the stomach).

In the one instance where there was no lightness in the head propelling me forward, the chest motivation was still there, and I made an agreement to eat half as quickly as I could.

In the past, when my Super Traders have done their motivation strategy, I don't remember too many instances where they clearly brought a strong value into play and that was the primary moving force. But it was the case for me.

Later, another variable came into play – frequency of having to eat the food. They fed me pomegranates. I gave them feedback that I really liked those and for about four days I got huge helpings of pomegranates for both breakfast and dinner. Pretty soon I couldn't eat them anymore. Too much of a good thing makes it negative for me.

Strategy 2: Moving Away From A Food Addiction

I've been in another situation with food for my health that is totally different. My friend Bruce Du Ve put me on a ketogenic diet where I was eating about four ounces of pork or beef each day and that's it. Here I'm doing the diet for the same value reason. I like the meat that I'm eating in the ketogenic diet (although it does become boring after a while) but I don't have to force myself to eat something to which I would normally say, "I don't like that."

Here, an entirely new sort of motivation comes into play. The ketogenic diet quickly shows you how much you are addicted to carbs and sweet things. For the first three to four days, there is a constant craving which I must ignore. That really isn't too difficult when and if I can keep away from the food I crave. But it's very hard when the food you crave is everywhere.

Picture the following situation. I have been on the ketogenic diet for about ten weeks. I'm at a workshop in London, sitting at the back of the room. The hotel staff is bringing in snacks for the workshop participants. These consist of cookies, brownies, puddings, and other sorts of sweet things. These are placed about three feet behind me and I can smell them. I definitely know they are there.

Bruce says that when you do this sort of diet, you eventually get to the point where you no longer crave this sort of food. In fact, you might not like it. But after ten weeks, I wasn't there – not even close. I could resist something tempting for about 30 minutes with me seeing and smelling it. 30 minutes of resistance was about my limit before I would act.

So, what happened with the ketogenic diet?

My health motivation was fully in place and I'd been able to maintain the diet for about ten weeks. Perhaps there were occasional slip ups, but I'd been good enough to lose about 25 pounds.

The food is placed behind me. I see it, and most importantly, I smell it. The smell is enough to produce cravings for the food. The average person has an addiction for sweet foods and refined carbohydrates that is probably as strong as the addiction others have to heroin or cocaine. I'm probably average at best in terms of my resistance.

The smell is almost compelling me to take some and eat it. The process in my head goes:

- Wow, I'd love some of that.
- You can't, it's not on your diet.
- But you can cheat just one time. Just a small cookie.

- You can't – it's not on your diet.
- This process is constant. There are probably two countermeasures and I have perhaps 30 minutes in which to pull them off.

"Option one: Move away from the food." That is not an option when I'm at a workshop and I'm the guest of honor. I must sit with the food right behind me.

Option two might be to find a distraction to keep me busy so this dialogue would not happen in my head. It would have to be a strong enough distraction that it would keep the thoughts and smell blocked for a significant period.

I tried several of these – telling the hotel staff to only bring healthy foods (they still brought two to three addictive foods).

Telling the hotel staff to take away the food as quickly as possible. But it would always be there at least two hours (and my threshold was about thirty minutes).

Eventually, I'd give in and have something. And then it's like giving an addict a little hit. Once you have some you can't stop. It only takes one cookie to take one out of ketosis.

I tend to be a move-toward person. I find that motivating myself to not move toward something I crave when it is around to be much more difficult than eating things that I don't like when there is no temptation for other foods around. At the point where I'd been at the Ayurvedic clinic for 22 days, I had no addictive food around to eat and I was not craving it at all.

In addition, on the ketogenic I'd also developed a minor "healing crisis" in that a cyst had appeared on my back and during the workshops it had opened and was starting to ooze. Having a healing crisis – which you can get on this sort of diet – also tends to overcome the impact of my primary value of getting healthy. Getting rid of the cyst requires some painful in-patient surgery – which I would prefer not to experience again.

Postscript

The day after writing this, I looked at my dinner and decided to throw it away. I had a sense of revulsion and acted spontaneously. However, I didn't go away from my motivating value here – my health. I happen to believe that fasting is good for you. So not eating the food, in my mind, is as healthy as eating it. What would be bad is eating some of the foods I normally crave.

The next day was my first trip to a shopping center. I saw several opportunities to eat food I love, but I passed them by. The craving wasn't that strong and the value of working on myself and health predominated.

 I also did a feeling release on the feeling of revulsion. My food just came in and I'm noticing some of that feeling just from the smell. Okay, smell is a part of this even though I haven't noticed smells. I will look at dinner and eat it or notice the feeling, do a feeling release, and then eat it.

One thing has now become clear for me. Motivation and liking are not the same. You can be motivated to eat foods you don't like. It's like the priest being so motivated by **his beliefs that he was willing to die a slow death where his feet were burnt off first** and then slowly consumed more and more of him. Eating foods that you don't like is nothing compared to that.

Today, working on myself is my highest priority so I need to get through this. I'm beginning to conclude that to some extent "liking of foods" may be hard-wired or a function of karma, because it's very hard to change.

I originally thought if people could like bourbon or cigars, then people could learn to like anything. But alcohol and nicotine trigger the pleasure centers of the brain. Ivy gourd and eggplant do not – at least, not mine

The following exercise is not necessarily a motivation strategy, but it could help you develop a strong one. Try it.

Exercise: Motivational Pattern

What do you want to be more motivated about – so much so that you really want to run and get it?

_____

_____

_____

_____

Do you know how to do it? If not, focus the rest of the pattern on becoming motivated to learn how?

Yes____ No____

What's valuable about it? Why is this important to you? How will it enrich your life?

_____

_____

_____

_____

Think about a time when you wanted to work on _____ but you became distracted – your mind went elsewhere.

As you think about what you put into the blank space, determine why that is important to you?

Your response – list as many whys or reasons as you can:

_____

_____

_____

_____

What is important about X – where X is each of the whys or reasons listed above? Why is that important? Make a list. In other words, you are making a list for each of the criteria above.

_____

_____

_____

_____

When you think about it (read the list you just generated), these are important. Why are they important? Make another list.

_____

_____

_____

_____

When you think about (referring to the last list), why are the things you listed important? Make another list.

_____

_____

_____

_____

When you get those, just the way you like it, what does it give you? In other words, you are moving up into higher and higher values, which might be levels of motivation.

_____

_____

_____

_____

_____

So, you get that _____ is important?

Is there anything even more important than that? Is that the top? You are going for the very top-most important thing – a top value. It should be obvious when you find it.

When you are certain that you are at the top, then step into that.

Take a deep breath and let that sense of (what you decided was more important) _____ fill your whole neurology.

What if this were the state that you were operating from every day?

When you are ready, look at doing (what you want to be motived to do) _____ from the perspective of that top value.

Is this strong enough to get your attention? Does it drive you?

Is this a big enough reason why?

So, when will you start working on that? _____

So, imagine that time in the future, when you are operating from this highest intention. What is that like? How is it for you?

If necessary:

> Now imagine your future with you operating out of this highest intention or value?
> What does that feel like?
> How does this impact your sense of who you are, your sense of self?

So, do you really want it? What if someone prevented you from having it or took it away? Would you want that? (You must feel a strong "no" response here to indicate it's highly motivating).

Will you remember it? _____

Van's Example:

I'm not sure that I can get myself to like the foods I don't like, but I'm pretty sure that I can motivate myself to experiment more and be willing to try more things. That's what I want to move towards? Something, for example, was just brought in for breakfast. I have no idea what it is, but I decided I wouldn't like it just because of the smell. If I can get myself to be eager to try it (not necessarily like it), then I will have progressed on this exercise. So, my test is right in front of me. I will also condense the exercise because I already know what's most important to me.

What do you want to be more motivated about – so much so that you really want to run and get it?

Being willing to experiment with foods; savor them; and understand (if I don't like them) what there is about the taste/smell that I do not like.

Do you know how to do it? If not, focus the rest of the pattern on becoming motivated to learn how?

Yes, this is pure motivation. I'll know it works by two criteria. 1) I'll be eager to try the food they just delivered to my room; and 2) when I got to a restaurant, I'll be willing to order at least one different thing.

Why is this important to you? How will it enrich your life?

First, it is working on myself – my highest value. Second, I'm working on something that I've always thought was just me; I'd never get through it; Third, there is some awareness to it that I think will really show I've moved up in consciousness.

Think about a time when you wanted to work on *food issues* but your mind went elsewhere. As you think about that, why is that important to you? In your response – list as many reasons as you can:

I've already listed my highest values. But it's important to show that I've solved an issue that has plagued me; it will make my wife happy (also a top 5 value); and I'll feel good for having done something I wasn't sure was possible.

What is important about X – where X is each of the reasons above? Why is that important? Create a list. In other words, you are creating a list for each of the criteria above.

The only new thing I get is how amazing I'll feel if I can get through something, I've never been able to solve.

When you think about (read the list you just generated). These are important. Why are they important? Create another list.

I'm already at the top.

When you think about (referring to the last list). Why are they important? Create another list.

I'm already at the top.

When you get those, just the way you like it, what does it give you?

I'm already at the top. I will have worked on myself and overcome something I thought was impossible. It's a new breakthrough for me and I will feel like anything is now possible.

So, you get that *"overcoming any personal issue and anything is possible"* **is important?**

Is there anything even more important than that? Is that the top? You are going for the very top-most important thing? It should be obvious when you find it.

Yes, that's it.

If that's the top, step into that.

Take a deep breath and let that sense of *"you can overcome any personal issue"* **fill your whole neurology.**

What if this were the state that you were operating from every day? *Great*

When you are ready, look at *eating today's food (that I have no idea about)* **with those eyes. Is this strong enough to drive your attention?** *Yes.* **Is this a big enough reason why?** *Yes*

So, when will the next time be when you are working on that?

In about a minute when I try breakfast here.

So, imagine that future time, operating from this highest intention? How is that?

If necessary:

> **Now imagine your future with you operating out of this highest intention.**
> **How does that feel?**
> **How does this impact your sense of self?**

I have one possible objection and that is, "What if I get something I don't like? Could I have had something I like?"

Response: You can send it back and try something else. Keep ordering until you get something you really like.

Now that makes it exciting.

Maybe you shouldn't have this? Perhaps I should take it away. (You must feel a strong "no" response here to indicate it's highly motivating). *NOOOOO!*

Will you remember it? *Absolutely.*

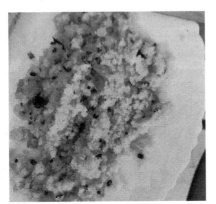

What happened: My breakfast consisted of two small bananas – not my favorite choice but fine and I enjoyed them. And this – what is shown in the picture. I have no idea what it was. When I tasted it, it was not something I liked but it was not something I really disliked either. And I thought with some flavor (and not so much pepper) I could like it more.

I was happy with those results.

CHAPTER 5

States, Metastates, Meaning, and Your Self-Definition

Let's make some important definitions to help us sort out propulsion systems. First, we will define pleasure as stimulating the senses, in a way that meets some sort of biological need, and in doing so makes us feel good about it. These are primary states of the senses. As such they might include:

- A prime steak cooked just the way you like it.
- A hot bath or a warm shower that relaxes you.
- Having a meal that totally stimulates the "best" aspects of your tastes and smell.
- Having a relaxing massage that invigorates you.
- Making love to the perfect partner in a way that gives maximum pleasure even before you climax.
- Sitting under a palm tree with a tasty drink with your eyes closed listening to the ocean waves.

These are all primary pleasures and have certain qualities in common: 1) They directly stimulate a number of your senses in a delightful way and have to do with the body directly; 2) The experience is in the "now" or the present moment; 3) They make you come alive; 4) They require no effort on your part; and 5) They are good for us – part of our survival mechanisms, and they feel pleasurable because we need to keep experiencing them to survive.

However, there is something else about pleasure that seems limiting. First, there are thresholds below which you experience very little and above which the pleasure becomes pain. When you have finished a good meal, for example, you don't want to eat any more. You are not hungry and eating more does not give you pleasure. In fact, you could probably eat to the point of feeling nauseous. When I got pomegranates twice a day for three straight days, they were no longer appealing to me.

In addition, these bodily sensations are short lived. Making love for hours usually doesn't work, especially for men. You eat a pleasurable meal until you are full and then it's not so pleasurable anymore. If one made love three times a day and ate the same wonderful meal three times a day, seven days a week, both would become boring, not pleasurable.

Finally, basic pleasure usually is not addictive. This has to do with the prior quality of pleasures being short lived and having a threshold beyond which they become a pain. *Addiction requires some higher-level meta-stating to give it a lot more meaning.* You'll understand that better when we cover addiction later in this book.

Now let's define meta-pleasures that are called happiness. What happens is we take a basic pleasure (or even a non-pleasure) and we instill it with all sorts of values, delight, importance, and significance. Then it becomes much more. We are essentially bringing higher level valuations about the primary state.

Richard Bandler, the cofounder of NLP, says that before you try to persuade someone,[1] you should get yourself in a ferocious state. Ferocious means MOTIVATED – you are ready to tackle anything. He'd look at a potential client, one whom he wished to motivate to do something, and say to himself, "Your Ass is Mine!" Or Richard might be sitting in an airplane and suddenly think to himself, "They are all strapped down; I could sell them anything!"

Part of the ferocious state, for Richard, involves thinking ridiculous things and believing them – for example, what he said to himself in the airplane. He says, "Go ahead and believe anything that will help you. It doesn't have to be true." His list might include:[2]

- Wake up in the morning thinking, "It's raining €500 bills." Finish the project and you can pick them up.
- Make things more and more exciting. If you don't, then things will just get duller.
- Sell feelings and totally believe in what you sell.
- Learn to love a challenge. When something gets difficult, that's when it becomes exciting.
- You can turn things into fun – there are no limits.
- When someone is doing something that works, figure out how they do it and then experiment with it.
- View cleints as "food to be devoured" Wouldn't they be even more delicious if they were covered with chocolate.
- View life in the greatest light. Everything works according to how it's created, and isn't today is the best day to be living life to the fullest?
- Attach wonderful feelings to anything and see what happens.

Later, Bandler talks about accessing the Puma State[3] and I've modified his words, hopefully without changing the meaning.

Float up in the air and see a huge puma below you. It's sleek with big white teeth, black fur, glistening. Now float down and become that puma. See out of its eyes. You are in a big canyon with high walls on either side and at the end of the canyon is your [client/project]. Look at them and think, "Your ass is mine."

First, try on some of Bandler's beliefs, and it doesn't matter if they are true or not. Then try on the Puma State. The results can be amazing. These are not primary states, they are what Dr. Hall would call metastates. In Richard's examples, we are not talking primary states, but things you imagine or create.

To illustrate, let's start by making a list of the things we enjoy. What do you really enjoy doing? What's fun for you? Make a list of at least ten things.

_____

_____

_____

_____

_____

_____

_____

What we define as being fun is rather unique for everyone. Let me give you a list of ten things that I enjoy. This list has no particular ranking of importance. In fact, some of these things I no longer do, but I defined them as fun and I would really enjoy them in the right context:

- Playing a round of golf where I'm totally in the flow and have a chance of a birdy (or better) on every hole when the ball lands on the green. For me that one is amazing.
- Skiing where I seem to be able to stay upright and go fast.
- Hang gliding where I'm totally in control and can sail on the wind for at least 20 minutes before it ends.

Now those are three things I no longer do. 1) The heat on a golf course tends to get to me and I don't play enough to have the experience anymore of always having a chance for a birdie. 2) After I broke my shoulder skiing and went through the pain of rehabilitating a frozen shoulder, I stopped skiing permanently. 3) Hang gliding requires expensive equipment and going to a place where that's possible. It's also dangerous, so while I might do it again, I no longer seek it out.

However, my list goes on, and it includes:

- Winning a poker tournament where there were at least 25 players.
- Playing certain games on my computer that give me an adrenaline rush;.
- Doing something creative, like writing this book, where the material literally just flows out of me.

- Visiting some place beautiful and historic where I get to learn new things. For example, in my last trip to England I visited Shakespeare's home; Winsor Castle; Leeds Castle; Oxford University; Cambridge University; Stonehenge and numerous other places and it was pure joy.
- Going on a romantic date with my beautiful wife.
- Experiencing a personal transformation.
- Helping someone else make a personal transformation and seeing them have that experience and their reaction to it.

You might look at my list and decide that some of those things are not fun at all. For example, if you define fun as scaling up a 3000-foot sheer cliff, I wouldn't agree. To me that's dangerous and terrifying and I'd never do it. You, in contrast might think that golf is a totally boring sport and wonder why anyone would enjoy it.

What you define as fun is basically a meta-pleasure. Such pleasures seem to have the following qualities:

- It's fun for you because of the meaning you give it. What's the context in which it is fun for you and what meaning do you give it?

- The experience requires us to devote a lot of attention and consciousness to the experience. What goes on is basically run in our heads. Playing golf at a level where my first putt on each hole is at least a birdy opportunity requires skill, practice, and a lot of attention.

- These metastates are different for each of us because we all bring our unique sense of values, beliefs, and frames of reference to them. It's not like pleasure where the primary qualities are "how much" and "to what degree."

Because we bring so many things to the metastate, it tends to be unique for each of us. I'm writing a book on propulsion systems. That has a unique meaning to me because of my values and interests. You might not even be able to imagine yourself writing such a book, much less putting yourself in a situation in which you constantly must look at your motivation (i.e., Why am I eating food that I do not like?).

When it comes to metastates, we are dealing with a system in which there is the whole metastate and many parts that come together for it to happen. When such Gestalts happen, there tend to be many emergent qualities. This tends to explain why some people like certain activities more than most could imagine. For example, a serial killer enjoys killing and acting out a certain pattern of behavior that 99.99% of the population could never imagine doing.

Lastly, there is usually a sense of flow that amounts to losing yourself when you are in such metastates. The person climbing a sheer cliff doesn't think about what she or he is doing until after they reach the top. While it's happening, there is a sense of transcendence and the mind is blank and it's the transcendence that is craved.

In summary, pleasure is a primary state that comes from the senses being stimulated in a particular way. Happiness is more of a metastate that comes from the significance we give to our pleasures and what happens.

Here is an exercise that increases personal power and blows out limitations.

Exercise: Becoming Bold and Ferocious

The following pattern was adopted from the Boldness Metastating Pattern given in *Propulsion Systems: NLP and Neurosemantic Propulsion Systems* by Dr. L Michael Hall.[4]

Step 1: Identify your block. What's stopping you? What stops you from doing something exciting, bold, and daring – something that you really want to experience, but then something holds you back?

So, remember a time when you really wanted to do something bold, you still feel you should have done it, but something stopped you. What was the primary level experience – the thing you wanted to do? For example:

- Invite someone to share an experience.
- Vacation in an exotic place.
- Do an act of kindness for "no reason."
- Do something weird in public just to push your limits.
- Really thrill a special person.
- Ask someone you are really attracted to for a date (if appropriate for your marital status).[5]

When you have all of these things, identify the key metamodalities involved by answering such questions as, "Where does the voice come from? Whose voice is it? What are the qualities of the voice? What are the qualities of the feelings involved? Where are they located? How big are they? What's the temperature? What other qualities do the feelings have? Vibration? Movement? Intensity?" Identify the qualities of any images you see, "Is it associated or dissociated? Where is the picture located (up, down, left, right)? Is it in color, 3D, panoramic or framed, a movie or a still? What stands out and seems important to you?"

_____

_____

_____

Step 2: What higher level (meta) experiences seem to get in the way?

- A voice said, "that's crazy" in a critical tone.
- Some image came up of a worst-case scenario that you imagined.
- Perhaps you got a bad feeling in your gut.
- Perhaps you just had a feeling of "I'd better not do that."

_____

_____

_____

_____

_____

Step 3: Determine the meaning you give it and then move through the sequence in a reverse manner.

Take each feeling sensation and allow them to become a picture or a voice. Ask the following:

- What would you look like or sound like?"
- What message do you contain?
- What meaning or significance do you have for me with regard to the experience I have imagined?
- What's the higher-level frame here?

Remember that higher-level frames always organize and govern lower frames and experiences. The frame runs the show. It creates both resources and limitations.

Whatever the meta-experience was, just keep increasing it until you have had enough. When it hits that point, just rewind it backwards – running everything backward in the representation of the memory. You might listen to the voice talk backward. Feel yourself walking backwards. Go back in time until before it existed.

Be there in that non-formed and non-structured time when you didn't have this particular issue. When you feel free of it, then fast-freeze that exact moment.

_____

_____

_____

_____

Step 4: Look at the limiting frame and determine if it's useful. Do some quality control on it.

In order to do the first three steps, you must go to a higher level – above and beyond it so that you can just observe the structure of your experience. From this position, check out the way you framed your limitation.

- Does it serve you?
- Does it limit you unnecessarily in any way?
- Does it make your life better?
- Is it in any way useful and thus serves you?

- Did it once have a positive function that no longer serves you?
- Once you see the limitations, make the higher level (meta-) decision, and say, "I will no longer accept this old frame! I will no longer tolerate this voice, image or feeling! I will recognize it and get rid of it."
- Say this strongly and congruently and let the old representation go away at a rapid rate of speed.

Step 5: When the old frame is gone (and you have a new one), then add some higher-level resources.

When the old frame has gone, add some new meta-frames. For example, hear a new voice that says, "You can enjoy yourself in a new a crazy way because it allows you to expand your skills and become even more effective."

- Feel this enjoyment as a blast that goes up your spine.
- Now hear yourself saying, "No problem, this will be fun and easy."
- Give yourself permission to feel bold and ferocious

_____

_____

_____

_____

Step 6: Feel a strong desire to move toward a more ferocious you.

Imagine yourself at the moment before the old limitation, before any taboo existed. But go there with your new resources. Feel the compulsion growing. Keep increasing it until you can feel it pull you.

Now begin to move forward in time with all of these new permissions, understandings, stills, and resources.

Let it grow even stronger as you move into your future, saying, "Oh, yes!"

_____

_____

_____

_____

Van's Example:

Step 1: Identify your block.
What's stopping you? What stops you from doing something exciting, bold, and daring – something that you really want to experience, but then something holds you back? So, remember a time when you really wanted to do something bold, you still feel you should have done it, but something stopped you.

I've got one. We were in Auckland, New Zealand, staying at the Skytower Hotel. They had an attraction at that hotel where you could jump off the top of the hotel and you'd almost free fall but they'd stop you before you went splat at the bottom. I really wanted to do that.

Step 2: What higher-level (meta) experiences seem to get in the way?

My wife said, "No, what if you get hurt? You've got workshops coming up next week. What if you get hurt and can't do the workshops? Do that some time when you don't have workshops coming up.

What stopped me was what my wife said, and me imagining that I might not be able to do the workshops.

Step 3: Determine the meaning you give it and then move through the sequence in a reverse manner.

With the kinesthetic and the feeling – allow them to become a picture or a voice. Ask the following:

- "What would you look like or sound like?"
- What message do you contain?
- What meaning or significance do you have for me with regard to the experience I have imagined?
- What's the higher-level frame here?

Remember that higher-level frames always organize and govern lower frames and experiences. The frame runs the show. It creates both resources and limitations.

Two of my higher-level values came up. My health and my business. I thought if I get hurt, I can't do the workshops.

Whatever the meta-experience was, just keep increasing it until you have had enough. When it hits that point, just rewind it backwards ... running everything backward in the representation of the memory. You might listen to the voice talk backwards. Feel yourself walking backwards. Go back in time until before it existed.

Be there in that non-formed and non-structured time when you didn't have the taboo. When you were free. FREEZE-FRAME that moment.

It didn't take much to increase it until I had enough and then I ran it backwards to before the taboo. It's not hard because before I cancelled my trip to Australia (after going to India), I was taking a trip to New Zealand after Australia. There were no workshops coming up (at least they were more than 30 days off) and I was planning to jump off the Skytower. The "what is," however, must not want me to do that because after I planned that I couldn't get a visa to Australia, and thus the New Zealand trip was also cancelled.

Step 4: Look at the limiting frame and determine if it's useful. Do some quality control on it.

In order to do the first three steps, you must go meta – above and beyond so that you can just observe the structure of your experience. From this position, check out the frame.

- Does it serve you?
- Does it create unnecessary limitations?
- Does it enhance your life?
- Have you had enough of that old frame?
- Did it use to have a positive function that no longer serves you?

Once you see the limitations, make the meta-decision, "I will no longer accept this old frame! I will no longer tolerate this voice, image or feeling!"

Say this strongly and congruently and let the old representation go away at a rapid rate of speed.

This one probably does not work well for that situation because the old frame was appropriate. I shouldn't risk getting hurt just before I'm scheduled to present. I probably would have done it without my wife saying something, but I now realize the wisdom in what she said. However, the next time I'm in Auckland, I'll make sure there are no workshops ahead of me and I'll jump.

Step 5: When the old frame is gone (and you have a new one) then add some higher- level resources.

When the old frame has gone, add some new meta-frames. For example, hear a new voice that says, "You can enjoy yourself in a new and crazy way because it allows you to expand your skills and become even more effective."

- Feel this enjoyment as a blast that goes up your spine.
- Now hear yourself saying, "No problem, this will be fun and easy."
- Give yourself permission to feel bold and ferocious.

Next time I'm in Auckland with no workshops ahead of me, I'll jump off the Skytower building. I can feel myself doing it and it is exhilarating.

Step 6: Feel a strong desire to move toward a more ferocious you.

Imagine yourself at the moment before the old limitation, before any taboo existed. But go there with your new resources. Feel the compulsion growing. Keep increasing it until you can feel it pull you.

Now begin to move forward in time with all of these new permissions, understandings, stills, and resources.

Let it grow even stronger as you move into your future, saying, "Oh, yes!"

I don't need to do this step because my wife's response (the taboo) was ecological. It was better for all concerned (me, my wife, and the clients at the workshop). For example, after I broke my shoulder skiing, I had to do a workshop and I could only use my left hand to write (I'm right-handed).

Exercise: Giving Yourself a Super Power Pleasure

The first step is to determine what's fun for you. Take something special from your fun list and describe it fully. What is there about it that is really fun? What are the sensory qualities and details? What makes that fun? Take that item through a submodalities checklist. You can just do one item. If you are not sure what details make it a super pleasure, then do a second one and notice the commonalities. Use the table below. This step may or may not be necessary. I did not use it in my example that follows.

Meta Modalities Checklist
What do you see?

Visual Qualities	Example 1	Example 2	Commonalities
Movie or still			
Panoramic or framed			
Color vs. black and white			
Brightness (1-10)			
Location (up-down-left-right)			
Associated/dissociated			
Distance of picture from self			
Color Intensity (1-10)			
Contrast (1-10)			
Movement (tempo)			
Angle viewed from			

What do you hear?

Auditory Qualities	Example 1	Example 2	Distinction
Volume			
Location of source			
Uniqueness of sound			
Voices? Whose?			
Speed			
Intensity			
Other			

What do you feel?

Kinesthetic Qualities	Example 1	Example 2	Distinction
Hot/cold (1-10)			
Movement			
Vibration			
Pressure (sharp, dull)			
Intensity			
Weight			
Size of feeling			
Other quality			

What do you taste?

Qualities	Example 1	Example 2	Distinction
Sour			
Sweet			
Salty			
Bitter			
Umami (savory)			
Strong/weak			
Warm/cold			
Crunchy			
Stringy			
Mushy			
Rubbery			
Slimy			

What do you smell?

Qualities	Example 1	Example 2	Distinction
Ashy			
Animal-like /musky			
Burnt/smoke			
Chemical/medicinal			
Chocolate			
Caramel			
Toast-like/cereal			
Earthy			
Floral			
Fruity/citrus			
Grassy/herbal			
Nutty			
Rancid/rotten			
Spicy			
Tobacco			
Woody			

Second, determine what higher-level meanings and significances you are giving to that item. Ask questions like 1) What's significant about that? 2) What does it mean to me? 3) What other positive meanings do I give to this fun thing that seems to make it really fun? Make a list.

_____

_____

_____

Now take each of the meanings in the prior list and note what each one means to you?

_____

Meaning 1: _____
Meaning 2: _____

_____

Meaning 1: _____
Meaning 2: _____

_____

Meaning 1: _____
Meaning 2: _____

Meaning 1: _____
Meaning 2: _____

You might repeat this process several times and keep adding to the list. Then when you are complete, notice what has emerged for you. What's the Gestalt?

What does this super-power pleasuring mean to you? What is its significance?

_____
_____
_____
_____
_____

The third step is to use your highest pleasuring. First, jump into this state, access it fully and completely. Be there in the state and feel all of this pleasure.

Fourth, become aware of these highest meanings of value and significance. Then ask yourself how you can take this state into some other everyday activity? How can you spread the joy around?

Finally, imagine fully being in this particular state, in some particular context, doing X, and take it into the future. (In other words, if I had this state fully and completely in just the way I want it, how will it alter my experience of, for example, work, relationships, learning. When you have the answer, spread your pleasure around and connect it to other behaviors.

_____

_____

_____

_____

Doing this exercise will enable you to 1) determine your pleasure strategy; 2) specify what you get out of the experience – conceptually. It identifies your meaning world -– the frames out of which you live to experience joy and pleasure.

_____

_____

_____

_____

Do I have enough meaning and value built into it to get me to use this behavior for triggering some other sense of happiness? What other meanings would I like to get out of it? Do I need to turn up my representation of pleasure?

_____

_____

_____

_____

Van's Example:

I'm going to pick a poker tournament that I won. It was an online tournament that had at least 2,500 entrants. It cost nothing to join and the winner won $25, and that winner was me. So, what did that mean for me?

(Huge Start). When playing poker, I originally had a goal of winning the World Series of Poker. However, I was in my 50s during this period and my memory wasn't that good. Frequently, when I folded my cards, I couldn't remember what the folded cards were and thus had no clue how I'd actually done in the hand at the end. This put me at a huge disadvantage in assessing the skills of other players. You need to remember what people had and how they bet; how often do they see the flop; determine if they are a big bluffer or pretty conservative. People who win the Main Event tournament usually have fantastic memories. Some have photographic memories. However, I learned that Chris Ferguson[6] had gone from zero money to $10,000 at the same site and that was my new goal. Thus, this win was a huge start. I feel this as a swelling (big and swirling feeling) in my chest.

(Survival) In the beginning, you are playing against a lot of people who have no idea about the odds or what constitutes bad play. That means one of them could get lucky and take you out by going all in when the odds were totally against them and getting lucky and winning.[7] I survived that. When it's over, I have a feeling of "yes," which in sensory details would be a strong upward moving feeling (sharp and powerful) in my chest.

(Persistence) I took about eight hours to win the tournament, so I survived that. I was a survivor. In eight hours, it's easy to get tired and do something stupid. Do that very often and you'll discover that you have no chance to win. This is like a slow rocking forward filling in my chest and head.

(Talent). It was huge for my ego. I knew I was good. This is an expansive feeling in my head. It feels full but airy. It feels like it keeps pushing outward.

(Proving Ground) I'd done something with huge odds against me. It was like a proving ground. This is very similar to the "yes" feeling I described earlier.

So now let's look at what meaning I give to each of these five things:

- Huge start: I could accomplish my goal. (The $25 was a very significant prize towards getting $10,000. I actually managed to turn it into $700 before I lost it all.[8]
- Satisfaction of knowing I did it.
- Survival. It meant I was sharp enough to survive. Luck was also with me.
- Persistence: I can stay the course I can win against really good players (those around at the end) as well as those who don't know how to play but could get lucky.
- Talent: Self-confidence. I was special and my skills were good.
- Proving ground: I was a really good player. My skills were good.

This is summarized in the next table. What is the key to this? It's pretty obvious to me that it's all about proving myself, knowing my skills were good, and feeling self-confident about what I can do in the future. I think winning a tournament with at least 2,500 players was almost as important to me as my original goal. I did something I thought was almost impossible and this showed me I could do it. I relived the immense pleasure and satisfaction (I experienced years ago just by doing this exercise.

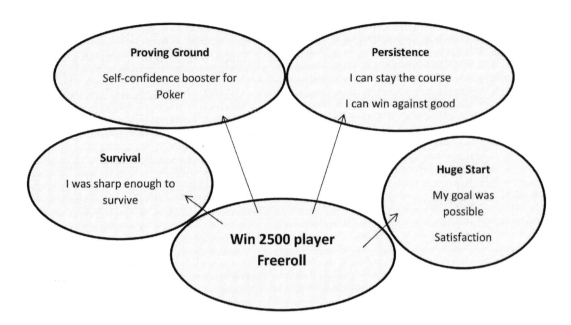

Use your highest pleasuring. First, step into this state, access it fully and completely. Be there in the state and feel all of this pleasure. Ask yourself, as you fully become aware of these highest meanings of value and significance, how you can take this state into some other everyday activity? How can you spread the joy around?

It's clearly and ego-based pleasure. I'm the best. I survived. I can do it. And it's easy to take that state (I can access it any time) and apply it to other situations. Also, I can probably spread the joy just by being in the state.

Imagine fully being in this particular state, in some particular context, doing X and future pace it? If I have this state fully and completely in just the way I want it, how will it alter my experience of things like work, relationships, and learning. So, when you have the answer, spread your pleasure around and connect it to other behaviors.

I'm applying it to being in India and finishing my full six weeks of treatment. I know I can do it. I can also apply it to finishing the next book ahead of me that will be a major task: *The Holy Grail of Trading: Systems Thinking and Understanding that You Don't Trade the Market – You Trade Your Beliefs about the Market.*

Doing this exercise will enable you to 1) determine your pleasure strategy; 2) and specify what you get out of the experience – conceptually. It identifies your meaning world – the frames out of which you live to experience joy and pleasure. Ask yourself, "Do I have enough meaning and value built into it to get me to use this behavior for triggering some other sense of happiness? What other meanings would I like to get out of it? Do I need to turn up my representation of pleasure?"

- There is tremendous self-confidence in this.
- There is a sense of accomplishment in this.
- There is a big "YES" to it.
- There is a resiliency to this.

Summary

Let's now summarize what we know about motivation and propulsion systems.

First, we have a key metamodality that tends to produce an evaluation or judgment. These evaluations tend to be hard-wired. Something "big" and "moving toward us quickly" feels dangerous. "Small and distant" feels safe. "Colorful and bright" tends to be compelling; "black and white" or "dim" is much less compelling and might even push you away. Thus, based upon metamodalities we might make an evaluation and that evaluation could cause us to take some sort of motivated action.

Most people are not aware of the sensory distinctions that are the basis of us evaluating things. As a result, we develop some sort of motivation strategy to make the critical metamodality happen. We use these strategies when we don't seem to be able to do something without making some sort of conscious effort. For example, if you need to clean up your work space, you might need a motivation strategy before you do it.

We have two kinds of motivation – "moving toward" and "moving away from." And a good propulsion strategy usually has us moving away from the undesirable and toward something we really want. It's usually a combination of both.

Propulsion systems tend to be unique to each person. Some people move toward dangerous things that could harm them. Others move away from success and making money. Some people are motivated by unique things and have strange, nonconforming behavior – such as the behavior of a serial killer who is driven to kill people in some unique manner.

What we want is always a state of being. We can control our states. We are driven toward positive states (hard-wired through metamodalities but influenced by meaning), and we are driven away from negative states (also hard-wired through metamodalities and influenced by meaning). These states are given meaning and significance, which influences propulsion.

Metastates significantly alter one's propulsion systems. There are certain key principles that seem to apply to metastates. These include:

1. Higher metastates control and organize lower ones. The higher frame gets empowered to dominate and permeate the lower level. When we think about a primary state, what we think about that state tends to dominate the primary state. It can defuse the lower state, magnify it, negate it, multiply it, create a trance, or even a paradox.

2. Someone or something will always set the frame of reference and whoever does that will govern the experience. (i.e., a part of you, someone else). Our very thinking is reflexive by nature.

Sometimes it occurs as a function of the cultural, linguistic, familial, and professional frames around us.

Sometimes it's primarily a function of the meaning you deliberately choose for it. And that's when it's very powerful for you.

3. The whole determines the parts and then from the parts, the whole emerges. So, a metastate might emerge from some parts interacting together. This might determine one's whole personality. *Example: Who we are is a collection of parts (little "i's") who tend to interact out of what emerges as self – whom we think we are. That self tends to interact and shape the parts. This process causes us to forget our True SELF, that Libby Adams calls "Big I."*[9]

4. We can always set up a higher governing frame of reference. There is magic to stepping outside and setting up a new frame. We can leverage our entire mind by stepping outside the system, tweaking one frame, and then transform everything.

5. Our experience or reality differs greatly at each meta-level. Nominalizations (love, for example) differ depending upon the meta-level. That is, as you think about that state, you move up one meta-level.

- I love X
- I love love. Now in the metastate there is no object.

6. Reflexivity (consciousness thinking about itself) gives consciousness systemic processes and characteristics. It sets up feedback and feedforward loops. It is non-linear thinking, instead of sequential.

- Reflexivity refers to our consciousness reflecting on itself. You fear the fearful state.
- It also creates feedback loops – the fearing of fear magnifies the fear.

7. When the higher levels are not useful or distorted, it can create a living hell. Things like self-condemnation and self-hating come from it. It is the structure of pathology and psychosis.

8. There are frequently strange paradoxes at the higher meta-levels – the most notable being that getting rid of unwanted thoughts and feelings involves welcoming them. In contrast, we can create very non-useful states through metastating even though our intentions are positive. When we fear our fear, it magnifies everything.

9. Frames are set through intention, energy, and lots of repetition. Just thinking about it doesn't change a higher-level frame. They must become intense enough, compelling enough, and habitual enough that they become a new frame of mind. It only registers when we use enough energy.

10. When we constantly operate at a metalevel, it becomes our primary state. It becomes habitual. Constant use makes them more stable. They become part of our neurology. Metastates become metaprograms.

What's Left to Learn?

Propulsion systems are a system. As such, they are full of feedback and feedforward loops. For example, the meaning you give a state feeds forward and fuels the metastate. But the metastate can feedback on the original state and totally change it.

The propulsion system is a lot more than the sum of its parts. Instead, there are emergent properties that come out when you put everything together. For example, winning the online poker tournament with more than 2,500 players gave me a huge sense of confidence about my ability as a player. Winning the tournament ended up being almost as significant to me as my goal of going from zero to $10,000. How many people can say they've won a poker tournament with 2,500 entrants?

There is a sense of oneself that plays into motivation. In the next chapter on metaprograms and propulsion systems, several metaprograms relate to the sense of self. In addition, there are also metaprograms that relate to how you judge things, probably a subset of self-monitoring. Finally, there are a number of metaprograms related to how you perceive the outside world. Some of these metaprograms, and how they relate to happiness and oneness will be explored in more depth in Chapter 6.

And of course, there are some metaprograms that seem quite unique. In the next chapter we'll discuss ten different metaprograms that I feel most relate to propulsions. It could be that given the systems nature of propulsion systems, every metaprogram that people have been able to dream up has some influence on propulsion.

We've already talked about values (your "Big Whys") and propulsion systems and we'll be discussing that in more detail in Chapter 7. Finally, there are some huge determinants such as your life's purpose and surrendering to Divine Will.

What's interesting is that everything in this volume is at best a useful model for how to function more effectively in the world. It will be very useful for someone with a strong ego-strength. It will have little use for someone with weak ego-strength.[10]

Notes

[1] This book is not about trying to persuade someone else or about sales. This is about self-propulsion, but Richard Bandler's ferocious state is about self-propulsion. In that state he is motivated to do anything.

[2] See references.

[3] The Puma State is mentioned in L. Michael Hall's book, *Persuasion Engineering-Simplified.* Neurosemantic Publications, Clifton, CO, page 18.

[4] Dr. L. Michael Hall. *Propulsion Systems: NLP and Neurosemantic Propulsion Systems,* this is a training manual published by Neurosemantics Publications, Clifton, CO: 2002

[5] Here I'm not suggesting that you have an affair that you know is inappropriate for your marital status.

[6] Chris was one of the owners of the site and has disappeared from the Poker scene when that site folded because he would be arrested if he came to the US.

[7] For example, you have AA but someone goes all in with 55. Then three other people call. Heads up you are about an 89% favorite to win against that opponent with any hand he might have. But with five people in the pot it drops down to about 55%. Those kinds of plays against me would happen and I'd have to survive that. Actually, someone could call my AA with a 72 off suit (the worst hand in poker). The flop could be 772, and I then have to get one more ace to win.

[8] This was not my goal, but it was still pretty good. My wife had originally given me $1,000 to play on the site. Playing sometimes five hours a day for over a year, I took the $1,000 up to as high as $1,700 and then eventually lost it all. I estimated that I'd paid them over $5,000 in fees for my play even though their fees were lower than Las Vegas casinos charge. I wasn't good enough to overcome that. Also, that site turned out to be a big scam (FULLTILT POKER). When the US outlawed Internet Poker (in most states), people were unable to get their money back from the site. So, it was just as well that I'd lost mine. I'd certainly had $1,000 worth of fun and it satisfied my excitement part and kept it out of the market.

[9] Adams, Libby. *Applied Learning and Implementation Strategies for Mastery of the "self."* International Academy of self Knowledge, 2002.

[10] Ego-strength is a metaprogram that is discussed in the next chapter.

CHAPTER 6

Metaprograms and Propulsions

Metaprograms are largely unconscious ways of behaving that become automatic for you as you grow up. Most of them just represent "preferences" for how to respond, but sometimes they become driver metaprograms, meaning you don't have a choice in how you respond – it's automatic. Dr. Michael Hall identifies over 60 metaprograms in his book *Figuring People Out*, and most people have 10 to 15 of them as driver metaprograms.

Since metaprograms are largely unconscious ways of behaving, an important step in gaining back some control is to become aware of them. One of the Super Trader lessons helps them become aware of them all – what their preferences are and whether they are driver metaprograms – meaning you have little choice. As you become aware of such programs, you suddenly have more choice in your life simply because awareness changes everything. Even becoming aware of your driver metaprograms is important because it's the first step to gaining control.

The ten key metaprograms relating to propulsion systems will be covered in this chapter, where you will learn how to evaluate yourself on each of these. And at the same time, I'll take you through my own answers on the various programs and we'll talk about how they impacted my decision to begin, and continue to do, the Ayurvedic treatments in India.

But let's talk about the most important one for propulsion systems here – do you tend to move towards things (carrot motivation) or do you tend to move away from things (stick motivation)? Let's do some exercises to see whether you are a carrot or stick person. Do you move toward what you want, or do you move away from what you don't want?

Are you A Stick or Carrot Person?

Below are some questions to evaluate yourself. In every question, be sure to really check what's important about that. You might say the car must have a good warranty because you might really be thinking about not getting one that breaks down all the time or the high cost of repair you had with your last car. To evaluate this test, notice whether your responses tended to be positive or negative. For positive values, put a plus sign in the space next to your answers. For negative values, put a minus sign in the space next your answer. Even though it might be stated positively, you might be moving away from something. For example, my dog must be hypoallergenic really means that you don't want to be allergic to your dog (i.e., move away from).

The illustrations below will help you decide whether your answer is positive or negative.

For example, for question 1, your responses might be:

- "I wanted a car that wasn't in the shop all the time like my last clunker." This is a negative response. If your reason sounds like that, then put a negative sign by it.
- "I really liked the design of the car." This is a positive response so put a positive sign by it.
- I want a red car (i.e., that sounds positive, but you really mean that your last car was black and got dingy looking and you think a red car will avoid that).

What are five things you look for when you buy a car?

_____

_____

_____

_____

_____

When I bought my Tesla Model S, I was looking for the following: 1) Was it fuel efficient? That was important because I planned to drive it around the country. 2) Was it high tech? 3) Did it have a lot of horsepower? 4) Was it sexy? And 5) Was there a nearby dealer I could trust? In my case, the first (not wanting to spend a lot of money on gas) and last (not wanting a dealer who'd rip me off in repair costs and who didn't show me respect) were both move-away. The other three were move-toward. So, I have three move-towards and two move-aways in my five responses.

Why do you want your most important goals in life?

_____

_____

_____

_____

_____

For question two you might say:

- "I want to be a successful trader, so I don't have a stupid boss breathing down my back." This is a negative response because the motivation is to get away from your boss. Put a negative sign by reponses like this.
- "I want the freedom to have my own hours, do what I want, and make unlimited income." This is a move-toward goal, so put a plus sign by it.

I've already discussed these reasons for me because they reflect my primary values. I am into self-transformation – to become a Siddha yogi. I want to help others transform. I want to write a perennial best seller that will help others transform. I want good health because if I live to be 100, which is part of my plan, I want those years to be productive, allowing me to achieve the other goal (this one is half negative because I don't want to be a vegetable or have issues with my brain). And I want a loving family that supports me and to whom I can give support.

Four of those are move-towards and one is mixed, so I have 7.5 move-towards and 2.5 move-aways in my responses.

Are you more likely to move toward what you want or away from what you don't want? List five things you've done lately. Were you moving toward a goal or avoiding something negative?

_____

_____

_____

_____

_____

For question three, if your answer reflects move-toward, put a plus sign by it. If your answer reflects move-away, put a minus sign by it.

- I gave my employees a bonus. (I want them to realize that they are appreciated and what a great place this is to work.) This is positive or move-toward.

- I gave my employees a bonus. (We probably lose one employee per year, and when one leaves, it costs a lot of money to find someone else who is new and good. I don't want to have to look again.) The same behavior is here, but because of the reason behind it, it is move-away.

Okay, what are five things I've done lately? 1) I came to India (move towards better health); 2) I canceled my trip to Australia because of visa problems, so that would be move-away, although there wasn't another choice within the time frame I had. 3) I booked a flight from HYD to RDU via Cathay Pacific. It was cheap. I really like that airline, so we'll call this one move-toward. 4) I booked flights to Delhi to see the Taj Mahal and visit one of my Super Traders who calls it an honor (so, move-toward) and to visit a friend I'm close to in Hyderabad (again, move-toward). And lastly, 5) I have scheduled the hair transplant surgery – my second. I'm moving toward having fuller hair and doing it for about 20% of the price I'd pay in the US. So, I now have 11.5 move-toward checks and 3.5 move-away checks.

If you were to buy a dog, what five qualities would you look for?

_____

_____

_____

_____

_____

For question four notice whether you are looking for positive or negative qualities.

- I must have a dog that doesn't shed – this is avoiding something so put down a negative sign.

- I want a dog that's really smart so I can teach it a lot of things and that's like a family member. This is a positive quality so you would put a plus sign by your answer.

This one is easy for me to answer. First, I love dogs in general. I like intelligent dogs. I like playful dogs. I like dogs who snuggle or rough-house with me (so physical). I like dogs who are somewhat independent and will take care of themselves. For example, Papillons (which I have) are good because they will exercise themselves. This is my first move- away from because I don't want dogs who need a lot of walks – and long ones. Papillons tend to exercise themselves. Lastly, I like a good-looking dog and there are a wide variety of dogs that fit this category for me.

So, here we have one move-away from category and four move-toward. My total is now 15.5 move-towards and 4.5 move-aways. I'm clearly a move-toward person.

Now add up your plus and minus signs. If you have 12 or more plus signs, then you tend to be a move-toward person. If you have 12 or more minus signs, then you tend to be a move-away person. If you have between 11 and 9 plus signs you are somewhat mixed – you are partially stick-motivated and partially carrot-motivated. The table below sums up this metaprogram.

Motivation Direction (Move-Toward versus Move-Away)	
This is our motivational energy when we act. Moving toward what we value, or, away from what we de-value and want to avoid.	
B. Explanatory Notes	
Move-Toward – have pull values; their goals move them toward the future. Have difficulty recognizing what to avoid. Motivated by carrots, not sticks. Achievers	Move-Away – have push away values; they avoid things in life. Have difficulty with goals. Problem Solvers
Balanced – can see possibilities and see and formulate problems while small and manageable.	

Evaluate all the other metaprograms related to propulsion

While the stick and carrot motivations may be the most important metaprogram in terms of propulsion systems, it is not the only one. Here are nine other metaprograms that will strongly influence your motivation.

2. Black-and-white[1] or "either/or" thinking

A lot of motivational metaprograms depend upon whether you are open or rigid to change. These include 1) Black-and-white thinking; 2) Seeing the world as being impermeable (static) versus constantly changing; 3) Thinking of nature as static rather than fluctuating; 4) A strong emphasis of following a fixed set of rules rather than giving yourself options; and 5) Being an early adopter or a later adopter. I think you can see the similarities here. As a result, we will only look at the first two metaprograms in this chapter.

First, **black-and-white thinking**. Black-and-white thinking means that you basically divide your world into two categories with very distinct boundaries. Here are some common examples.

- You either believe what I believe, or you are wrong.
- You are either for me or against me.
- Women are meant to serve men. They either do it or they don't.
- If you are not a fan of my team, then you are the enemy.
- You are either a Republican or a Democrat.

Explanatory Notes	
Continuum Thinking Enables us to engage in a more refined discerning awareness as we see degrees and possibilities.	Black-and-White (Either/Or) Thinking Is appropriate for some things that are major categories such as male or female, day or night.
Discriminate at much finer levels. Work with fuzzy logic. Sometimes creates decision problems. Speak more definitively.	Makes clear distinctions or boundaries. Enables quick decisions. Is where we all go when we experience extreme stress. Does not allow the gray areas of life.

Can you see how this can shape your motivation? It puts people into two camps and those in the wrong camp are basically enemies, so, of course, this sort of thinking will shape your behavior.

I'm a continuum thinker. In fact, as a black-and-white thinker, I probably would not be able to do what I'm doing now in India. First, I'd believe that my beliefs are right and if they didn't serve me food I liked, I'd probably leave. I would either like it or not. I wouldn't be sitting around thinking, "What is there about the qualities in this food that I don't like?"

What are you – a continuum thinker or a black-and-white thinker? And how did this impact your ability to motivate yourself? Is it useful? A black-and-white thinker would say, "Of course, it's useful, because they would have trouble seeing how it was not useful.

_____
_____
_____
_____
_____

3. Solid, Impermeable versus Changing or Permeable Metaprogram

The next metaprogram relates to how you see the world. Is it solid, real, and unchanging? That's one perspective. Or is the world constantly changing so that nothing seems certain?

If you are familiar enough with my writings, my stance on this one is obvious. Think about the statement I frequently make that "your beliefs shape your reality." And furthermore, "no belief is true, they are just true in a context." If they are true in a wide context, and they bring value to you and others who follow them, then they are useful. If the context is narrow and they don't bring much value, then they are not useful.

This belief dramatically shifts my propulsion systems because my top value is to work on myself and it gives me the structure for doing so. Find useful beliefs and useful maps. The more maps you have, and the more useful they are, the more you will stand out as a genius in any field.

Not knowing for sure can be "not useful" in some contexts because it brings hesitancy and uncertainly. And if you combine that uncertainty with low self-esteem, it spells problems. But that's not what I do. I'm in India doing Ayurveda. I'm pretty sure my Inner Guidance brought me here, because I made a resolution never to come back to India. Do I know that the Ayurvedic treatments will improve my health? No, I don't. I think they will, but I won't know much until they are over. Am I concerned that I'm wasting my time? Well, the cost of my trip here, including all the Ayurvedic treatments and my room and board was more than paid for by what I saved on the hair transplant. Plus, I wrote a book that might have taken me months to complete in about 3.5 weeks – at least for the first draft. The time was worth it even if I get no changes in my health from the clinic experience.

My position is that I know nothing for certain. So, I'm permeable, but I trust my Inner Guidance. I have faith in the perfection of the what is. Even though my position is "I don't know," I also trust in my path. That's a powerful position and there is no hesitancy. The action seems automatic and I just witness it happening. Thus, I'm permeable but without the hesitance and doubt that most people would have with this metaprogram. I see change as being great and part of a Divine Process unfolding.

Durability (Permeable versus Impermeable)	
The quality of our mental constructs – solid, firm, impermeable, while others deal with much more permeable constructs. This means that other influences can permeate and influence the person's thinking.	
Impermeable People	Permeable People
• Can tolerate many subordinate inconsistencies without modifying the overall construct. • Have rigid belief systems. Will think in terms of definitiveness, "no question."	• Their constructs are easily changed. • Have many dimentions that are easily revised. • In anchoring states other memories and feelings from other events immediately permeate them.
	• Will demonstrate terms of hesitation or doubt.

Look at the questions below and use them to assess yourself on this metaprogram. Are things impermeable, not capable of revision, or are things permeable, easily revised? How does this impact your way of being? And how does it impact your motivation and ability to propel yourself in some direction?

As you think about some of your mental constructs, your ideas about success and failure, of love and forgiveness, of relationships and work, of your personal qualities, do you find the representations of what you know permanent or unstable? How can you tell?

Think about something you know without a doubt about yourself. Now think about something you are uncertain about. How do these sets of representations vary?

How well are you able to hold and maintain an idea or representation?

Do you understand how many of the concepts you hold are just "nominalizations" – processes that you have turned into a noun and given qualities as if they are fixed?

___

___

___

___

4. Others Reference Thinking

This metaprogram is about how you reference your attention. Do you use your own standards and references to determine what is appropriate, or do you want feedback from others?

Here you might want to reference a fashion show. My wife used to watch one called *What Not to Wear*. Designers set the standard for what we should wear. That standard must change every year, or they won't make as much money. Narrow ties are in and wide ties are out – except when they come back into style. Here you'll hear comments like, "That's so 80s." Or, "You are like someone who was born in 1920 and stayed there."

Elicitation Questions:

- Where do you put the most attention – on your own thinking and choosing, or externally on others, events, rules, and so on?
- In relationships, do you find yourself primarily attending to your own needs or to the needs of others?
- If there is a conflict of interest, do you focus on your needs or those of others?
- How hard or easy is it to attend to others? And to yourself?
- What do you first seek to attend to or take care of?

_____

_____

_____

_____

Attention (Self-Referent versus Other-Referent)	
Tells us where we invest our attention. Self or others. To look for authority (internally or externally), where do we posit the locus of control of judgment? Who/what do we use as our reference point?	
Description: Internal Referent Perceiving • Evaluate internally based on what they think is appropriate. • Are self-motivated and they make their own decisions. • Choose and validate their own results. • Can easily decide for themselves. Will ignore feedback and not take it that seriously. • A manager just must provide them with standards.	Description - Other Referents • Need and want lots of feedback. They feel disrespected without it. • Need input from external sources. These people focus primarily on others. The more they think they know, the more closed minded they can be.

In my case, I'm a very strong self-referent person. **I tend to believe that most beliefs that people hold are not useful at all.**[2] They tend to be the beliefs of the brainwashed. I lean towards looking for what successful people do and for what's new and different. These two strategies give me useful beliefs and more options. You can probably imagine that I would not be in India doing Ayurveda if I listened to what others said.

How does that relate to being in India? The last time I went to India, I swore I'd never come back again. I really don't like the food. But most importantly, India has way too much red tape. For example, yesterday I went to see the hair transplant doctor at a large hospital in Kochi, India. I had a 10am appointment, but no one told me where to go. Fortunately, I had a driver who spoke a little English and stayed with me the whole time. I've included the details in the footnote,[3] but I was in the hospital for 3.5 hours just to get my surgery scheduled. It was almost three hours past my appointment when I saw the doctor, and this was just to decide whether or not to use him. In the US, I would have been in and out in about 15-20 minutes.

However, several things sort of came together and the next thing I knew I was scheduled to be in India for six weeks. As far as I was concerned the only explanation was because my Inner Guidance wanted me to be here. My Inner Guidance, by the way, is an Inner Source, not an external one. I'm not talking to God outside myself, but inside – you could call it my Higher Self.

You may or may not be familiar with your own Inner Guidance, although everyone has a connection to God inside. It's a huge transformation when you find it. However, even before I had a strong Inner Guidance, I was still guided by my own standards – not some external authority standard.

I just watched a video in which a teacher asked her students (about 10-12 years old) what they wanted to be when they grew up and why. Most of them responded with some profession like doctor or lawyer. But one boy wrote down happiness. The message of the video is that most people adopt the goal and aspirations of others, but that should not be your guidance. Why do you do anything? The answer is to get to a core state like happiness. But if you follow an inner standard, you can go to that core state first and then the other things are just trivial.

Now please evaluate yourself. Do you tend to do what others want or are you guided by your own inner standards – whether divinely inspired or not. Whatever your answer may be, how does it impact your propulsion systems? Be honest with yourself. Don't just put down an answer because it's the way you wish it would be or think it should be. What's true for you right now?

_____

_____

_____

_____

5. Pessimism

When something comes up, do you tend to see an optimistic or pessimistic scenario playing out, or neither. For example, it's March 9, 2020. The Dow Jones Industrials were down over 2000 points this morning and it triggered the circuit breakers so the market was shut down. The market is down almost 20% in less than a month. What's going to happen? (What did you believe would happen as you were experiencing this period of time?)

In my case, I remember October 1987. That was very similar and then there was an immediate spring back after Black Monday and that was the end of the crash. But here we have a possible pandemic that (while I don't believe it's serious) could shut down the economy for a while. In addition, oil prices are crashing. BTC is also down and that's unusual because historically it has zero correlation with other markets. Where am I? I'm really in an "I don't know mode." Just follow my rules and see what happens.

One of my key beliefs is that I'm guided by my Inner Guidance and that there is a perfection to the what is. If I'm not seeing that perfection, then I'm not trusting that Inner Guidance and realizing that I'm being taken care of constantly.

I've also noticed that when I think of some of the worst things that ever happened to me – or at least they seemed like it at the time – they turned out to be very significant and turned into some of the best things that ever happened. My divorce was a great example of that one. However, seeing this sort of perfection requires a deep trust and surrender to reach. Some people cannot do that, and they tend to resist what happens and end up being a victim of it. Go with the flow, accept and you will experience that perfection. Resist and you will experience yourself as a victim.

Now it's time to evaluate yourself. Again, be very honest with yourself. Are you generally optimistic, pessimistic or neither (also a possibility if you think what happens is random)? Which is most true for you? And how does that impact your self-propulsion? Use the following elicitation questions to help you decide.

Elicitation Questions:

- When you encounter a problem or difficulty, do you first consider the worst-case scenario or the best?
- Does your mind more naturally go to problems and difficulties or to opportunities and positive challenges?
- Do you see the glass as half empty or half full?
- Do events that you judge and give a negative meaning to make you negative?
- Do you tend to give things a negative meaning?
- Do you tend to make a lot of negative judgments?

Scenario Thinking Style	
How we look up difficult, challenging situations. Do we first see the obstacles or the opportunities to master a challenge?	
Explanation: Worst-Case Scenario (Pessimistic)	Explanation: Best-Case Scenario (Optimistic)
• Makes us pessimistic and skeptical with a focus on finding and having problems.	• Makes us optimistic in an inspired way; look for good things.
• Skeptics who focus on problems. Skill at problem solving and quality control. Sharp eye as a proofreader. Seligman (1975) focus on learned helplessness and the 3 Ps. • Personal – it's about me. • Pervasive – It impacts everything in my life. • Permanent – it will last forever. • Blame themselves for failure and are victims.	• Have a strong expectation that things will turn out right despite setbacks. Visions and dreams pull them forward. • Failures are something they can change and improve upon. • With too much of this they live in illusions and can become crippled with anything negative.

6. Necessity and Impossibility

"Necessity" and "impossibility" are one extreme of modal operators in which you either believe you must do something (no choice) or you can't do it (again no choice). Can you see how this would impact your propulsion systems? If you believe you cannot do it, you won't. Why would you? Because you believe that it can't be done.

If you believe you have to do it, then you again have no choice. It's imposed upon you that you have to do it. Now contrast with the opposite modal operators that say "I want to" – which means you have a choice. Or which say "I can" – which again imply you have a choice.

Again, there is no question where I stand with these. I have few limits that I know of ... I can even eat this food that I don't like. It's not mandatory that I do it. I choose to do it. I could also choose to throw it away or to not eat it. Or I could choose to do both of those options.

How do you run your life? Do you set up boundaries where you cannot go/do? Do you have requirements in your life that say you must do something? Ask the elicitation questions and when you have answered the questions, notice how your responses impact your propulsion systems.

Elicitation Questions:

- How did you motivate yourself to go to work this morning?
- What did you say to yourself to get yourself moving?
- When you think about work what do you say about it?

- Why did you select your current job?
- Why have you chosen that school or that schedule?

_____
_____
_____
_____
_____

Modal Operators (Necessity; Desire; Possibility; Impossibility)	
How we conceptualize the world. World of 1) demands; 2) world of desires; 3) world of limitations; 4) world of possibilities.	
Necessity Explanation: • Person operates from compulsion, control, law; must, have to, should.	Desire Explanation: • "want to" "love to" "get to" Lead to motivation and drive.
Impossibility Explanation: • I can't, shouldn't, mustn't; you shouldn't miss work or show up late.	Possibility Explanation: • I can, will, may Look for new opportunities and expand their options.

7. Perfectionism in Achieving Goals

In terms of accomplishing goals, you can be pessimistic, optimistic, and a perfectionist. We have already talked about pessimism so let's look at another huge roadblock, perfectionism. Our society trains us to want to be perfectionists. You need to get 94% or so on a test in school in order to get an "A." If you were unlucky and had a critical parent, you might come home, show your Dad the 94%, and he just looks at you and says, "Why didn't you get 100%?" The bottom line is that you can never please him, so you develop a self-critical part of yourself to try to win his approval. This part thinks, "I'll criticize myself before Dad does, perhaps I can anticipate everything before he does and maybe I can please him." This then becomes your way of being.

And if you have this problem, it's difficult to accomplish anything because you are always trying to make it perfect. And perhaps you get discouraged.

Obviously, that is not me. I tend to be optimistic that I'll accomplish what I set out to do. My goal in India is to improve my health. I have a long list of potential health improvements – my biggest desire is to sleep better and to have more energy. If I can accomplish that, I'll be delighted. I've also asked about healing joint pain – I only have it when I try to run, but I haven't been able to run for about 12 years or so. My skin gets itchy, I have a cyst on my back that might need more surgery and I have a couple of skin tags. I'm optimistic that these will all be healed or improved. If they are not, then perhaps I'm here for another reason – the hair transplant for which my savings will pay for the cost of the trip, or to get this book written? Or perhaps something else entirely. Who knows, but I'm optimistic.

If I were pessimistic, I probably would not have come. If I were a perfectionist, then I wouldn't be happy unless all the health issues get fixed. As far as I'm concerned, I'm here for a reason. I think that has to do with health, but perhaps not. I trust my Inner Guidance.

Read through the elicitation questions below and then assess yourself. Again, be honest. Notice how whatever style you pick will impact your ability to propel yourself toward goals or to accomplish necessary tasks.

Elicitation Questions:

- Think about a goal you set, and how you went about making it come true.
- You need to accomplish something of significance – how will you go about doing that?
- Imagine that you have more than 20 Super Trader lessons to complete. How do you go about that?
- Was the process of achieving it a pleasant or unpleasant experience for you?

Goal Striving (Skepticism; Optimism; Perfectionism)		
How we think and make choices about goals; We love the goal or hate it.		
Skepticism Explanation: • Hates goal setting. • Defeatist attitude. • Expect the worst to happen.	Optimism Explanation: • Does best he can and leaves it at that. • Take goals in small steps. • Fun moving toward the goal. • Goes with the flow well.	Perfectionism Explanation: • Goal is never good enough. • This person is never satisfied. • Set high standards and judge themselves harshly for failing. • Future orientation that is excessive. • Tend to procrastinate.

There are a lot of metaprograms around the ego. How much do you value yourself (self-esteem)? How much self-confidence do you have? Obviously if you don't have self-confidence, you won't be motivated to do things. How strong is your self-integrity? What is your ego strength? We will discuss a couple of these metaprograms here, but they obviously all relate to motivation.

8. Low Self-Esteem

Again, let me answer the elicitation questions as an example for you. The answer to the first question is that I value myself as a person highly. It's not based upon accomplishments – although it used to be. It's now based upon my relationship with my Inner Guidance.

But I have to caution you about my responses here because my meditations and the program I'm doing with my Internal Guidance are all designed to get rid of my sense of "I" so that there is no resistance ever to following Inner Guidance. However, I think that can only happen when you have a high self-esteem to begin with.

Now, rate yourself honestly by going through the elicitation questions below. And when you rate your sense of self-esteem, notice how it impacts your propulsion systems.

Elicitation Questions:

- Do you think of your value as a person as conditional or unconditional?
- When you esteem yourself as worthwhile and valuable, do you base it upon something you do, have or possess, or do you base it upon a given (i.e., your inherent humanity, man in God's image and likeness).
- How solid or weak is your personal sense of your innate worth or dignity?
- How easily can you say, "I am lovable, I am precious."

_____

_____

_____

_____

_____

Self-Esteem (Low Conditional versus High Unconditional)	
Explanation: Conditional (Low Self-Esteem) <ul><li>Self-esteem is placed on a conditional foundation.</li><li>Self-esteem is linked to temporal conditions, like a treadmill of achievement.</li></ul>	Explanation: Unconditional (High Self-Esteem) <ul><li>Self-esteem is high.</li><li>Self-esteem comes from no particular conditions and is strong.</li></ul>

9. Self-Monitoring is Low and Externally Based

This metaprogram refers to the ability to go inside and recognize how your thoughts and feelings control your experience. If you work on yourself a lot (for many years, in my case), then you begin to realize how much you create it all for yourself.

However, some people think that everything happens externally. They have a lot of problems monitoring their thoughts and feelings. As a result, they experience the world as happening to them rather than them creating their experience.

I don't think I need to answer the elicitation questions as an example because this metaprogram is similar to the others and my stance is quite obvious: I create my entire experience. It's an extreme stance, although useful for me. Read through the questions in the table and notice where you stand on self-monitoring. How does that impact your ability to use propulsion systems?

Elicitation Questions:

- What are you feeling right now? What are you thinking?
- What mental and emotional patterns are your strengths?
- What are some of your weaknesses that you want to deal with?
- How much do you monitor yourself as you feel stressed or relaxed, self-conscious or self-forgetful; angry, fearful, joyful, social, or sexual?

_____

_____

_____

_____

_____

Self-Monitoring (Low External versus High Internal)	
This has to do with the ability to go inside and recognize what one is experiencing in terms of thoughts, feelings, and impulses (and even things like sub modalities). It's the ability to take one's own psychological pulse.	
Explanation: Low Self-Monitoring (Low External)	Explanation: High Self-Monitoring (High Internal)
• These people will have difficulty telling you how they feel or think. • Typically, they will say, "I don't know." • At the extreme they may not even know how to go inside to discover their thoughts. • They may be more skilled socially or more extraverted in recharging their batteries. • Super Trader Program likely to be difficult to do.	• These people know their own thinking, emotions, needs, impulses, choices and their inner world. They are highly attuned to themselves. • If at peace they will be able to empathize with others. • If inwardly conflicted, they will have a painful self-awareness they want to escape from.

10. What We Deem to Be Important (Values)

I sometimes think that Dr. Hall really stretches things by including values and Myers Briggs types in his metaprogram classification. And the same time what we deem to be important, our values, are critical to motivation. They shape what you move towards or away from dramatically.

I've discussed my values extensively in this book and it should be clear to you how they shape my motivation. Chapters 7 and 8 of this book will help you determine your own values. Your values shape your motivation. They should be the focus of your propulsion systems.

Elicitation Questions:

- What is important to you?
- What is the most significant thing about X? (Substitute a number of things for X such as a job, relationship, project, or where you live).
- What do you invest your time and energy into?

_____

_____

_____

_____

_____

Values (What we Deem to be Important)
Values are a nominalization, so what is the verb behind them? What we treat or view as being important. They are abstractions of importance. We imply a state or value to our representation of something. We trust in it and act on it. They organize our life. So, we encode our thoughts into some metaprograms and then we have a thought about its significance or importance. That is, we value every metaprogram we use habitually. Whether you mismatch or think globally, you will value it.
Maslow (1950) created a hierarchical list of emotional value that plays a critical role in our lives: 1) survival; 2) security; 3) love and affection; 4) belonging; 5) self-esteem and regard; 6) self-actualization. Others might include: 7) power; 8) control; 9) achievement; 10) affiliation; 11) transcendence; 12) ease; 13) pleasure; 14) romance; 15) sex; 16) knowledge; 17) religion; 18) harmony; 19) challenge. Values are whatever we believe to hold significance. Clare Graves (see Chapter 8) created groups of people according to his model of evolving values over time.

Conclusion

After reviewing these ten different metaprograms and the impact that they have on my propulsion systems, I'm not sure that every metaprogram[4] doesn't either hinder or help my propulsion systems. Here we've focused on those that make motivation difficult, but doesn't the opposite metaprogram tend to promote motivation? Of course, it does.

In the last chapter of this book, we'll be setting up your motivation template. While you are doing that keep in mind what you've learned about metaprograms and your propulsion systems.

Finally, values are so important that I've devoted the next two chapters to them.

Notes

[1] Black and white thinking works as follows: 1) you see something or hear something and you like it; 2) it comes from a source you believe; and 3) suddenly it becomes truth for you. For example, the Netflix show *The Crown* is the story of the reign of Queen Elizabeth II and it is molded around known historical events. However, no one knows what really goes on inside Buckingham Palace or Windsor Castle, so the rest is just historical fiction. But for many people watching, what they see suddenly becomes fact. Similarly, when Donald Trump is the president of the United States he makes many statements on Twitter. Most of his statements cannot be fact checked, but some people hear them, like what they hear and then it becomes the truth.

[2] I have had this idea for as long as I can remember, and it was certainly reinforced when I started to do modeling work. If you want to be great, do a massive change in your belief systems.

[3] First, I had to go to the International Desk to get a card. The card cost me about $9 to get. To put that into perspective, I had a driver with me for 5.5 hours and his total cost was $19. I put my address on the card, including NC as my state, and I was told, "We don't have a state called North Carolina in our system. Why don't you say you are from California or Florida because those are in our database?" Thus, my card says Cary, NC 27518 Florida USA.

Next, I had to wait about 90 minutes more to be put near the doctor. After an hour we were told he was in a meeting. Then we waited about 15 minutes more outside his door. Then I saw the doctor. He said I needed to schedule the surgery at the Surgery Desk. She quoted me a price that I didn't understand. I think she said something like 2 lakh. I thought that might be

200,000 rupees, but I wasn't sure so I asked, "How much is that in dollars?" She said that I needed to go down to the International Desk and they'd explain. I said, "Just write down how much and I'll translate myself," but she sent me to the International Desk. It took another 15 minutes for them to tell me it was about $3100 – so it was about 210,000 rupees. Then back upstairs to say that price is okay and to have her schedule it. And then I still didn't have the doctor's phone or email so I could communicate directly. That took another 15 minutes to get. RED TAPE! In the US, the same information would probably take 15-30 minutes to get from the time of the appointment. But the surgery would cost $20,000 not $3,000.

Having done the surgery, I would describe it as flying economy class around the world. At the end of the trip, I'm happy with the savings, but I would probably never do it again and I would go business class in the future. It was crude at best and I'm not even sure I like the results yet. Over a year later, I don't think they did enough.

[4] See References: This book lists 60 metaprograms, all of which could impact motivation in some way. It also has excellent chapters on how to expand and utilize them. I strongly recommend it if you are interested in a lot more detail about metaprograms.

CHAPTER 7

Values and Your Propulsion System

Values are probably at the top of the list when it comes to impacting propulsion systems. In addition, their impact also depends upon your awareness of them. For example, if your awareness is very low, then you could be on automatic pilot and just react to what happens in the world. You don't have any particular motivations, so you don't get anywhere. You are run by your metaprograms – and you are certainly not aware of them.

Eliciting your values is like finding your destiny. It becomes a whole new step-up in awareness. Suddenly you can go after what you want. If you are mostly a move-away person, then you realize this, and can start to build your own propulsion systems that not only push you away from what you don't want but they also propel you towards what you do want.

Value Elicitation Exercise:

The first, and most important step in completing this chapter is to do a value elicitation. This is the same exercise that is in the Peak Performance Home Study Course in volume 3 (Chapter 3). If you have done this exercise before, then simply copy your values in the space below. Note whether they are move-toward values or move-away values by putting a plus or minus in the space to the right.

_____ _____

_____ _____

_____   _____

_____   _____

_____   _____

_____   _____

_____   _____

_____   _____

_____   _____

If you have not done the exercise, then it is given below. Do it now. First, you should already know if you tend to generally move toward or away from things. Do the appropriate value elicitation if you are dominant in one direction, but for most of you, do both the positive and the negative value elicitation.

Be sure that you participate fully in this exercise. If only one part of you participates and determines your values, then you will not find any conflict in your values. For example, I asked one of my clients, who had distinct conflicts in his life, to do this exercise. When he showed it to me, there were no obvious conflicts in his list of values. The reason was that the part of him that wanted to change remained in control during the exercise. That part listed its values. The part producing conflict, the part of him that caused him to overwork himself each day at the markets, elected not to participate. So be sure to determine who is doing the exercise (the part that wants to change; the part that's curious about you and your life; or a part that doesn't want change at all). So, while doing this question, periodically ask, "What part of me am I getting responses from and is there any other important part that should participate?"

This may be a common problem for readers. One reader reported that he was able to get over this particular problem by listing his traits instead of his values. When he did so, he was able to determine distinct conflicts in his traits. If you find no conflict in your values, yet your behavior indicates that you do have conflict, then use this alternative approach.

Value Elicitation (Move-Toward)[1]

Many conflicts that you may experience involve a conflict in values. One step toward eliminating such conflicts is the value elicitation exercise.

Your values are like a bar code. If you change one bar, you get a different computer reading. If you change one value, you get a different life. Your bar code of values is the hierarchy by which you run your life. If you can successfully elicit your own bar code, you have a guide for successfully running your life.

1. What is absolutely essential for you to have in your life? Answer this question with a list of at least ten words or phrases. I have included a list of suggested values at the end of this exercise in case you have trouble, but I suggest that you don't use the list unless you absolutely need to.

2. Now prioritize your list. Look out in front of you, and create a void. What's more important to you _____ or _____? Put one word on one side and another word on the other side of your visual screen and decide which is more important. If you had to do without one of the two values, which one would you pick? Go through your entire list comparing each item with every other item. For example, suppose your list of values consisted of the following:

Love	Peace
Sex	Intelligence
Money	Honesty
Adventure	Sense of importance
Security	Investment success

You first ask yourself what is more important, *love* or *sex,* and you come up with *love*. Then you ask what is more important, *love* or *money*, and you answer *money*. You then ask what is more important, *money* or *adventure*, and you answer *money*. Then you ask what is more important, *money* or *security*, and you answer *security*. Next you ask what is more important, *security* or *peace*, and you answer *security*. You continue this until you complete the list.

What is more important? Love or Avoiding Poverty?

TABLE 7-1: SUGGESTED POSITIVE VALUES			
Acceptance	Decisiveness	Humor	Relationships
Achievement	Determination	Imagination	Relaxation
Activity	Dignity	Independence	Resourcefulness
Adventure	Discipline	Initiative	Respect
Affection	Efficiency	Intelligence	Responsibility
Affiliation	Encourage-ment	Intimacy	Risk
Aging	Endurance	Investments	Security
Approval	Energy	Justice	SelfAcceptance
Belief	Enthusiasm	Knowledge	SelfEsteem
Calmness	Excellence	Leadership	SelfKnowledge
Career	Exercise	Love	SexFulfillment
Caution	Faith	Maturity	Sharing
Change	Flexibility	Morality	Simplicity

Commitment	Focus	Motivation	Sincerity
Common Sense	Forgiveness	Objectivity	Strength
Communication	Freedom	Open-mindedness	Structure
Compassion	Friends	Opportunity	Success
Competition	God	Optimism	Support
Confidence	Growth	Organization	Trust
Consistency	Guidance	Parenting	Understanding
Contentment	Happiness	Patience	Values
Contribution	Harmony	Perfection	Wealth
Control	Health	Persistence	Winning
Cooperation	Honesty	Philosophy	Wisdom
Coping	Hope	Purpose	
Courage			

If you ended the list with *security* as the most important value, then the value *money* (the value that was most important before *security*) would be the next logical place to start looking for your second most important value. You would then systematically compare *money* with all the other values on your list except *security*. Continue this process repeatedly until you have all ten values ranked.

3. Take your most important value (*security* in our example) and ask yourself what is important to you about that particular value. Again, you should come up with a list of about ten words or phrases.

4. Prioritize this new list using the same method that you used in step two. That is, make a binary comparison of each two-word pair.

5. Repeat steps 3 and 4 for every value on your list. You should now have a prioritized list of about 100 words.

6. Determine your evidence procedures. For each word on this list ask yourself the following questions:

   a) How do you know when you have _____ (fill in value)? What are some of the ways you know you have it?

   b) How do you know when you do not have _____ (fill in value)? What are some of the ways you know you do not have it?

This six-step procedure could take you several days to complete. Completing it is well worth the effort, because it will give you a road map to your life. Most importantly, it will give you a means by which you can see potential areas of conflict in your life before they become serious.

The value elicitation procedure can have great benefit in all aspects of your life. For example, if you are having trouble with your marriage, I would suggest that both you and your spouse do steps three through six for the value *relationships*.

Value Elicitation (Move-Away)

Negative values are important because what you resist tends to persist. That is, the negative values that you most resist, tend to stick around in your life.

1. What is absolutely essential for you to avoid in your life? Answer this question with a list of at least ten words or phrases. I have included a list of suggested negative values at the end of this exercise in case you have trouble, but I suggest that you not use the list unless you absolutely need to do so.

2. Now prioritize your list. Look out in front of you, and create a void. What's more important to you – to avoid _____ or to avoid _____? Put one word on one side and another word on the other side of your visual screen and decide which is more important. If you had to do without one of the two values, which one would you pick? Go through your entire list, comparing each item with every other item. For example, suppose your list of values consisted of the following:

Table 7-2: Some Possible Move-Away Values	
Failure	Rejection
Clutter	Depression
Hopelessness	Getting high/drunk
Being out of control	Emptiness
Feeling inferior	Feeling unappreciated
Criticism	Anger
Fear	Being wrong
Seeing "what's" wrong with everything	Feeling helpless
Being a victim	Feeling unloved
Feeling alone or abandoned	Feeling abused

You first ask yourself what is more important to avoid, *failure* or *rejection*, and you come up with *rejection*. Then you ask yourself, what is more important, to avoid *rejection* or to avoid *clutter*, and you again come up with *rejection*. Then you'd ask yourself, what's more important, to avoid *rejection* or *depression*, and you decide that *depression* is now worse. Now you ask yourself, what's more important, avoiding *depression* or *hopelessness*. You decide that depression is worse. Now you ask yourself what's more important, to avoid *depression* or to avoid *getting drunk/high*. You think that *depression* is worse. You continue this until you complete the list.

Let's say that you end up with emptiness as your most important value to avoid. Prior to that, the next worse one was depression. So now you start comparing depression (the negative value that was most important below emptiness) with the remaining items in the list. Continue this until you have ranked all ten negative values.

3. Take your most important value (*emptiness* in our example) and ask yourself what is important to you to avoid about that particular value. Again, you should come up with a list of about ten words or phrases.

4. Prioritize this new list using the same method that you used in step two. That is, make a binary comparison of each two-word pair.

5. Repeat steps 3 and 4 for every value on your list. You should now have a prioritized list of about 100 words.

6. Determine your evidence procedures, using the same questions that you did for the positive values. For each word on this list, ask yourself the following questions:

   a) How do you know when you have _____ (fill in value)? What are some of the ways you know you have it? _____

   b) How do you know when you do not have _____ (fill in value)? What are some of the ways you know you do not have it? _____

Value Elicitation (Mixed: Move-Toward and Move-Away)

What is absolutely essential for you to have in your life (from the move-toward exercise)? Answer this question with a list of at least ten words or phrases. I have included a list of suggested values at the end of this exercise in case you have trouble, but I suggest that you not use the list unless you absolutely need to do so.

What is absolutely essential for you to avoid in your life (from move away-from exercise)? Answer this question with a list of at least ten words or phrases. I have included a list of suggested negative values at the end of this exercise in case you have trouble, but I suggest that you not use the list unless you absolutely need to do so.

Now put both lists together and prioritize it. Look out in front of you and create a void. What's more important to you – to avoid _____ or to avoid _____? To have _____ or to avoid _____? To have _____ or to have _____? Put one word on one side and another word on the other side of your visual screen and decide which is more important. If you had to do without one of the two values, which one would you pick? Go through your entire list comparing each item with every other item. For example, suppose your list of values consisted of the following:

Some Possible Mixed Values	
Move-Toward Values	**Move-Away Values**
Happiness	Rejection
Family	Depression
Spirituality	Getting high/drunk
Freedom	Emptiness
Money	Feling unappreciated
Honesty	Anger
Loyalty	Being wrong

Then you ask yourself, what is more important, to avoid *rejection* or have *happiness*. You might decide that you'd be happy if you avoided rejection, but do your best to decide whether you want happiness or to avoid rejection. Let's say it is now happiness. Then you'd ask yourself, what's more important? Happiness or avoiding depression? And you decide that avoiding depression is the most important. You will continue like this until you complete the list.

Let's say that you end up with your family as your most important value to have. Prior to that, your next most important value was avoiding depression. So now you start comparing depression (the negative value that was most important below family) with the remaining items in the list. Continue this until you have ranked all your negative and positive values.

- Take your most important value (*family* in our example) and ask yourself what is important to you about that value or to avoid about that particular value. Again, you should come up with a list of about ten words or phrases.
- Prioritize this new list using the same method that you used in step two. That is, make a binary comparison of each two-word pair.
- Repeat steps 4 and 5 for every value on your list. You should now have a prioritized list of about 200 words.
- Determine your evidence procedures, using the same questions that you did for the last two exercises. For each word on this list, ask yourself the following questions:

How do you know when you have _____ (fill in value)? What are some of the ways you know you have it?

How do you know when you do not have_____ (fill in value)? What are some of the ways you know you do not have it?

For each of your top values, notice what roles you have in obtaining them. List that role in a table. Some of your evidence criteria for certain values might also have roles as well. Use this information to make a list of your most important roles.

Notice when you prioritize your values, whether the positive or negative ones come to the surface. If it is negative ones, then I suggest you start focusing on the positive aspects of your life. For example, at the end of each day, write down all the things that you feel grateful for in your life.

Van's Example: Value Elicitation

I'm mostly a move-toward person, but I will do the mixed value elicitation as I expect that's what most of you will do. In addition, if I was told, "Do this or you are going to die a horrible death," I would do whatever was requested (probably). But is that because I'm avoiding the negative or because I'm moving toward the more pleasant alternative? It's about 50-50. However, if there were a possibility of a horrible death versus violating my top values – for example, doing something (I can't think of what) that would set back the consciousness of humanity into the Dark Ages, then I would pick the horrible death.

What do I absolutely move toward in life? Here is my list.

Van's Move-Toward Values
Adventure
Creativity
My business
Learning success models
Being a big picture guy
Spirituality/Self-transformation
Helping others transform
Family
Financial freedom
Intimacy
Time to relax and do what's fun

Some of those 12 that I listed could probably be grouped together, and we will get to that later. Now what are my top move-away values?

Top Move-Away Values
Negative energy in others
Rejection
Chaos
Detailed busywork
Manual labor
Avoid poor health as I get older

The next step is to take my entire list and prioritize it. So, what you do is take item 1 (which is adventure) and compare it with each of the others until I find one that is more important.

Then, I take the new most important value and compare it with what else is on the list until I find what's more important than that. And I keep going like that until I find what's most important for the entire list of both positive and negative values.

Then I repeat the process for the second most important value (and I can use the second most important item I found in the first go around and then repeat the process with that.

So here is my example.

	Adventure	Creativity	
		My business	
		Learning success models	
		Big picture guy	
1		Spirituality/ Self-transformation	Helping others transform
			Family
			Financial freedom
			Intimacy
			Relax and do what's fun
			Avoid negative energy in others
			Avoid rejection
			Avoid chaos
			Avoid detailed busywork
			Avoid manual labor
			Avoid poor health as I get older

From this table, my most important value is spirituality and self-transformation. But I highlighted those values in yellow that I had to think about before deciding that spirituality was the most important.

Now to find the second one, I primarily have to start at the last one to stand out (creativity), or the first highlighted one (helping others transform). I already know that helping others transform themselves is more important to me than creativity. It would be my top value if I didn't think I had to transform myself a lot in order to help others.

So, let's do another table with that one.

1	Spirituality/Self-transformation	
2	Helping others transform	Family
		Financial freedom
		Intimacy
		Relax and do what's fun
		Avoid negative energy in others
		Avoid rejection
		Avoid chaos
		Avoid detailed busywork
		Avoid manual labor
		Avoid poor health as I get older

So, this one is easy; helping others transform comes out on top as my number two value.

For the third one, I have to decide whether creativity or family is more important. I believe that family is the most important so we will start with family in a new table. This is something interesting to me because I thought I valued creativity more.

1	Spirituality/Self-transformation		
2	Helping others transform		
3	Family	Financial freedom	
		Intimacy	
		Relax and do what's fun	
		Avoid negative energy in others	
		Avoid rejection	
		Avoid chaos	
		Avoid detailed busywork	
		Avoid manual labor	
4			Avoid poor health as I get older

This one is easy, as I get my first move-away fvalue. I'd always thought of this as a positive value, but I'm much more interested in not having problems as I get older than in moving toward great health. As a result, I have discovered something that I was unaware of until now.

Since family already was at the top except for the last one, family is my fourth highest value.

For the fifth one, I need to compare creativity with financial freedom. And this time, creativity is more important than financial freedom. I'm assuming I have enough financial freedom to be able to be creative, but I happen to believe that my financial freedom comes from creativity so creativity is more important.

1	Spirituality and Self-transformation		
	Helping others transform		
	Family		
4	Avoid poor health as I get older		
5	Creativity	My business	
		Learning success models	Part of my creativity
		Big picture guy	Part of my creativity
6		Financial Freedom	
		Intimacy	Part of family
		Relax and do what's fun	
		Avoid negative energy in others	
		Avoid rejection	
		Avoid chaos	
		Avoid detailed busywork	
		Avoid manual labor	

In this round, I think learning success models and being a big picture guy are part of my creativity. Thus, I will eliminate them and make them part of creativity. In addition, I think intimacy is part of family life, so I will eliminate that. Here, a few of the negatives start to impinge. I think all the negatives could prevent me from being creative. However, I'm going to assume here that I am creative, and in that state, I wouldn't even notice the negatives.

My values so far are as follows:

1	Spirituality/Self-transformation
2	Helping others transform themselves
3	Family
4	Avoid poor health as I get older
5	Creativity
6	Financial freedom

At this point, I probably need to start again with my remaining values. Here is the new table starting with adventure.

	Adventure	My business	I actually think my business fits in with the top five values as a subset of helping others transform
		Relax and do what's fun	
7		Avoid negative energy in others	Avoid rejection
			Avoid chaos
			Avoid detailed busywork
			Avoid manual labor

My 7th value is avoiding negative energy in others (and that's probably to avoid rejection as well).

I'm pretty sure my eighth value is to avoid manual labor and my ninth value is to avoid detailed busy work (falls under working for others).

Adventure would be the 10th value

That leaves relax and do what's fun as number 11. This might be classified as do "feel good" things which might be doing what's neither important nor urgent. Like watch television, go to a movie, read a fun book etc. However, I think it's strong enough to be my 11th value.

Then the last one is avoiding chaos. I'm ranking this as number 12. It's still on the list, but some of my other values tend to neutralize it.

The following table summarizes my top 12 values.

1	Spirituality/Self-transformation
2	Helping others transform themselves
3	Family
4	Avoid poor health as I get older
5	Creativity
6	Financial freedom
7	Avoiding negative energy in others
8	Avoid manual labor
9	Avoid detailed busywork
10	Adventure
11	Relax and have fun
12	Avoid chaos

The next step is to come up with a list of about ten things for each value (what do they mean). The step after that is to prioritize them, so I will do both together.

The next table gives the first four items with their subsets.

1	Spirituality/Self-transformation	Become one with my Inner Guidance and so that she will give me what I ask for when I ask.
		Be very happy for no reason and experience the joy of unconditional love.
		See the perfection of the "what is."
		Become a witness so that nothing disturbs me, and I am at peace.
		Quiet mind with no chatter.
		Raise my vibration so that I can better impact others.
		To take the oneness with my Inner Guidance to a higher level so that She anticipates my needs and gives them to me before I have to ask.
		To be an example for others.
		The incredible knowledge I get through the conversation that I have daily, after my mediations with my Inner Guidance. For example, we are currently discussing Gregory Batson's book *Mind Versus Nature*.
2	Helping others transform themselves	To solve problems such as global warming. That means influencing Level 5 entrepreneurs (according to the Graves' value scale) for whom power is more important than love.
		To raise the vibration of others as a means of solving global problems.
		To raise the consciousness of a billion-plus people to at least 5 on the VTI scale described in Chapter 8.
		Game of giving away 100,000 copies of Trading Beyond the Matrix.
		Writing a book that explains the illusion and the wonderful game we can play when we get that we make it all up.
3	Family	Companionship.
		Intimacy.
		Having a hostess around who has extraverted qualities that I don't.
		Having someone who loves to take care of me.
		Best friend.
		Someone to take care of and guide.

		Finding out about family from ancestry.com.
		Being grateful that my family is small as I think family tends to be Karma teachers rather than spiritual teachers.
4	Avoiding poor health as I get older	Having the mobility to carry out my other values.
		Having a sharp brain throughout my life.
		Feeling energy and passion throughout the day.
		Being able to run a 10K (but that stopped perhaps 15 years ago).
		Not taking prescription drugs that ameliorate symptoms but can make your overall health worse.
5	Creativity	Developing success models.
		Being a big picture type of person who can see the essence of something.
		Getting concepts like Maya at a different level so I can explain it to others.
		Writing books.
		Developing workshops.
5a	My business	A vehicle for creativity.
		Source of financial freedom.
		Vehicle for the top two values (transformation of myself and of others).
		Being a visionary leader.
6	Financial freedom	Gives me the ability to do everything else.
		Is a measure of my transformation and the ability to manifest in the world.
		Game to play.
		Model for others.
		Infinitely Wealthy Person can teach Infinite Wealth.
7	Avoiding negative energy in others	Mixed because if I need to do this, it means that others can impact me.
		Sign I need more self-transformation.
		Avoid conflict.
		Avoid hurting others.
		But I get to set boundaries.

8 and 9	Avoid manual labor Avoid detailed busywork	Only work for myself.
		Make sure I have people who are good at doing the things that I don't like to do.
		Don't do anything I don't want to do if I can find someone who makes less money per hour than I do who can do it for me at that rate.
10	Adventure	Spend about three months per year traveling to places I've never been.
		Do things that stimulate me (but make sure no chance of injury). I stopped skiing after I broke my shoulder, and it took almost a year to rehab the frozen shoulder that developed.
		Do things that are different.
		Be a first adopter.
		Doing things that are beyond my comfort zone, just to see what its like on the other side of that zone.
11	Relax and have fun	I've earned the right to do nothing if I want.
		Take a nap if I need it.
		Watch TV.
		Be a Green Bay Packers fan/owner.
		Go to movies or watch on TV.
		Read a good book.
		Take my wife to a nice dinner.
12	Avoid chaos	Avoid extremely messy/smelly situations (I had some of this with my ex-wife).
		Be organized on my computer.
		Be organized in my workshops/books.
		Be organized in my thinking process.

I find it very difficult to prioritize among these subcategories because, in some cases, they are steps or just different meanings for what the primary value means. So, I will leave my organization the way it is.

The next to last step is evidence procedures for each one of the subcategories. How do I know when I have it? How do I know when I don't have it?

Evidence for the Subcategories		
	Evidence I have	**Evidence I don't have**
Become one with my Inner Guidance so that She will give me what I ask for when I ask	Prayer Journal and daily dialogue.	Impatience when I ask and don't seem to get what I ask for.
Be very happy for no reason and experience the joy of unconditional love	I feel really good.	I have problems.
See the perfection of the "what is"	I feel really good.	I have problems. I lack gratitude.
Become a witness so that nothing disturbs me and I am at peace	At peace.	I find myself caught up in my thoughts rather than witnessing them.
Quiet mind with no chatter	At peace.	Aware of head chatter.
Raise my vibration so that I can better impact others.	I'm attracting more people to transform. We are seeing greater transformations.	Low income in business People resist self-work
To take the oneness with my Inner Guidance to a higher level so that She anticipates my needs and gives them to me before I have to ask.	I have the courage to travel someplace with nothing, and when I get there, all our needs are met.	The courage to do so is lacking. I don't have the faith.
To be an example for others.	Feedback.	No feedback.
The incredible knowledge I get through the conversation that I have daily, after my mediations with my Inner Guidance. For example, we are currently discussing Gregory Batson's book *Mind Versus Nature*.	I can see the discussions in my daily journal with my Inner Guidance.	Conversations are short and boring.

Evidence for the Subcategories		
	Evidence I have	**Evidence I don't have**
To solve problems such as global warming. That means influencing Level 5 entrepreneurs for whom power is more important than love. See Clare Graves' Values.	I'm totally at peace, and they either seem meaningless, or they don't seem to exist for me.	They still exist, and I think about them.
To raise the vibration of others as a means of solving global problems.	I become famous for helping others.	I'm pretty anonymous.
To raise the consciousness of a billion-plus people to at least Level 5 on the VTI scale described later in Chapter 8	I become famous for helping others.	I'm pretty anonymous.
Game of giving away 100,000 copies of Trading Beyond the Matrix.	I can count the books. Currently, in mid-2019, we are on 6000.	
Writing a book that explains the illusion and the wonderful game we can play when we get that we make it up.	That book is printed and in my hands. People say that what it does for them is what I intended.	
Companionship	Kala and I do things together.	I'm alone.
Intimacy	Intimacy sharing and physical contact.	Distance and no physical contact.
Having a hostess around who has extraverted qualities that I don't.	We have regular VTI parties.	Parties stop.
Having someone who loves to take care of me.	Kala is always doing things for me.	Kala no longer does much of anything.
Best friend.	We share and talk all the time.	We don't share and talk.
Someone to take care of and guide.	I see/feel the changes in my wife.	She is emotional and upset.
Finding out about family from ancestry.com	I see my large family tree. I find a new major insight.	I don't see anything, and the tree is gone.
Being grateful that my family is small, as I think family tends to be Karma teachers rather than spiritual teachers.	I have my wife and my son and my niece (and her husband and son).	Many people around and chaos.

Evidence for the Subcategories		
	Evidence I have	**Evidence I don't have**
Having the mobility to carry out my other values.	Can go where I want and do what I want.	Unable to go/do.
Having a sharp brain throughout my life.	I continue to do what I've always done and enjoy it.	Tip of the tongue phenomenon becomes greater; driving seems harder and harder.
Feeling energy and passion throughout the day.	I'm excited to do what I do.	I feel too drained to do anything.
Being able to run a 10K (but that stopped perhaps 15 years ago).	I can run without knee pain and thus train.	I run and start to get knee pain. I get to walk instead.
Not taking prescription drugs that ameliorate symptoms but can make your overall health worse.	I'm not taking any prescription drugs, and I haven't for about ten years.	I'm taking prescription drugs.
Developing success models	I come up with a new idea that will help people (i.e., improvement to Super Traders program)	A long period (at least a year) goes by with no new ideas.
Being a big picture type of person who can see the essence of something.	Someone talks, and I can summarize what they are saying and their viewpoint in a few words.	I get bogged down in details.
Getting concepts like Maya at a different level so I can explain it to others.	I read, meditate, and talk with the Divine and get new ideas all the time.	No new ideas for at least three months.
Writing books.	I'm working on a new book (outline state or actual chapters written).	Nothing is being written and I have no desire to do so.
Developing workshops.	I have an idea for a new workshop (one based upon this book).	No new ideas or impetus to get them.
A vehicle for creativity.	All of the above.	Nothing new happens.
Source of financial freedom.	I get a salary that is more than I need to live off of.	VTI no longer pays me any money/VTI has no income.

Evidence for the Subcategories		
	Evidence I have	**Evidence I don't have**
Vehicle for top two values.	I am juiced and do my meditations daily.	Stagnancy. Mentally/emotionally.
Being a visionary leader.	Continually have new ideas to apply.	I no longer interact with VTI.
Gives me the ability to do everything else.	I don't have to think about whether I can do/buy something.	I'm concerned about money.
Is a measure of transformation, and the ability to manifest in the world.	Goals beyond what I need are met; I want to give money away.	Things don't seem to change or improve.
Game to play.	Measure of siddhi power.	
Model for others.	I can give lots of personal examples.	I can't give personal examples.
Infinitely Wealth Person can teach Infinite Wealth.	Excited to teach Infinite Wealth.	I want to stop teaching that class.
Mixed because if I need to do this it means that others can impact me.	My life is quiet.	I sense negative energy from others.
Sign I need more self-transformation.	My life is quiet.	
Avoid conflict.	My life is quiet.	
Avoid hurting others.	My life is quiet.	
But I need to set boundaries.	No sociopaths in life. No one taking advantage of me.	
Only work for myself.		Someone else keeps giving me orders.
Make sure I have people who are good doing the things that I don't like to do.	Happy employees doing what I don't want to do or have time to do.	

Evidence for the Subcategories		
	Evidence I have	**Evidence I don't have**
Don't do anything I don't want to do if I can find someone who makes less money per hour than I do who can do it for me at that rate.	I can ask the question, and the answer is typically the name of a person who qualifies.	
Spend about three months per year traveling to places I've never been.	Scheduled in my calendar.	Not scheduled.
Do things that stimulate me (but make sure no chance of injury). I stopped skiing after I broke my shoulder, and it took almost a year to rehab the frozen shoulder that developed.	Brings excitement.	I'm bored traveling.
Do things that are different.	Does it extend me a little bit?	Is it too comfortable?
Be a first adopter.	AI, electric car ...	Not willing to try what's new.
I've earned the right to do nothing if I want.	I do nothing or something fun that's not important or urgent, and no one cares.	I feel stressed.
Take a nap if I need it.	I take regular naps.	
Watch TV.	I watch at least one hour a day.	
Be a Green Bay Packers fan/owner.	Watch packer games and have fun.	
Go to movies or watch on TV.	Two to three movies per week.	
Read a good book	Have list of next books to read.	No interest in next book.
Take wife to nice dinner.	We go out each week.	No dinner date for at least a week.

Evidence for the Subcategories		
	Evidence I have	**Evidence I don't have**
Avoid extremely messy/smelly situations (I had some of this with my ex-wife).	House is so bad I have to leave.	
Be organized on my computer.	I can find things quickly.	I can't find anything.
Be organized in my workshops/books.	I can go in and just give a workshop or start writing.	
Be organized in my thinking process.	New ideas.	

While I haven't totally completed all of his, I think you get the idea of how it is done. Since I'm a move-toward person, I'm more interested in evidence that I have rather than evidence that I don't have.

Finally, the last step is to determine the roles you play in life. Look at your values list (and also the subcategories) and determine the key role that you play. In some cases, you might just have one role for a particular value. In other areas, you might have multiple roles. Below is the table where I determine my roles.

Role	Value/Sub-Value
Spiritual Master	Spirituality/Self-transformation
	Become one with my Inner Guidance and so that She will give me what I ask for when I ask.
	Be very happy for no reason and experience the joy of unconditional love.
	See the perfection of the "what is."
	Become a witness so that nothing disturbs me, and I am at peace.
	Quiet mind with no chatter.
	Raise my vibration so that I can better impact others.
	To take the oneness with my Inner Guidance to a higher level so that She anticipates my needs and gives them to me before I have to ask.
	To be an example for others.
Guru	Helping others transform themselves.
	To solve problems such as global warming. That means influencing Level 5 entrepreneurs for whom power is more important than love.
	To raise the vibration of others as a means of solving global problems.
	To raise the consciousness of a billion-plus people to at least 5 on the VTI scale described in Chapter 8.

	Game of giving away 100,000 copies of Trading Beyond the Matrix.
	Writing a book that explains the illusion and the wonderful game we can play when we get that we make it all up.
Best Possible Husband	Family.
	Companionship.
	Intimacy.
	Having a hostess around who has extraverted qualities that I don't.
	Having someone who loves to take care of me.
	Having someone I can support in her personal growth and seeing what happens (and how our life is better) when she evolves in consciousness.
Best Friend	Best friend.
	Taking care of my dogs.
	Someone to take care of and guide.
	Finding out about family from ancestry.com.
	Being grateful that my family is small as I think family tends to be Karma teachers rather than spiritual teachers.
Passionate Person	Avoiding poor health as I get older.
	Having the mobility to carry out my other values.
	Having a sharp brain throughout my life.
	Feeling energy and passion throughout the day.
	Being able to run a 10K (but that stopped perhaps 15 years ago). Thus, I'll change this to some exercise at least three days per week.
Success Guru	Creativity
	Developing success models.
	Being a big picture type of person who can see the essence of something.
	Getting concepts like Maya at a different level so I can explain it to others.
Best Selling Author	Writing books.
	Developing Workshops.
Visionary Leader	My business.
	A vehicle for creativity.
	Source of financial freedom.
	Vehicle for top two values.

	Being a visionary leader.
Wealth Magnet	Financial freedom.
	Gives me the ability to do everything else.
	Is a measure of transformation, and the ability to manifest in the world.
	Game to play.
	Model for others.
	Infinitely Wealthy Person can teach Infinite Wealth.
Peace Maker	Avoiding negative energy in others.
	Mixed because if I need to do this, it means that others can impact me.
	Sign I need more self-transformation.
	Avoid conflict.
	Avoid hurting others.
Boundary Setter	But I need to set boundaries.
	Avoid manual labor and detailed busywork.
	Only work for myself.
	Make sure I have people who are good doing the things that I don't like to do.
	I don't do anything I don't want to do if I can find someone who makes less money per hour than I do who can do it for me at that rate.
World-Class Adventurer	Adventure.
	Spend about three months per year traveling to places I've never been.
	Do things that stimulate me (but make sure no chance of injury). I stopped skiing after I broke my shoulder, and it took almost a year to rehab the frozen shoulder that developed.
	Do things that are different.
	Be a first adopter.
Laid Back Dude	Relax and have fun
	I've earned the right to do nothing if I want.
	Take a nap if I need it.
	Watch TV.
	Be a Green Bay Packers fan/owner.
	Go to movies or watch on TV.

	Read a good book.
	Take wife to nice dinner.
World Class Organizer	Avoid chaos.
	Avoid extremely messy/smelly situations (I had some of this with my ex-wife).
	Be organized in my computer.
	Be organized in my workshops/books.
	Be organized in my thinking process.

So, to complete my value elicitation, here are my 14 roles in life.

	My Roles
1	Spiritual Master (SM)
2	Inspirational Guru (IG)
3	Best Possible Husband (BPH)
4	Best Friend (BF)
5	Passionate & Healthy Person (PHP)
6	Success Guru (SG)
7	Best Selling Author (BSA)
8	Visionary Leader (VL)
9	Wealth Magnet (WM)
10	Peace Maker (PM)
11	Boundary Setter (BS)
12	World-Class Adventurer {WCA)
13	Laid Back Dude (LBD)
14	World Class Organizer (WCO)

Now contemplate your life. What have you done with your life? Do your values reflect what you have done? Do your values reflect who you are? If the answer is "no" to either question, then either there is some deep undercurrent to your life that's not reflected in your values, or you did a very poor job at determining what your values were.

How about your roles? Are there any roles you have in life – personal or business which you have not listed? Think about it, and if you come up with one, notice why.

How Do You Spend Your Time?

Steven Covey, in describing the habits of highly effective people, suggests that you look at how you spend your time. In addition, he classified time spent into two categories:

- Is it important to achieving your dreams, or does it have no relationship to achieving your dreams (not important)?

- Is it something that is urgent (it requires your immediate attention) or is it something that is not urgent?

The net result is that you end up having four categories of how you spend your time.

Doing what's not important and what's not urgent: This is usually when you just do things to feel good. My role of "laid back dude" just wants to do this sort of thing. And that's okay. There is a place for it, but that's not all I want to do. For some people, this might be where you hide from the world.

Doing what's urgent and not important: There are several ways to classify this group of things. First, they are distractors. For example, do you answer the phone immediately when it rings? If so why? It might just be a sales call. Or do you answer it if it is someone you know? Again, why? Perhaps we can say you have delusions about what's important, and these things cause you stress.

The next category of tasks is those things that are both urgent and important. These are things you have to do right now. They are important for meeting your goals. In many cases, you have to do them right now because you put them off until they became urgent. And if that's the case, you are spending your time fighting fires.

And finally, the last category is the things that are important but not urgent. In my opinion, transformation and growth stem from working in this quadrant. For example, right now, I'm working on writing this chapter of my book. I absolutely don't have to do it right now. But I think, in the future, it will help my Super Traders and a lot of other people. I'm going to show a lot of people how to achieve their dreams. We might even do a workshop on the topic. It's important, but I could do it six months from now or tomorrow. It doesn't have to be now.

Time Awareness Exercise

You have one more exercise to do. Do it while you are completing the rest of this book because it will take a week to do.

Find a timer (on your computer, your phone, or perhaps on your smartwatch). Set it to go off once each hour. At the end of the hour, you are going to do something that's important but not urgent. Namely, reflect back on the hour and ask the following questions.

What did you do during the hour? Which of the roles you listed was busy during that time period? Was there some role that you were not aware of? If so, then make a record of it.

For each of the roles you notice during the hour, how was your time spent. Go down to as small as 15-minute intervals. Which of the four categories did you spend most of your time?

There is no need to do this while you are sleeping. Just notice when you went to bed and when you got up. You can call sleep as being important and not urgent time spent on your health (unless you were sleep-deprived, and then you might say it was both urgent and important).

When you are finished, you should have a table that lists the time spent doing each role; any new roles you might observe during your week of observation; and how much of the time for that role was in each of the four categories.

Here are two tables, one you can use as a template, and the second one is a brief example of two of my days.

Activity	Time	Role	Category Hours			
			I	II	III	IV

Here is a a record of how I spent yesterday in the format of the table above. It's not close to being representative of how I spend my time as it doesn't include any of my trips or any of my workshop days.

Activity	Time	Role	Category Hours			
			I	II	III	IV
Sleep	1-7 a.m.	PP			6 hrs	
Bemer®	7-7:40 a.m.	PP				40 min
Meditation & conversation with Divine	7:40 -9 a.m.	SM				80 min
Shower and Misc.	9-9:30 a.m.	PP				30 min
Walk	9:30-10:30 a.m.	PP				1 hr
Emails etc.	10:30-12 a.m.	SG	45 min	45 min		
Work on Book	12-4 p.m.	BSA/IG/SG				4 hrs
Emails	4-4:30 p.m.	SG/WM			30 min	
Fool around	4:30-6 p.m.	LBD/WCA	90 min			
Check markets	6-6:30 p.m.	WM				30 min
PP for Streaming Video	6:30-8 p.m.	IG				90 min
Dinner	8 -9 p.m.					1 hr
Watch TV Fool around	9 p.m.-12 a.m.	LBD/WCA	3 hrs			
Walk dogs	12-12:15 a.m.	BPF			15 min	
Sleep	12-7 a.m.	PP				7 hr
Bemer® and sleep	7-8 a.m.	PP				1 hr
Meditate and converse with Divine	8-9:30 a.m.	SM				90 min
Shower	9:30-10 a.m.	PP				30 min
Fool around	10-11 a.m.	LBD	1 hrs			
Emails and lessons	11 a.m.-1 p.m.	IG/SG			1 hr	
Lunch	1-2 p.m.	PP				1 hr
Interview	2-3 p.m.	SG			1 hr	
Fool around	3-5 p.m.	LBD	2 hrs			
Work on book	5-7:30 p.m.	BSA				2 hrs
Dinner with wife (go out)	7:30-9:30 p.m.	BPH, PP				2 hrs
Watch TV	9:30-11:30 p.m.	LBD	2 hrs			
Walk dogs	11:30-11:45 p.m.	BPF			15 min	
TOTALS (hours)			10.25	0.75	9	25.20

Again, this is a small sample of my time – just two days. I spent 10.25 hours that might be called wasted time. If I had something important to do, I could easily take away from this time. I spent 45 minutes looking at emails that seemed urgent but were not that important. I spent about half of my time doing important/not urgent things. This is where one really accomplishes a lot. I spent 9 hours doing urgent, important things, 6 hrs of that was sleeping when I was somewhat sleep-deprived (so I also called it urgent).

Develop a spreadsheet that looks something like this and keep track of your hours.

Activity	Time	Role	Category Hours			
			I	II	III	IV

Next, when you have collected several weeks' worth of data (and it might be useful to do it for a month or two), then fill out the next table. I've done it as an example just looking at my small sample of data.

Role	Total Time	Category I NI/NU	Category II U/NI	Category III U/I	Category IV NU/I
1 – SM	2.833				2.833
2 – IG	6.5			1.0	5.5
3 – BPH	2.0				2.0
4 – BF	0.5			0.5	
5 – PP	23.167			6	17.167
6 – SG	7.0	0.75	0.75	1.5	4.0
7 – BSA	7.5		0.75	0.75	6.0
8 – VL	0				
9 – WM	1.0			0.5	0.5
10 – PM	0				
11—BS	0				

12 – WCA	4.0	4.0			
13 – LBD	10.5	10.5			
14 – WCO	0				
15					

From this table, I can begin to see how much time I devote to each role and how much of that time is in each category. It's quite revealing.

I've spent no time here being a visionary leader (VL), but that comes in spurts. I've spent no time being a peace maker (PM) – but that's not something I seek out. I've spent no time being a boundary setter (BS), and that might be quite representative. Finally, no time being a world-class organizer – I might have forgotten things I did in other time periods.

If you find that much of your week was spent doing something unusual, then continue your record-keeping for at least another week. For example, there might be a week each month in which I'm involved in workshops. That's certainly not representative of a typical day, so I need to spend more time. Another time, I might be on one of my trips. That's not necessarily typical of my normal day. Do enough weeks to represent how you spend time in your life.

When you have done this exercise, especially filling in the time, you might become aware that there are roles that you want to play and are neglecting. Note if any are obvious to you in the space below.

Here is what I noticed.

Exercise is not a big deal in my life. It could be; I'd love to run if I could run without hurting my knees. I also have a lot of problems when it's hot outside, but, given the time and overcoming my tendency to get wiped out by the heat, I'd love to play golf again. That would mean an extra 8 hours of time each week for golf (twice each week). It could be PHP, but we'll call it the Exercise is Fun (EF) role.

I don't make an effort to socialize much. Probably what happens when you are an 89% "Introvert" on the Myers Briggs. But I could make that a useful role. I already have the role of best friend – but that's part of my relationship with my wife. However, I will keep it under the role BPF.

I'm really an animal lover. I consider my dogs my friends, so I called some of the time BPF, but we will change that role to Animal Lover (AL). We just got a third dog. All are Papillons, but this one is a little female (only nine weeks) who is quite dominant, so she is not likely to take a lot of nonsense from our two older males.

Lastly, I want more of a philanthropist role. It doesn't take a lot of my time now, but I'd like to increase that. So, we will call that Great Philanthropist (GP).

I don't expect that Boundary Setter (BS) and World Class Organizer (WCO) will get a lot of time in my life, but perhaps they will be.

Here is the table of my roles redone. You should redo yours as well at this point.

	My Roles
1	Spiritual Master (SM)
2	Inspirational Guru (IG)
3	Best Possible Husband (BPH)
4	Best Friend (BF)
5	Passionate & Healthy Person (PHP)
6	Success Guru (SG)
7	Best Selling Author (BSA)
8	Visionary Leader (VL)
9	Wealth Magnet (WM)
10	Peace Maker (PM)
11	Boundary Setter (BS)
12	World-Class Adventurer (WCA)
13	Laid Back Dude (LBD)
14	World Class Organizer (WCO)
15	Exercise is Fun (EF)
16	Animal Lover (AL)
17	Great Philanthropist (GP)

Thus, I now have 17 roles for which to delegate my time. When you finish this chapter, make a note of your observations and learnings in the space below.

_____
_____
_____
_____
_____
_____
_____
_____
_____
_____
_____

Note

[1] You might find it useful to do the positive values, and then the negative values, and then the mixed.

CHAPTER 8

Useful Models for Values

The material presented in this book about propulsion systems is a set of useful beliefs. These beliefs are not necessarily true. These are just made up, but useful concepts. If you use them, they will help you become happier and more successful. That's probably the best we can do. The four models presented here should be treated as models that are useful but not necessarily true. But if you start doing that with everything you believe, then your awareness and level of consciousness will skyrocket.

Key Models for How Values are Organized

In this chapter, I'd like to present four models that could reflect how values are organized. Those models are Abraham Maslow's Needs Hierarchy, Clare Grave's Emergent Cyclical Levels of Existence Theory (ECLET), the David Hawkins's model of consciousness, and the Van Tharp Institute (VTI) model of consciousness.

Maslow's Needs Hierarchy

Maslow would probably say that you start with needs and progress to values. Maslow wrote three books on the topic and his ideas were very controversial at the time because they dealt with non-observable concepts in a period when behaviorism[1] ruled psychology. However, the model presented is quite useful.

Maslow believes that **physiological drives** are the starting point for a motivation theory. These needs include breathing, food, water, sex, sleep, the maternal instinct, homeostasis, and excretion. Take any one of these away for long enough, and you will have a very motivated person. Maslow even goes on to say that if the body lacks some chemical, the individual will develop a very specific appetite for foods containing that chemical.

He also says that survival needs will dominate over other basic needs. Thus, a person who lacks all the levels of Maslow's hierarchy: food, safety, love, and esteem, will probably spend his/her time looking for food. Maslow also says that someone dominated by a physical need will redefine many things in his life. For a hungry man, for example, the ideal future would be to find a place where there is a lot of good food.

The basic philosophy behind Maslow's theories is once basic needs are satisfied, then higher needs tend to emerge. When hunger is satiated, it becomes unimportant. A new physiological need, if unsatisfied, would emerge.

When all the physiological needs are satisfied, then **safety needs emerge**. These needs, if not satisfied, would serve to organize behavior. The person would be safety-seeking. At this point, even his/her world outlook becomes one of seeking safety. The person then wants everything to be orderly and predictable, with no hidden dangers. Some of the common metaprograms, discussed in the prior chapter, will tend to emerge when one is deprived of safety early in life. These might include:

- A preference of the known and the familiar, and a distrust of change.
- Having a known religion or philosophy that organizes the universe and explains it nicely.
- A tendency toward black-and-white thinking – it's safe or it's not safe.
- Dependency, finding others (especially those who seem to be powerful) to rely on for safety.
- Establishing obsessive-compulsive organization so that no dangers will appear. This means having rules or procedures in place that emphasize safety.

At the next level, once the physiological and safety needs are met, Maslow says that "love" or "belongingness" needs arise. These include both giving and receiving love. If these are lacking, the person will desperately search for a life partner, friends, or even children. He or she wants to belong to a group. This will dominate his/her life to the extent of forgetting that he was once hungry or insecure. Here Maslow emphasizes that love does not mean sex, but that sex can become part of the love need.

The fourth level of need, according to Maslow, are the esteem needs. People need a stable, firm, and high evaluation of themselves (i.e., based upon achievement and respect of others). There are two classifications here. The first gives a wide definition of esteem as it includes strength, achievement, adequacy, self-confidence, independence, and freedom. Can you see how certain metaprograms might come out of not having these things?

The second definition comes from the esteem of others. It includes prestige, reputation, recognition, and appreciation. When these come about, it leads to changes in other metaprograms – self-confidence, self-worth, ego strength, self-integrity. Of course, not having these things leads to a sense of inferiority and helplessness.

For Maslow's fifth need, self-actualization, he says, "What a man can be, he must be." It's the desire for self-fulfillment. It's like finding your purpose in life and then doing everything you can to fulfill it. For example, many people have creative urges that must be fulfilled – the desire to paint, write, or create music. This only comes from people who are basically satisfied in all their other needs (which he says is rare in our society or any other human society).

One might tend to think that when one type of need is 100% satisfied, then the next need emerges. Maslow explains that that is not the case for most people. When basic needs are satisfied, say 60%, then safety needs might be satisfied 20%, and love needs 10%, and perhaps esteem needs 5%. It's not as if one need must be fully satisfied for another to emerge.

There are certain requirements for all the basic needs to be met. These include freedom to speak, to express oneself, to do as one wishes as long as no harm is done to others, freedom to seek justice, and environmental conditions in which there is basic honesty and orderliness. If these conditions are not met, says Maslow, it is almost as if a basic need is not being met.

Maslow gives some additional insight into this theory in his *Theory of Motivation* book. He says that people who have been satisfied in their basic needs throughout their lives, particularly in their early years, can withstand a large degree of thwarting of those needs. For example, this probably describes me, and if I am motivated enough, I can certainly deprive myself of some of the basic needs. Here in India, I'm deprived of food I like, but I'm using self-awareness to determine what causes me to like or dislike certain foods. At other times, I've managed to fast for some time, all for the sake of becoming healthier.

Maslow makes a few other points that are worth mentioning. Not all behavior is motivated. Some of it just happens. You can hear a word, and an image implied by that word comes to mind. That, according to Maslow, is not motivated behavior. The classification system is based on functions, purposes, or goals – not necessarily motivated behavior.

Conclusions: Maslow's theory nicely explains that when many of these different needs are thwarted, it leads to automatic behavior that we have called metaprograms in the prior chapter. Examples include:

- No safety, then go for the familiar and avoid change and risk.
- No safety, then go for procedures that help with safety.
- No safety, then join groups that promise security if you follow them. You become dependent upon them.
- No esteem from self, then develop low self-confidence, and low-ego strength.
- No esteem from others, then develop low self-worth and low self-integrity.

Maslow's theories flourished during the time of "Behaviorism" in psychology. In such an environment, topics like needs, motivation, self-actualization, happiness, and purpose were not considered to be objects of study. For example, studying rat behavior was how you learned about behavior in general, and you can't ask a rat what his purpose in life is.

Clare Graves' ECLET

Clare Graves taught psychology at Union College in Schenectady, New York, where he developed an epistemology model of human psychology. He claimed that the inspiration came from his undergraduate psychology students. Graves was highly influenced by Maslow's thinking, but he was aware of the negative press that Maslow got. There are rumors that 1) he burned his work just before he died, and 2) that he was working on a book just before he died but never finished it. Both rumors are contradictory and we may never know.

Graves collected data from over 1,000 men and women, aged 18 to 65 between 1952 and 1959. And from the data he gathered, developed what's known as the *Emergent Cyclical Levels of Existence Theory* (ECLET). He believed that humans developed new psycho-social coping systems to solve their problems and cope with the world they encountered.

He also believed that humans are forever emergent with new, open systems in response to evolving problems. Both progression and regression are possible with his model. He also believed that these cycles alternated between self-expression and self-denial. Maslow, when he learned of this model, said it was much more sophisticated than his own.

Graves' levels are given in the table below. In Graves's model, individuals swing through Maslow's levels: Physiological, Safety, Belongingness, and Self-Esteem. However, he imposes a new third level of Power (see the table below), and then his sixth through eighth levels are:

6) Information
7) Understanding
8) Beauty and Self-Expression.

The table below shows the eight levels:

Clare Graves ECLET Levels	
Self-Expression	**Self-Denial**
Level 1: Maintaining physiological stability with physiological motivation, no particular value system, and automatic thinking.	**Level 2:** Tribal living to maintain safety. The motivation is assurance, and the primary value is safety. The thinking is autistic thinking. The value system consists of tribal traditions. You were expected to sacrifice yourself for the good of the tribe and even give your life as a sacrifice to the gods.
Level 3: Is about power and there is some self-awareness. The primary motivation is exploitation with people acting like psychopaths. The value system is about power and dominance. This is the feudal system of the Middle Ages and the King represents the ultimate alpha male.	**Level 4:** Developed to counteract the madness of level 3. Here there is some sort of book that tells people what to do. It could be a religious text or a corporate manual. The primary motivation is security – do what the book says, and you'll have peace. The value system is about sacrificing oneself now for later rewards or salvation. The thinking is absolutist – the book is always right. Level 4 was the only way to control level 3. Thus, the Church tended to dominate sociopathic kings.

Clare Graves ECLET Levels	
Self-Expression	**Self-Denial**
Level 5: Thinking reacted to the tyranny of level 4 and to avoid that dualistic thinking of we're right and you're wrong. The credo was to conquer it all, but everyone who's smart enough has a chance. Here the motivation is independence using science to conquer the world. Thinking is now very multiplistic. *Science became the backbone of level 5 thinking* – brought about by the need to conquer nature and control everything.	**Level 6:** Thinking arose in reaction to level 5 dominance of huge corporations, etc. Their goal was to live within the human element with an affiliation motivational system. The specific motivation was love and affiliation to develop community, allowing each person just to be.
Level 7: Comes about because level 6 has no way to get anything done. *We now have systemic thinkers who wish to restore viability to a disordered world.* Level 7s have an existential motivational system with the specific motivation of developing self-worth. The end goal is existence through acceptance.	**Level 8:** Comes about because level 7 tends to foster existential dichotomies. Now we have an end value of communion through experience with an end goal. This stage just started in the last 30 years and is very rare. Those who talk about it have no experience of it and thus cannot describe it. It's said to be about ontological being.

Several books have come out about Grave's ECLET in an attempt to apply it to how to influence others by learning how people think. Two notable examples are *Spiral Dynamics*[2] and Adriana James's book, *Values and the Evolution of Consciousness*.

Let's look at each of these levels in a little more detail:

Level 1: Level 1, according to Dr. Adriana James, represents the consciousness of pure survival. This type of thinking started at least 100,000 years ago. It represents pure animalistic type survival with no self-consciousness but with heightened sensitivity to the environment. It's each person for himself in a dog-eat-dog world.

I'm not sure that level 1 makes sense. If a woman gives birth, she's probably at least with a man and possibly other family members. In contrast, this grouping seems to assume that we were all loners at first. The overall model seems more complete to assume a level one existed or exists, so perhaps that's why it is there. Another contradiction, in my opinion, is the level one people are assumed to have a heightened sensitivity of the senses at this level, which I have always assumed, tends to occur primarily with advanced spiritual states.

Level 2: Level 2 thinking sprung up about 40-60,000 years ago when mankind began to assemble into tribes for safety. Family and the clan became the key to living and the tribal leader was always right. It's thought to be a sacrificial way of life where the concerns of the tribe are everything. Newcomers are treated with suspicion and you need to be born[3] into the tribe to belong. The tribe will have multiple gods reflecting all the manifestations of nature. The focus of authority is the tribe or clan itself, with the tribal leader representing the clan. The thinking is somewhat like the following quote from an Aboriginal leader:

> "Decision making is made in harmony across everyone involved and is steered by the circle of Elders …the title (Elder) is very much respected and an extremely special privilege."[4]

American Indians would also fall into this category.

Proponents of the Graves Model consider this to be a very low level of consciousness. Alternatively, if you look at Hawkins levels of consciousness, as described in the next model, these people might be at very high levels of consciousness. That is my belief. For example, Benjamin Franklin in 1770 wrote that "Happiness is more generally and equally diffused among Savages than in civilized societies. No European who has tasted savage life can afterwards bear to live in our societies."[5]

Level 3: Level 3 thinking is all about power and it probably started with the agrarian age about 6,000 years ago. Some tribes used to sacrifice members to the gods and the members considered it an honor to sacrifice themselves for the tribe.[6] Graves might think that some young people might rebel at this idea and start level 3 – every man for himself in search of power and dominance.

At level 3 we get almost pathological behavior of "What's in it for me?" and "What can I do to seize power?" The whole feudal system of the Middle Ages was based upon this model. The king granted power to certain nobles in exchange for taxes and men to fight in war, the noble had his own land and allowed peasants to work the land in exchange for a mere subsistence level of existence. What was produced on the land belonged to the nobleman. Even wildlife was the king's or the nobleman's property. Poaching was usually punished by death. You don't kill your noble lord's deer.

Great conquerors are prototypes of level three. Names come to mind such as Alexander the Great, Attila the Hun, Genghis Khan, Erik the Red, Ragnar Lothbrok, William the Conqueror (really a viking), and in more modern times, Adolf Hitler and Joseph Stalin. Here you also have the alpha male or the alpha female, the dominant person – not because of wisdom but because of strength and power.

Level 4: Level 3 thinking can only be tamed by level 4 thinking, which appeared about 3,500 years ago and started to become significant about 400 AD. Suddenly, there appeared a right way of thinking. It was usually symbolized by a book – often a religious text. The book described how to behave and thus provided a way to tame level 3s. Throughout much of European history, there were kings and popes. Both had authority, but the pope could condemn the king to eternal hell for not following the rules of the book. If you follow the rules of the book, then you might not live a happy life and much sacrifice was demanded, but you were told that you would find salvation in the afterlife. Priests had a lot of power in that they could help you get into heaven if you contributed to the church. Level 4 was able to curb the powers of level 3, but it was a lose-lose situation. Following the rules didn't bring happiness, but not following the rules brought about extreme measures, including such things as the Inquisition.

You can find level 4 in many groups today. According to Adriana James, anything with an "ism" at the end of it falls into this path. Nazis might have been led by a level 3 thinker, but they established a level 4 way of thinking. Socialism, Fascism, and Capitalism all have similarities, according to James. But she takes it even further, including Buddhism, Taoism, Tantrism, etc. and just about any form of government existing today. Also, in level 4 thinking, there are two sets of rules – one belongs to the ruling class and the other one belongs to everyone else. In the US, members of Congress get their own retirement system and don't have to pay into social security. Spend one term in Congress and your retirement is set for life.

What's more interesting is how some power elite groups have taken over level 4 thinking. James describes the medical profession as an example. Only one way of thinking is tolerated – allopathic medicine to treat symptoms. People who work outside the system are not tolerated, especially those who try to find alternative methods to treat cancer. Chemotherapy, radiation, and surgery are the only allowed methods to treat cancer. These are not successful and you are not allowed to know how ineffective the methods are. Alternative healers who establish a successful practice treating cancer are driven out of business, and if that doesn't work, they are often killed.[7] A level 4 system has one primary goal – to maintain itself and its doctrine.

Level 5: Level 4 brought about a tyranny, supported by the book of rules. For example, from the time of Aristotle until the 17th century, knowledge came from the thinking of the early Greeks and had to agree with scripture (the book) or the King. To go against that thinking was heresy. This was the authority paradigm as a basis for knowledge. The book or the pope or the king is the authority for what is. This authority paradigm is still practiced today as the teacher or professor is assumed to have the knowledge to pass on to students. Investors look to the "talking heads" on CNBC as authorities on what the market is doing.

Science (and adherence to the scientific method) started around the 17th century and became the backbone of a new Level 5 thinking that fueled the Industrial Revolution. Now we have free-thinking, trade, commerce, and the scientific method. Notice that if you strongly believe in the scientific method, you are fully into level 5 thinking.

Suddenly control is back in the hands of the individual, and we get personal power, individual freedom and control. Level 5 wants to destroy religious dogma in return for freedom, independence, and massive mastery of the world. Man has dominion over the world, can kill off whole animal species, can use up the world's resources, and pollute the planet.

We suddenly become fascinated with presenters who have programs on *Personal Power*[8] and how to get it all. Suddenly you have huge corporations that start to dominate the world – big oil, big agribusiness, big pharmaceuticals, and today, those companies that dominate the internet and artificial intelligence.

Let's look at allopathic medicine and big pharmaceutical companies as an example of level 4 and level 5 thinking working together. Big pharmaceutical companies represent level 5 thinking and they will do whatever they can to preserve their trillion-dollar industry. They don't want drugs that heal people; they want drugs that ameliorate symptoms so that people can take them for the rest of their lives, paying huge prices every month.

Just as an example, James quotes the following statement from a sales representative at a pharmaceutical company. *"If you are stupid enough to buy my product without checking it out, it's your problem. I have my mind and you have yours. I am using mine, what about you."*[9]

A friend of mine who is into alternative health procedures once heard the CEO of a pharmaceutical company say: *"At age 65 or so, people retire and take themselves out of the economy. And at that point, we get to take them out and put their house back into the economy."*[10] But here at level 5, it's all about profits and control. Level 5 is also supported by level 4 agencies such as the Food and Drug Administration (FDA) and the American Medical Association (AMA) – which go by the book and punish those who don't follow in line. A level 5 company can find this very useful in helping them maintain their dominance.[11]

The primary concepts that come out of level 5 thinking include market economy, utilitarian political philosophy, the commercialism of technology, the scientific method, the use of machines to increase productivity, and the absolute right to "life, liberty, and the pursuit of happiness." Does this sound familiar? It's what dominates our culture today.

What's interesting about this level is that the money elite take over control from government. Government still exists, but the rich rule it all. Think about central bankers who control a country's money supply. The US Federal Reserve is not a part of the US government. Instead, it is controlled by the richest families in the world – think Rockefellers, Rothschilds and DuPonts. They believed:

"politicians are too weak and too subject to temporary popular pressures to be trusted with control over the money supply."[12]

But my favorite statement is a quote from Baron Montagu Norman, a former Governor of the Bank of England, who is pictured on the left. He said something I've thought of for years, but this statement seems to confirm it. Norman said:

These truths are well known among our principal men, who are now engaged in forming an imperialism to govern the world. By dividing the voter through the political party system, we can get them to expend their energies fighting for questions of no importance. It is thus, by discrete action, we can secure for ourselves that which has been so well planned and so successfully accomplished.[13]

Laura Shinn, in a 2014 *Forbes* article, pointed out the richest 85 people in the world have as much wealth as the lowest half of the population consisting of over 3.5 billion people.[14] That's now changed; four years later in January 2019,[15] the 26 richest people have as much wealth as the poorest 3.7 billion people combined – showing just how fast the money is moving to the wealthiest people. And it reported in the Oxfam Report in January 2017 that the 8 wealthiest men in the world (i.e., about 1% of the world's billionaires) own as much as the poorest 3.7 billion people in the world.[16]

What's interesting is that during the first six months of COVID-19, we have produced more millionaires than before. And the richest people in the world have just moved up in status. For example, Jeff Bezos was worth about $119 billion in December 2019. But by the end of August 2020, he was worth over $200 billion. Also, a number of the top five people have moved up dramatically. All this has occurred in an atmosphere in which the GDP has gone down by an annualized rate of 32% — based upon the second quarter of 2020.

In the 2020 Forbes list of the 400 wealthiest people on the planet, you need 2.1 billion to qualify. In the ten years since the financial crisis, the number of billionaires has doubled. Today there are about 2,200 billionaires around the world today (most of them don't make the Forbes 400 list). Between 2017 and 2018, a new billionaire emerged every two days. The world's population is now 7.8 billion, which means that is one billionaire for every 3.5 million people on earth.

Notice that if there are 2,200 billionaires and about the top 1% of them own as much as the bottom 3.7 billion people, then what percentage of the world's wealth is owned by the world's 2,200 billionaires?

Year	Richest People Owning Half the World's Wealth
2014	85 Richest
2015	(no online data for this year that I could find)
2016	61 Richest
2017	43 Richest (also saw one article saying top 8)
Jan 2019	26 Richest

In 2019, it was estimated that there were about 42 million millionaires on the planet – which means that there is one per 183.7 people on the planet. Just to show the extremes in the US, in 2018, there were 11.8 million households in the US with over a million in net worth (not including their primary residence) or about 3% of the population. In November 2020, according to the US Debt clock (usdebtclock.org), there are 18.37 millionaires, which means it has gone up to 5.5% of the US population.

The rich families from the end of the 19th century, control much of the power of the world.[17] They tend to own the central banks, which are allowed to print money out of thin air. However, the top 26 richest people are not from these families (at least most of them). Mark Zuckerberg, the founder and primary owner of Facebook, thought about developing a stable cryptocurrency that people on Facebook can use as money. That cryptocurrency, called Libra, would have been a stable currency, backed by stable fiat currencies. That made countries and central banks very nervous because it could kill the US Dollar. It would have tipped the power structure from the old rich to the new rich. Zuckerberg, of course, was forced to back down from this idea. Zuckerberg still has a Libra currency coming out, but on a much less ambitious scale, so we will see what will happen.

Notice your thoughts about all of this. Is it unfair, and you think the government should do something about it? If so, you are probably a level 4 thinker. Is your thought that people are learning how to make it? Then you are probably a level 5 thinker.

Try using *The Secret Daily Teachings* app for a few months, it's available on the App Store, Google Play and Amazon. You basically get a big check every day, and your job is to spend it. If you do, you get a bigger check the next day. The biggest check is $200,000, and then you get a $200,000 check each day. When I first got those, I bought a huge office building and about a million dollars' worth of crypto assets and toys such as my own helicopter. After a while, at least for me, there is a sense that the only thing to do with it is to give it away. Now, I might use $200,000 to:

- Help adopt homeless pets and care for them.
- Feed 40,000 Brahmins in India.
- Give the money to the Salvation Army.
- Help feed and save children around the world.
- Help prevent all sorts of cruelty to animals.

$200,000 per day is an income of $73 million per year. I absolutely would not know what to do with it except give it away, and I'd probably hire someone to take on that task and give me a weekly report. In fact, I got bored giving away money with the Secret App, and I stopped using it.

The United States now has more level 5 thinkers than anyplace else in the world, but they still constitute only a small majority of the population. Television shows like *Shark Tank* foster this sort of thinking and the show is appropriately named. Although the ideas sound "American," they create all sorts of problems. Huge corporations arise that become trillion-dollar businesses. They have no interest in anything but protecting their profits, so it doesn't matter that 1) they also create an elite class of people and 2) do things that will eventually kill off much of humanity through global warming as well as cause the sixth great mass extinction (the Anthropocene extinction) which is ongoing.[18]

Level 6: Consequently, the level 6 thinker was born, going back to a group thinking with the idea that we should all love each other and treat each other with respect. At the same time, there is a rebellion that says we should hate the extremists who are killing off the planet (i.e., the level 5s).

Level 6 says that everyone has the right to believe what they want. As a result, everyone has the right to be heard and understood. Level 6 also understands that 1) knowledge constantly changes and there is much we do not understand; 2) science does not give a model of reality that is adequate; and 3) is open to all possibilities. Level 6s realize that consciousness changes everything.

Level 6 is motivated by the need for peace and cooperation (as opposed to achievement). They are into natural healing – linking health to diet, emotions, and the overall balance of the body. Consequently, they are in conflict with level 4 organizations such as the AMA, the FDA, the Department of Agriculture, and the Centers for Disease Control and Prevention (CDC).

The level 6 thinker pays attention to the inner world (consciousness, thoughts, and emotions) as well as to the well-being of others. The emphasis here is on what might be called prana or the life force energy in people. The goal is to raise the kundalini (life force) to change the body and consciousness. They understand the notion that "consciousness" is non-local, and this completely contradicts the motivations of those at level 4 and 5 – to make a superior human or become immortal by putting consciousness into another body.

And finally, in level 6, there is a movement towards oneness. We can all flourish as individuals, accept our differences and move toward oneness. Level 6 is about searching for enlightenment.

The problem with level 6 is that it is not very functional. Everyone gets to have their input and each viewpoint is valued. Because everyone is different, decisions cannot be made, and a level 6 society would be bankrupt.

Level 7: About the middle of the 20th century, science found that its paradigms of what was real kept changing. Suddenly, we had general relativity and quantum mechanics. The old models didn't work anymore and *systems thinking began*. Systems thinking is really the tool of the level 7 thinker. Notice how fast new levels are now appearing. Proponents of Graves's theory seem to be a bit confused about the start dates. One of them has its existence only beginning about 1990 – about 30 years ago while the other suggests that it began 70 to 100 years ago.

We now have systems thinkers who believe that the whole is more than the sum of its parts, that there are multiple causations on many levels, and that the observer is part of all of this – the subjective is at least as important as the objective. Level 7 has an existential motivational system and its goal is developing self-worth and the end goal is existence through acceptance.

My belief is that most of the people writing about level 7 and level 8 have no idea what they are talking about because they have no experience of it – they probably are level 6 thinkers at best.

Adriana James talks about level 7 thinkers being interested in conquering deep space and colonizing it as a way of solving our problems. She points out that space exploration has gone into deep secrecy. For example, in 1973, all moon exploration was scrapped from public view for absurd reasons. Furthermore, she points out that the Department of Defense reported that $2 trillion was missing as of 2001 and that grew to 8 trillion in 2015 – where the money went is "unknown."[19] – but she assumes it might have to do with incorporating Alien technology and the military use of space by level 7 thinkers.

Van's Viewpoint on Level 7: Level 7 is probably where I am – if level 7 even exists. I say that we can solve the level 5 and 6 problems by raising consciousness, especially our own. That fits me. We have found our purpose in life and it's about giving to others and helping them grow, but the key is about expanding the consciousness of all human beings. That also fits me. There is now some realization that perhaps consciousness is a major field that physics doesn't (but should) study and that consciousness creates it all. The goal then is to go back to the source of creation, to attain Siddha yogi status, and then bring that back to the everyday world. However, I believe that there are probably 7.7 billion paths to enlightenment – one for everyone on the planet.

I would probably say that level 6 is about systems thinking, while level 7 is about what I call *Beyond the Matrix Thinking* – here, our entire experience is illusion, and the goal is to find what's useful (brings value to our self and to others) and to get in touch with our Inner Guidance to get closer to reality.[20]

Level 8: Level 8 is assumed to have just started. According to the proponents of the Graves model, level 7 has to produce some sort of problem. They claim that level 7 tends to foster existential dichotomies and that level 8 is now about ontological being. This doesn't make any sense to me and it's clear to me that level 8 was developed just because it was a necessary part of the model.

Van's Viewpoint on Level 8: Level 8 is about joining the group again, so to me, there is one place for it to go – God Realization. God Realization happens when a person becomes one with his object of devotion. Ramakrishna is a classic example. He was a Bhakti yogi, devoted to the Hindu Goddess, Kali, and eventually became one with her. Then to prove that anyone could do it, he became one with Jesus and then one with Mohammad. Yogananda was another example of a God-realized human being. To me, as someone who is striving for it but has yet to see it, God Realization is the state of pure unconditional love, which means that you see love (the Divine) in everything.

When you are one with the Divine, you surrender and are led by your Internal Guidance. You see the perfection of everything, have no idea what will happen next, and just do what you are guided to do. Level 8 might be the highest level one can attain in a human body (although Graves' proponents would say that more levels will emerge). However, growth in consciousness is a never-ending journey. What I describe as levels 7 and 8 are just the beginning here."

Why Use the Graves' Model?

First, the model gives us a reference point from which to understand our motivations and behavior. No one is purely on any one level, but the various levels are useful in understanding motivation. It potentially gives us a more complete picture of why someone is the way they are. Remember, it's **useful fiction**. It's a map, somewhat useful, but totally made up.

The model can also be used to look at the challenges of the human race because it has societal implications. It can perhaps predict where we are headed (this is a level 5 statement), partially because the model has one fundamental assumption – that people cannot skip levels. You must master levels 1 through 6 to become a level 7. We must be honest in observing ourselves and note the level from which we are operating.

It also explains why other people can seem so different. I wonder, for example, why people are not willing to work on themselves. But you must be at least at level five for this to be meaningful. Working on yourself is meaningless to levels 1-4 – according to the model. At level 5, people will be attracted to Tony Robbins style of self-work because it's about personal power for them.

According to the model, most people in the world are at level 4 or getting to that level. The United States has the most level 5s (and it's why so many people on the Forbes 400 list are from the United States). Donald Trump, before his wealth was put into trust when he became president, ranked at number 259 on that list. However, I've also seen him ranked at about 715 – with about 3.5 billion. He is clearly a level five and hated by level 4s and level 6s. According to James, levels 4 and 5 make up roughly 70-80% of the US population. Level 6 comes out around 10% (and growing fast); everyone else is either level 3 or lower.[21] I have no idea where this comes from – 90% of the US population is at least level 4 – I tend to doubt it.

Another implication of the model is that these levels are beyond the choice of the individual. A level 5 thinker would want such a choice because of his achievement motivation. Even though he/she measures achievement in terms of power and money, he/she would read this material and automatically want to be a level 7 but with materialistic aims.

While we have no choice of where we want to be, people operate out of the level at which they seem to get the answers to life's problems. All levels have some sort of advantage and create new problems. Moving to a new level means that they have done so by moving out of a level that no longer works. Here the assumption of problems and advantages comes from a dualistic model of the world. That doesn't exist at my conception of level 8. However, even God might decide to create and then discreate and that might be seen as moving from one level to another.

As you become enlightened and realize the perfection of the "what is," you stop having problems. And through doing so, the entire Graves model breaks down.

It should be obvious that there is a back and forth swing between individual orientation or self-expression (odd number levels) and communal orientation or self-denial (even number levels), although that becomes more blurred at higher levels. Life is about relationships and there are clear relationships at each level. Thinkers at each level have both conscious and unconscious views about those at other levels. Maslow was aware of the Graves model before he died, and he believed it was a clear improvement on his own thinking.

Dr. David Hawkins' Levels of Consciousness Model

David Hawkins, in his 2002 book, *Power Versus Force*, claimed he'd developed a method of determining truth from falsehood. Using kinesthetic testing, people remained strong if something was true but weak if something was false.[22] Hawkins could then develop a model and test the levels of consciousness with kinesthetic testing.[23]

George Goodheart Jr. developed Applied Kinesiology in 1964[24] as a technique for holistic health practitioners. He could ask, "Is this substance good for you?" or "Is this remedy good for you?" He believed the body does not lie. Level 4 scientists believe it to be pure fiction. Hawkins later claimed that your consciousness had to be above 200 for it to work;[25] he claimed that most of the human population was below 200.

The next development was Behavioral Kinesiology. Dr. John Diamond,[26] a psychiatrist, discovered that works of art, music, and games affected the body and could be measured through kinesiology. Rap music makes everyone go weak, while classical music makes everyone go strong. Drummond, as a result of his work, believed that everything we interact with either strengthens or weakens our life force. Diamond claims that it takes extensive training to properly do behavioral kinesiology.

David Hawkins, already a psychiatrist with a successful career, got his Ph.D. through testing his hypothesis of the universality of muscle testing. If it's good for one person, then it's good for another. He tested his hypothesis by giving 100 people a sealed envelope either containing organic vitamin C or NutraSweet. Even though no one knew the content of the envelope, those with vitamin C were strong and those with NutraSweet went weak. In Hawkins' opinion, kinesiology could be used to determine "truthfulness."

You can make a statement about anyone and test it. You can look at a scientific theory and test it. The belief here is that the kinesiology response transcends your own knowledge and goes into an infinite field.

Hawkins's model says that you can measure human consciousness through such testing and that it goes from zero to 1,000 on a logarithmic scale. Because this is a log scale, there are huge differences between, say 500 and 1,000. Hawkins says that 1,000 is the limit for a human being, but beings such as Archangels could have levels over 100,000.

Within the scale, there is a clear demarcation between constructive consciousness and destructive consciousness at the level of 200. Anything above 200 is constructive and anything below 200 is destructive. When he first developed his scale, Hawkins said that the human race was something like 190 on the scale and that the only thing that kept us from destruction was the number of people above 600 who were using their power to balance it all out. One person at 600 will balance out 10 million below 200.

Gandhi, for example, calibrated by Hawkins at 700 and was able to defeat the British Army, which calibrated at 175 – which is equivalent to the emotion of pride. Below 200, people are into force to get what they want (i.e., think Graves level 3) while people who calibrate over 200 people have power – hence the title of his book. I used this model for many years because I thought it was useful, but I now believe it also has many limitations.

Power Versus Force

Hawkins was by no means the first person to develop levels of consciousness. It's part of Scientology, Dynamism, the Sedona Method, and several other sources. Hawkins may have easily borrowed the concept and just applied muscle testing to it. I'm pretty sure Scientology had levels of consciousness before Hawkins came up with his model. The following table shows some clear levels of demarcation for the levels of consciousness model.

David Hawkins' Model of Levels of Consciousness With Clare Graves Levels Superimposed			
Level of Consciousness	Description	What Happens	Commentary
700-1000 **Graves Level 8?**	Enlightenment One = everything Self-gone	Those who have a huge impact on mankind Power/ Expanding	Hawkins believes you need to go through a huge painful transformation to pass 600.
600 **Graves Level 7**	Peace	Complete surrender to the divine; quiet mind.	*One person in 10 million reaches this level.* It's good, I suppose, that one person at this level balances out 10 million below 200. Thus, if he is right, then there are about 780 people in the world at this level.
540	Joy	In harmony with divinity	

David Hawkins' Model of Levels of Consciousness
With Clare Graves Levels Superimposed

Level of Consciousness	Description	What Happens	Commentary
500 **Graves Level 6**	Love	The spiritual domain emerges here, but below 500 is the physical domain *0.4% of the population reach here*	At this level, you must get that everything causes everything else. Hawkins says top scientists (like Einstein) who are into linear thinking cannot reach 500 on the scale but ranked at 499.
400 **Graves Level 5**	Intellect/Reason		Subjective not important Predict and control is the motto.
350	Acceptance	You are the creator of your experiences	Minimum level for trading success.
250	Neutrality	Unmotivated	Not attached to outcomes.
200	Courage	Neutral, no longer a victim of others	*78% of the population rank below this level. Contrast this with the estimate from the proponents of Graves model that say that level 4-5 people make up 70-80% of the population.*
175 **Graves Level 4**	Pride	Force/Contracting	Level 4 fanaticism
150	Anger		Unfulfilled desire
125 **Graves Level 3**	Desire		Wanting and addiction
100	Fear		
50	Apathy		Homeless, living in poverty
30	Guilt		
20	Shame		Most people who commit suicide rank here and it is close to death.

What is the Value of Hawkins' Model in our Discussion of Propulsion Systems?

I don't consider any of these models to be real, just useful. Consciousness might be equivalent to awareness and how do you measure that? Why is it a log scale? Perhaps that makes it impressive, but I'm not sure how useful it is. If everything is one, as higher levels might suggest, how can there be levels of consciousness? Are we talking about levels out of the illusion of the Matrix? If so, that would make Hawkins statement that kinesthetic testing ranks at 600 a false one.

Nevertheless, the model is very useful for the following reasons:

It gives me a reason for talking about transformation and a way of measuring it. We don't use kinesthetic testing since I don't believe in it, and it might take a lot of skill to master it. Instead, Hawkins says there is a direct correlation between happiness and consciousness, and it's useful that way. Happiness is a great high-level value to have. I can show the progress of my traders in terms of happiness. This can be done as a group average and it can be done individually. Below is one graph in which one of our students, graduating from Super Trader I, who tracked his lifetime happiness. Notice the impact of the Super Trader program.

The Hawkins model is also useful because it is a strong framework for the transformations we do. It gives a backbone to what we are doing with personal transformations. It also gives a useful explanation, without being too over-the-top, about categories of values.

The Van Tharp Institute (VTI) Model of Consciousness

While the Hawkins model has been very useful, there are certain aspects of the Hawkins model that are not seen as useful. First, I don't like the idea of ranking truth and falsehood. Hawkins has a book by that name, *Truth Versus Falsehood*, and to me it's just a book of meaningless judgments. Like below 200 is not true, and above 200 is true, but 600 is more true than 200? How about the idea that the map is not the territory and perhaps the first level of truth is realizing that everything in our experience is an illusion? When you get that, you perhaps begin to get some truth and it certainly doesn't begin at 200. What if the ultimate truth is just oneness and only the unchanging is true? I don't think you could predict that at all from the Hawkins model of consciousness.

Second, Hawkins states that 600 on the consciousness scale is like having a sense of oneness and the peace of God. However, to go beyond that, you have to go through a painful, dark night of the soul. So far, that has not been my experience. However, once you get to peace, the sense of self is gone and there should be no reason for a dark night of the soul experience.

Lastly, all of Hawkins' beliefs are based upon muscle testing, and I'm not convinced of the validity of such muscle testing at all. For example, I went to an Ayurvedic practitioner who was also a chiropractor and believed in muscle testing. He took my pulse but most of his conclusions were based upon muscle testing and then seemed to disagree with what other Ayurvedic practitioners were saying.

As a result, I decided to come up with my own model of consciousness. Is the model true? No, because the map is not the territory and anything expressed through language leads us to illusions because it causes us to divide the world into subject, object, and verb. However, try out the model. You might find it very useful. It is very useful to me right now; therefore, I plan to use it. The VTI model divides consciousness into ten stages. The constructive consciousness doesn't occur until you realize that 1) the map is not the territory, 2) everything in your experience is made up and projected, 3) and if you are going to live in the world, you might as well make up something that is useful for success and happiness.

The next figure shows the four levels and the ten stages:

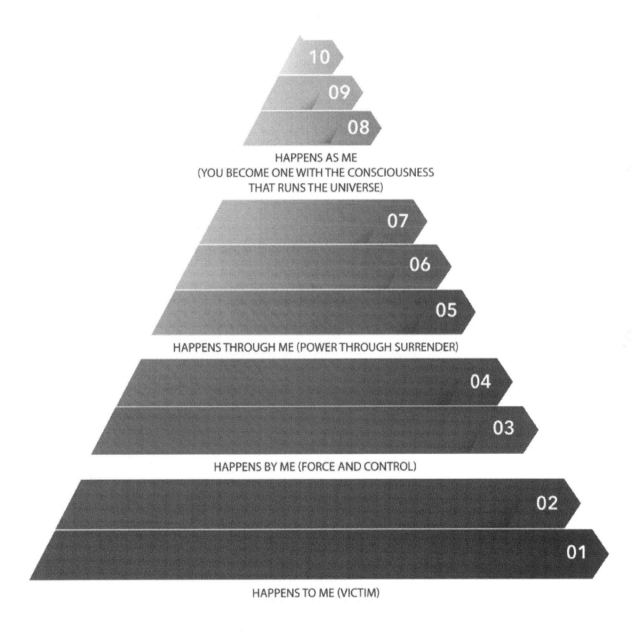

First, let's look at the four levels in consciousness. At the first level, you are just a victim and your experience is that stuff happens to you.

At the second level, you are looking for control through force. Stuff happens by you. You make it happen by sheer intention, will, determination, and action. It is the realm that we call personal power.

The dividing line between constructive and destructive consciousness occurs at about level five, where you at least realize that everything is made up. This stage facilitates the third level of consciousness where you begin to surrender to the power of the universe and allow it to act through you.

Finally, the last level is when you merge with your Inner Guidance and realize the oneness of everything. Now, since all there is oneness, if something happens, it is you.

The Bible is full of words like "sin." Jesus forgives us for our sins. You must cleanse yourself of sin to go to heaven. However, the original meaning of the word "sin" was "to miss the mark." Think about it this way, if you believe yourself to be separate from everything as language conditions us to do, then you are missing the mark. You are sinning. If you believe you are a noun, separate from everything else, then you are sinning. But as soon as you realize that, you can begin to step away from sin. Unfortunately, you have to get this realization experientially. I cannot convey it to you in terms of language, which separates things into subject, object, and verb.

For example, *A Course in Miracles* is a channeled work in which the author is Jesus. In that work is a slightly different version of the Lord's Prayer, which goes as follows:

> *Forgive us our illusions, Father, and help us accept our true relationship with You, which there are no illusions and where none can ever enter. Our holiness is Yours. What can there be in us that needs forgiveness when Yours is perfect? The sleep of forgetfulness is only the unwillingness to remember Your forgiveness and your Love. Let us not wander into temptation for the temptation of the Son of God is not Your Will. Let us only receive only what you have given and accept but this into the minds You have created and which You love. AMEN.*[27, 28]

The Ten Stages of Consciousness of the VTI Model

Victim Level of Consciousness: The ten stages of consciousness are as follows. The self-destructive stages are 1 and 2, which fall into the victim category. The belief at this level is that "stuff happens to me."

> Someone on **stage 1** operates on a level of "I'm just an insignificant being, living on a rock hurling through space. Life is meaningless, so what's the point. Here one might be dominated by emotions of shame, guilt, apathy, fear, and a sense of hopelessness. I would expect very low levels of happiness at this level, say between minus 55 to minus 20.[29]

> **Stage 2** people still feel they are insignificant and a victim, but here perhaps lady luck or the gods will intervene and help you. Thus, they might be dominated by negative emotions such as anger, desire, and pride, but some of the hopelessness is gone. Happiness scores are still very low, probably somewhere between minus 19 and plus 10.

Personal Power Level of Consciousness. The next three stages constitute the personal power level because you sense that things happen through your personal control. I would say that these stages are not so much self-inhibiting, meaning your ego-self, as they are Self-destructive, meaning your Higher Self. On these three stages, it's pretty much you versus the world but with some chance of doing well.

> **Stage 3** is where the individual starts to feel worthwhile. Here he/she has courage, satisfaction, personal pleasure and is starting to get personal power. Happiness scores probably fall between 10 and 35.
>
> **Stage 4** might include someone who is a level five on the Graves scale. The mindset is on power and ruling the world or being the richest person in the world. This stage has willingness through intention and probably has happiness scores between 35 and 55. There is still a lack of awareness at the level of all of the unconscious presuppositions that rule one's life. Leaders of state and some of the richest people in the world probably fall into this level. This shows that money and power are not good measures of consciousness. At this level, you can probably become a successful trader as you should be out of fear and greed and into acceptance of whatever happens to you as a trader.

People at the personal power level of consciousness will often manipulate those on the victim level of consciousness and might very well fall back into the victim level. For example, Donald Trump created a story about how the election was stolen from him and got a lot of people at the victim level to agree with him.

Awakened Level of Consciousness. Everything changes as we move into the Awakened Level of Consciousness, stages 5, 6, and 7. Here you are tapping into Oneness and surrendering control to your Inner Guidance. At this level, you may begin to develop what Patanjali calls Siddhi powers, but they are also a distraction on the journey and a way to bring your former sense of self back into existence. "I can levitate" or "I can manifest what I think about" are examples of such temptations.

> **Stage 5** might be called a neutral stage and there is a huge step between stage 4 and stage 5. At stage five, you become interested in how successful/happy people think. This is the point when you finally understand that you can make up useful, meaningful models that are useful in a wide context that will increase both success and happiness. It is also possible, but not for everyone, that you will become quite aware that your model of the world, your subjective experience, is all made up. Here happiness scores are between 55 and 70. This is the minimum level of happiness that I want for those who complete the transformational phase of the Van Tharp Institute (VTI) Super Trader program.
>
> At **stage 6** one realizes that there is an infinite number of perspectives, and despite that, the "what is" is actually perfect. It's just the unique perspectives that believe they are right and thus cast judgment upon the other perspectives as being inferior. Here you begin to experience true joy and happiness. You have your purpose in life, and you are surrendering to it. At stage 6 you are scoring at the top of the VTI happiness test.
>
> **Stage 7** takes this even further because now you are surrendering to your Inner Guidance and you just go with the flow produced by that surrender. Happiness scores are rather meaningless at this stage.

Enlightened Level of Consciousness. The final three stages of consciousness are what I call the enlightened level of consciousness. Here everything happens through oneness. Your experience happens as you rather than through you. The enlightened level include stages 8 through 10.

Jesus' two primary commandments were 1) to love thine God with all thy heart and 2) to love your neighbor as thyself. And these commandments are a call for people to operate at the enlightened levels.

Stage 8 involves seeing oneness in everything and realizing that it is who you really are. That's really the definition of unconditional love – seeing love/God in everything. And you cannot see it in yourself until you see it in everything else. At stage 8, you realize that who you really are is an unchanging witness that is always present and always the same.

Most people have the potential to go up to **stage 9**. In fact, enlightened beings claim that it is the destiny of all to get there. Everyone is chosen, but few are called to do it at any given time. At stage 9, you can totally move into the consciousness that is the basis for everything. Within that consciousness, you have access to full Siddhi powers, and you are feeling enlightened. You can go into a cave somewhere and spend the rest of your life in meditation or you can bring it back to the world.

There is a **stage 10**, but if you get there, you probably just disappear. At stage 10, you have lost all attachment to the physical world and what's left is likely to just turn to light and disappear. The founder of Tibetan Buddhism, Padmasambhava Rinpoche (also known as Guru Rinpoche and referred to as the second Buddha) lived in the 7th century. He is the founder of the Nyingma School of Buddhism and also Dzogchen. One of the emphases of Dzogchen is to attain the rainbow body. There are thought to be three levels of the rainbow body: 1) The minor level where you die and your body shrinks quite rapidly until only the fingernails and toenails remain. There are pictures on the internet of such people if you Google the topic of "rainbow body;" 2) The major level of the rainbow body is that your body simply turns to light and disappears. At this point, you stop being attached to anything in this world. And 3) The most advanced level is where you turn to light but remain on the planet. This perhaps was Jesus when he was resurrected. The gospels claim that you could touch the resurrected Jesus, but perhaps he could change from a light body to a physical body as needed. Guru Rinpoche, his 25 disciples, and many of their disciples all turned to light – or so the legend goes.

Tarthang Tulku, a Tibetan monk who has resided in the United States since 1968, says that when people turn to light (and disappear), all that remains are whatever clothes they were wearing. As a result, people would mark the spot where this occurred with a stick. Tulku says that there is a mountain in Tibet (Monk's Robes Mountain) where there are over 100,000 such sticks.[30] And another website[31] says that there are over 160,000 people who have achieved the rainbow body. Furthermore, the internet has recent examples of such transformations and some pictures.

My friend Stuart Mooney[32] says that other people who are close to this stage of consciousness stay on the planet only by attaching their consciousness to something here. Ramakrishna, for example, was attached to fish curry and could spend the day talking about it. Maharishi Mahesh yogi, the founder of Transcendental Meditation, stayed on the planet by being attached to his master and constantly thinking of his master.

We at the Van Tharp Institute have used both the Hawkins and VTI models of consciousness. For example, most people have heard from the media that fear and greed are bad for trading and get people into trouble. Anyone who knows that concept can relate to fear and greed being levels of consciousness below 200 on Hawkins' scale and they are in the victim level on the VTI model. If you are attached to losses, you will produce them because what you resist persists. If you are attached to profits, you will take to them quickly, and thus limit them. Instead, you need to be able to accept both. Acceptance falls in at 350 on the Hawkins scale and thus is probably a minimum level of awareness necessary for success. And that probably falls at stage four on the Van Tharp Institute scale.

Attaining higher levels of consciousness can be a life purpose or an ultimate value, as can the process of helping others do the same. Those two statements fit with my top values. It is as if the model comes with a built-in purpose for life.

Notes

[1] In Behaviorism you can only study what is observable to the eye such as behavior or the stimulation you give to produce the behavior.

[2] Beck, Don E and Cowan, C. *Spiral Dynamics: Mastering Values, Leadership, and Change*. Blackwell Publishing, a division of Wiley: New York, 1996.

[3] Most humans today have Neanderthal blood in them, so human tribes didn't intermingle?

[4] James, Adriana. *Values and the Evolution of Consciousness*. Sidonia Press: Henderson, NV, 2016, p. 120.

[5] https://www.thomhartmann.com/blog/2005/01/original-wisdom-stories-ancient-way-knowing. Hartmann,Thom (2205, January). *Original Wisdom: Stories of an Ancient Way of Knowing*. https://www.thomhartmann.com/blog/2005/01/original-wisdom-stories-ancient-way-knowing

[6] Tribal sacrifice, in my opinion, is not what happens in Aboriginal or Native American societies. It is almost the opposite, everyone chips in to help each member so that everyone has enough.

[7] James, Adriana. *Values and the Evolution of Consciousness*. Sidonia Press: Henderson, NV, 2016, p. 180

[8] If you understand my thinking, you should know that this is not how Van Tharp thinks. We have a course on Systems Thinking (which is a step above the analytical thinking of science) and my next book, tentatively entitled Beyond the Matrix Thinking, which (in my opinion) is a step beyond Systems Thinking.

[9] James, Adriana. *Values and the Evolution of Consciousness*. Sidonia Press: Henderson, NV, 2016, p. 262

[10] Personal discussion with a leading alternate health practitioner.

[11] Level 4 thinkers would totally disagree with everything said here. In addition, this is just my opinion, and not rules for to use to guide yourself through life.

[12] Gladstone, chancellor of the Exchequer in 1952. Quote in Carroll Quigley, *Tragedy and Hope: The History of the World in Our Time*. 1966, p. 53

[13] Speech addressing the US Bankers Association in 1924. Reprinted in the Idaho Leader, USA, on Aug 26,1924. James, see chapter reference notes, p 272.

[14] https://www.forbes.com/sites/laurashin/2014/01/23/the-85-richest-people-in-the-world-have-as-much-wealth-as-the-3-5-billion-poorest/?sh=3141cee17531. James, op cit, p. 242. We're not saying they own half the world's wealth, just the equivalent of the wealth of the poorest half of the population.

[15] Elliot, L.(2019, Jan). *The world's 26 richest people own as much as poorest 50%, says Oxfam*.The Guardian. https://www.theguardian.com/business/2019/jan/21/world-26-richest-people-own-as-much-as-poorest-50-per-cent-oxfam-report

[16] https://www.oxfam.org/en/research/economy-99. I don't know if this is true but it's probably close to being accurate. And what difference does it make whether its 8 or 26 – it's still lopsided.

[17] The Vanderbilts, the Rothschilds, the DuPonts, the Morgans, the Rockefellers, etc. represent the old rich. The new rich include Jeff Bezos (first person to be worth over $100 billion), Bill Gates, Warren Buffet, Bernard Arnault and family, Carlos Slim Helu and family;, Amancio Ortega, Larry Ellison, Mark Zuckerberg, Michael Bloomberg, and Larry Page. The names of the old rich do not appear in the top 500 richest people on the planet.

[18] Nearly half of the animal species surveyed had lost 80% of their population between 1900 and 2015. https://www.theguardian.com/environment/2017/jul/10/earths-sixth-mass-extinction-event-already-underway-scientists-warn

[19] James, Adriana. *Values and the Evolution of Consciousness.* Sidonia Press: Henderson, NV, 2016,, pp. 322-323.

[20] The Van Tharp Institute has an eLearning course entitled Trading Genius 2: Systems Thinking and Beyond. Here I present about 30 hours of material that pretty much gives my stance on Systems Thinking and Beyond the Matrix Thinking.

[21] http://www.artofwellbeing.com/2017/09/05/gravesmodel/

[22] You make a statement and someone applies pressure to the extended arm. If it remains strong then the statement is true and if it goes weak, the statement is false.

[23] Any model, just because it uses language, it just a model. The map cannot represent the territory. As such one should conclude that it is clearly false, yet kinesthetic testing tends to say that some models are true. Kinesthetic testing calibrates at 600—the level of nonduality—which means the technique itself transcends a complete intellectual (i.e., linear) understanding of the phenomenon. Thus, according to Hawkins, when one does muscle-testing in the above fashion, one is accessing the timeless, spaceless database of consciousness itself. So, does this mean it's accurate or is this just Hawkins' method of justifying what he is doing and saying?

[24] See chapter reference notes

[25] I once designed a workshop for my Ultimate Trader program to do this sort of testing. It was a complete failure, but I was not aware of the requirement that those being tested needed a consciousness level above 200. Nevertheless, I've been suspicious of it since that time.

[26] https://drjohndiamond.com/biography/

[27] Schucman, Helen. A Course in Miracles. 3rd ed. Mill Valley, Ca: Foundation for Inner Peace, 2007, p. 350, 12:1-7

[28] A Course in Miracles, [T-16. VII.12]

[29] VTI has a happiness test that we use to get a rough estimate of your level of consciousness through your happiness score which range from minus 55 up to plus 85 http://happinesstest.vantharp.com/.

[30] Tulku, Tarthang. *Keys of Knowledge*. Dharma Publishing: Berkeley, CA, 2016, p. 171.

[31] Urbanic, Sarah. Rainbow Body Phenomenon - The Highest Level of Attainable Consciousness and Enlightenment. Mot Mag. https://www.motmag.com/awakeandaware/2017/8/5/rainbow-body-phenomenon-the-greatest-level-of-attainable-consciousnesss

[32] Stuart Money (author of *American Buddha*), private conversation October 2020.

CHAPTER 9

Purpose and Your Inner Guidance

Purpose is probably the pinnacle of one's propulsion system. One of my primary goals for people doing our programs is to have them attain a huge self-transformation that involves them finding their purpose. To complete the transformational phase of our Super Trader program, students must document five major transformations that they have made. For many people, two of those five, although no particular transformation is required to do so, include 1) connecting with their Inner Guidance and 2) finding their purpose in life.

In this chapter I want to give you examples of our students who have found their purpose, plus several examples of how it's impacted someone's life. In addition, we'll conclude with an exercise to help you find your purpose. We do this in our advanced Peak Performance class (Peak 202) and, for some people, it may require connecting to one's Inner Guidance (which also happens in that workshop) to actually get their purpose.

Some Examples of Purpose:

The following examples of purpose come from Super Traders who have gone through the five major transformations required toward the beginning of the Super Trader program. They come from varied backgrounds and probably represent all the world's major religions.

NF: My purpose is **to increase my level of consciousness and then spread this through the world.** This will include trading successfully, then using this as a platform for publishing, and finding a way to bring an enhanced level of consciousness to the world. **My Dream Life is to be My SELF or my SOUL, following my Purpose.**

JS: I have unlocked my purpose in life – which is **to majorly help awaken humanity and the planet, and to be a conduit of love, light, abundance, and happiness for as many as possible.** This is a hugely powerful purpose, and it has underpinned many miracles so far.

SM: I believe the purpose of life is **to be happy, and I feel that within me**. My decisions on most matters are influenced by core beliefs and values. I feel more at peace with myself and content with who I am. I have become acquainted with the essence of me as SELF. I am cherishing every moment of my life. Through this journey of time, **I am discovering my SELF and the world around me and following the passions of heart with God-given free will**. Now it is a completely different picture; I am full of energy and life. My days are filled with activity that shows the direction of my journey in life.

SJ: One particular experience was showing me **my primary purpose – awakening**. My Divine showed me what it was like in an awakened state and how my life would be beyond this. It was the most amazing experience. I realized that **life was not about trying to get the most "stuff." It was about how rich my soul was and how I could get closer to who I really am.**

AL: From the program, I have learned that I am an individuated part of God and that **my purpose is to create my own experiences (e.g., manifest) and to serve my Personal Mission**. So, before, my mental state was to wait for things to happen to me, and now it is up to me to create what happens to me.

RM: My Purpose: **Reveal God Self to god self. That means: show to my little "i's" (my parts) as well as to other people's little "i's" that there is a Higher Self in all of us, one with each other, and one with God. That Purpose defines my values, which determine my goals, which define my plans, which drive my actions. The entire structure seems like a pyramid to me, which is a lot more solid than everything I have relied on before**. In the past, I used to have goals, plans, and mostly unconscious values. Now I have the entire pyramid, and there is a whole different feeling of how my life goes. There is a backbone to my life – my Purpose, that seems so crisp now – and having it makes everything look different, smoother, clearer.

MG: I wanted to be at the top of my classes at school and university, get a scholarship to do a PhD., get my PhD., be a famous research scientist, become a partner at the consulting company I worked for, be a top network marketer, etc. I think these goals were substitutes for a real purpose in my life. I then discovered that my purpose was: **"Be Love and Peace and spread that consciousness around**." That works perfectly for me now. It defines a state of being that I want to be at, and it also gives me a purpose that has an outward focus and is bigger than just myself. It means that I will do things that promote love and peace in others or for others.

DW: In the Super Trader program, I found my true Purpose: **"To find Peace and Love and share it with others."** The simplification was enabled by 1) a connection with God and 2) an understanding of Self. The state of Peace and Love is enabled by the growing of consciousness. The mind doesn't grow, but rather, the pathway is cleared to Universal Mind. Love is living Oneness; it is Self-Love and forgiveness. Courage is only a temporary condition until Self-discovery leads to the realization that there is nothing to fear.

AM: Up until about three years ago, I had no clearly defined purpose. Then during a Mankind Project New Warrior Training Adventures course, I came up with my mission: "To create a world of Joy and Abundance, by letting go and letting the real man inside shine through." After the start of the Super Trader program, this became: "To co-create a world of Joy and Abundance, by being at one with my Divine Guide and allowing God's love to shine in and through me." However, I felt this was interfering with my Oneness journey by seeing my Divine Guide as external/separate from me. The two opposing thoughts just weren't sitting comfortably. Therefore, my purpose then changed to: **"I create a world of Joy and Abundance by being my SELF and allowing Truth to shine in and through me."** This sat much better.

KA: Before the Super Trader program, I had a vague sense of my purpose in life – but nothing concrete. I had a pretty good idea of what I didn't want in life and a pretty good sense of what I wanted my day-to-day life to look like; however, I hadn't put it all together in a nice neat little package. I somehow knew that I liked to help people and I had a very good idea of how I don't want to do that (i.e., I don't want to be a social worker or a psychotherapist or run a non-profit charitable organization). I know that I love trading and have wanted to be a trader for a long time. I also know that I like writing, psychology, and doing self-work. So, I came up with the following life purpose: **"To achieve my highest potential so that I can help others achieve theirs."** The statement immediately resonated with me, and I knew that trading fit into it as a means to an end.

CL: My purpose is to is manifest Buddha's Nature and ride this life as it goes.

BE: The purpose of my life is to create peace, love, happiness, and abundance and share it with others. To summarize, my life is now guided by my purpose and by my Divine. I let them lead the way, and I just focus on executing what I'm supposed to. It's a much more relaxed, stress-free, and happy way to live life!

RH: In a Peak Performance 202 workshop, I participated in the purpose-finding exercise even though I already had a purpose figured doing the exercise might strengthen that purpose but instead, during the exercise, I heard that **my purpose was to love as God loves.** My immediate reaction was, "I can't do that. I can't even come close. I'm human!" The new purpose lingered, however, and I began to consider that perhaps, possibly, I could strive to love as God loves – as best as I could. Van helped by sharing a teaching from "A Course in Love." The book explains that loving like God means seeing God in all things and people. So yes, I now believe a human - divinely inspired - can love as God loves, and this is my purpose here.

> THE TWO MOST IMPORTANT DAYS IN YOUR LIFE ARE
> THE DAY YOU ARE BORN AND THE DAY YOU FIND OUT WHY.
>
> Mark Twain

Now let's look at several examples of what these people went through to find their purpose.

How I Found My Purpose: RM

What it Used to Be Like: At the time I made this profound and lasting shift, I had already made four major transformations. The biggest problems remaining, even after that, were: fear of failure and fear of success.

Yes, I felt that God wants me to succeed. Yes, I was a lot more aware of my relationships, and my reasons to succeed were going to impact them as well. Therefore I had a stronger "Why?" Yes, I was hugely more aware of how the Matrix works. And yes, I was a lot more functional, powerful, and 100% responsible.

Still, I just could not find the root of my remaining fear of failure. "What if I actually fail, in the end?" was a recurring thought. "What if I succeed beyond a "safe" level?" was another, in a typical manifestation of the fear of success. Deep inside, something was still missing, even after the wonderful Super Trader1 journey made so far.

In truth, even before this shift, I already felt transformed for the better in so many ways. I felt quite congruent inside. However, there was nothing to be congruent to outside of myself. I felt I lacked a clear purpose, something to be aligned to, feel attracted by it, and motivated to pursue. Over the years, I did buy books about finding my passion but barely read the covers. And when I attended seminars, I took notes, listened closely to the speaker, but that was it. There was no result from any of those attempts (which now I recognize as not being serious attempts at all, due to a big resistance, likely caused by self-sabotage).

What Happened: One of the Van Tharp Institute programs was renowned for helping people finding their purpose, so I prepared myself to be really ready when I took it. I dedicated time before the course started, to watch the introductory material and read what was asked of me, even more than once. And when it started, my highest priority was to do all my "homework" and do it thoroughly. I believe that attitude and seriousness to work on myself while continuing to do the Super Trader 1 lessons were very helpful in getting the results!

How it happened? On the second day of the program, we did an Alignment procedure, and during it I got the first glimpse of what it means to do something when living from a higher state of consciousness, being inspired by my Higher Self. The experience was very short, extremely clear, and made a permanent impression. Then, on the third day, we clarified the purpose intuited on the second day so that my conscious mind integrated it as well.

So, what is my purpose? **To reveal God Self to god self**, which means to show to my parts (little "i's") as well as to other people's little i's that there is a Higher Self in all of us, one with each other, and one with God.

Today, several months later, I feel the same, maybe even more, passion towards living on purpose. The shift is not just that I found a pleasant-looking statement that I call purpose, but how every concept learned in Super Trader 1 (and before) fell into place. It is a feeling of alignment to something outside of myself that for a very long time, I longed to happen. The fear of failure and fear of success were both completely gone after I realized that all I need to do is to step into my purpose, and follow the flow. From that standpoint, there is neither success nor failure, just feedback, and movement.

Worth mentioning is that I fully understood how my purpose requires full, complete trust in God's Will. Also, I had another unexpected shift: freedom (which is something I was chasing for a long time) became synonymous with "aligning my free will with divine will. Even as I write this, I'm still surprised by the 180-degree shift, as far as what freedom means to me now. With my previous map of reality, this new definition of freedom would have surely been assigned the meaning of "complete lack of freedom." But, based on the new map, I see freedom as an enabler of a broader perspective: "I have nothing of my own, yet I have access to everything God has."

What Life Is Like Now: The increased congruence between values, goals, plans, and actions strengthened, as now all of them stand on top of a purpose. **That purpose defines my values, which determine my goals, which define my plans, which drive my actions**. The entire structure seems like a pyramid to me, which is a lot more solid than everything I have relied on before. In the past, I used to have goals, plans, and mostly unconscious values. Now I have the entire pyramid, and there is a whole different feeling of how my life goes. There is a backbone to my life – my purpose, that seems so crisp now – and having it makes everything look different, smoother, clearer, better.

I think the proper feeling to describe my life after this transformation is: "having a deeper meaning, being in alignment with a power greater than myself." Congruence is one way to label it, but it is a congruence between God and me, instead of congruence inside myself.[1]

Discovering My Purpose: MG

What It Used to Be Like: I think that for much of my life, I did not really have any clear idea of what my purpose for existing was. For a long time, the nearest I got to a purpose was something like I was here to experience life and try to have a good time. This fit in quite well with my beliefs about God at that time. If God either did or did not exist was not important. Also, if the universe was run by the laws of physics, then why would we need a purpose for living other than just experiencing life and enjoying it?

I did have goals related mainly to my career at the time. I wanted the following:

- To come top of my classes at school and university.
- To get a scholarship to do a PhD.
- To get my Ph.D.
- To be a famous research scientist,.
- To become a partner at the consulting company I worked for.
- To be a top network marketer, etc.

Some goals I achieved, some I did not. I think they were substitutes for a real purpose to my life. They did give me a reason to get out of bed each day, but even when I did achieve some of them, I did not feel satisfied for very long. I would have a moment of glory, and then it was on to the next goal in the hope that it would satisfy me more and be what I really wanted. I also had other goals, like lots of travel, having stuff, having lots of relationships, etc. It was really all about boosting my ego.

I felt like I was on a treadmill, with a carrot dangling in front of my nose to keep me going and that my life was being run by everyone except me. I started to feel that what I really wanted was to just be myself and run my own life, but I did not see this as a purpose. I felt I had no idea what my purpose was. I kept thinking I should be able to find a purpose that was bigger than just me. When I worked as a consultant, I had helped business people come up with mission statements for their organizations that sounded impressive (even if no one took much notice afterwards), and I thought I should be able to do the same for myself.

About 10 to 12 years ago, I did some workshops on self-esteem and purpose and came up with "Be myself." On one level, that felt right, but I thought it was too inward-looking and did not seem to go any further than my old idea of enjoying life.

What Happened? The first time I did the Peak Performance 202 workshop, just before joining the Super Trader program, I realized that being was much more important than doing and having, which I had focused on for most of my life. I got a little more clarity during the Super Trader lessons where I had to define some goals but still could not come up with anything that really convinced me or made my life worthwhile.

When I repeated the Peak Performance 202 workshop, I got a big breakthrough. Someone at the workshop said her purpose was just one word: "Love." This resonated very strongly with me, and I played with it for a few moments before deciding that my purpose could also be one word: "Peace." That really felt right for me. Peace was what I had stumbled on doing shiatsu and at other moments of my life when I felt life was perfect.

This purpose was still inward-looking, but it felt worthwhile. I thought I needed to achieve that state of being before I could go any further. I felt that once I achieved that purpose, a further purpose would come to me, so that felt right for the time being. However, I still wasn't completely sure, so for the 28-day course we do as part of the program, one of the goals I set was to define my purpose.

Between the workshop and the course, I read *The Why Are You Here Café*, which is about finding your purpose. More than anything else, it helped me understand why my previous attempts at finding a purpose had been unsatisfactory and why my life up to this point had felt so frustrating and without purpose. It told a story of the green sea turtle which swims with the waves and rests when waves go the opposite way. I have spent most of my life swimming whichever way the waves went.

Through a meditation done on the second day of the course, I came up with "**Be love and peace and spread that consciousness around.**" That works perfectly for me now. It defines a state of being that I want. It also gives me a purpose that has an outward focus and is bigger than just myself. It means that I will do things that promote love and peace in others or for others.

What Life Is Like Now: I now feel that my life does have a worthwhile purpose and that I am not just here to have a good time. I realize that I need to know I have made a difference and that permanent things for the better have happened because of me.

I also learned that I would achieve my purpose by setting and achieving goals that brought me closer to it. I had known this from my consulting days, but it had always seemed academic then. **Now I have a connection between my goals and my purpose.**

At this stage, my main goals are 1) becoming a Super Trader graduate, 2) becoming the best trader I can be, and 3) to raise my consciousness level to Love and Peace. Beyond that, 4) my goal is to raise money through trading to support organizations or people whose goals are compatible with my mission. At this stage, I don't see myself setting up or running such organizations. However, **the power of a clear purpose is that I can add other goals later that enable me to achieve my purpose**. Finding my purpose means that I will need to revise the goals and objectives I defined early in the Super Trader program.

An interesting observation is that before Super Trader, my purpose of "Being me" was really being the separated me or my little-me. And my life was mostly driven by my parts. **My purpose now is "Being ME," and my life is driven by my Higher Self.**

The Power of Knowing My Purpose in Life: BE

What it used to be like: For the entirety of my school and work life, if something needed to get done, people came to me. That was the essence of my life, and it became much worse as I transitioned into full-time employment. I was the king of the to-do list, and my life revolved around crossing things off my list as fast as possible. As a result, I worked ridiculous hours. Since I worked from home most of the time, I never really unplugged and would just work with the family right beside me. There was never an end. There was always something that needed to be done.

I had lots of goals and desires but no real priorities. Work always came first, but even there, I was more focused on crossing things off my list than working on what was the most important item. I was nearly always the first person done with an assignment, but I had no real life outside of work either because I'd just start another assignment.

I'd also spend time working on things that weren't important at all. I didn't push back when people asked me to do things they should be doing either; I just added those things to my list. I was a people-pleaser, always looking to make a good impression and have people like me.

Even though I was successful in my career, all of this left me feeling unfulfilled. I wasn't unhappy, but I wasn't happy either. I knew I didn't want to keep doing this (working, working, working) for the rest of my life, but I didn't see a light at the end of the tunnel either. I was also comfortable and not willing to take on risks I felt might jeopardize the standard of living I was used to. I was 100% stuck in the rat race.

Moreover, given the nature of the parts I ultimately dealt with in my other Super Trader transformations (must succeed / afraid to fail, control, perfection), I felt I was carrying the weight of my world on my shoulders alone. I didn't even realize how exhausting it was, not to mention the additional stress and anxiety. I had created an army of one. It was a reasonably successful army, but not a happy one, nor a scalable one that could grow and become even more successful.

What happened: When I started the Super Trader program, identifying my purpose was a top priority. I knew, given my nature to execute things I focus on, that knowing my purpose could be the spark that set me on the way to bigger things. I was also aware of the path to finding my purpose would likely come through the 28-day course that is part of the program. When I started, I was very excited but also had some anxiety about being able to come up with my purpose in just one scheduled session. Ok, not a little anxiety, A LOT! What if I couldn't do it? How could it be that easy? I'd spent a lifetime trying to figure out what my purpose was and gotten nowhere. To say that I was skeptical about someone helping me figure it out in a day would be an understatement!

Well, it took me about 5 minutes with some help – Incredible …

The purpose of my life is to create peace, love, happiness, and abundance, and share it with others.

I now had my purpose and I was pumped! I also understood the importance of using my purpose as the guiding light for all my actions. I started using it to prioritize everything I did daily. Because my purpose covers every aspect of my life that's important to me, I started prioritizing non-work things ahead of work for the first time ever. It was liberating. It also made me more productive. I stopped working on things that I didn't need to be working on in the first place. And I had no guilt about not doing them either because I knew they were not in alignment with my purpose. I also started telling people "no" when it involved something they could or should be doing themselves. All of this was truly transforming to me.

What life is like now: Looking back on it, I hadn't even realized how big identifying my purpose and developing that connection with my Divine was for me. I developed a tremendous amount of self-confidence because I generally knew what I should be doing in life. I was no longer concerned about individual outcomes because I understood there was a master plan for me. So long as I acted in accordance with my purpose, everything was going to be great. Finally, having that regular dialogue with my Divine lifted a huge burden from me. I no longer felt I was carrying the weight of the world on my back. I had a partner, and He's guiding me to follow God's Will. My trust in my Divine and my purpose replaced my fears and doubts about the future.

Every morning, I write down my purpose in my journal. It's a simple reminder and helps ensure I start the day with the proper mindset.

Each evening, I prioritize what I'm going to do the next day based on how things line up with my purpose. If a task or an activity does not fit within my purpose, it does not make the list, period. I already had a system for getting things done and tracking my performance. Now it's just supercharged with a purpose.

Every day I simply focus on doing what I've planned to do. I'm not stressed about the past or worried about the future because I understand God has a plan for me. As long as I'm doing things in accordance with my purpose, I'm on track.

I have no concerns about individual outcomes. This is most common for me in work where sales calls don't work out, customers choose someone else, etc. I just treat these as learning experiences, log my gratitude for the learning opportunity and move on with whatever is next. No stress, regrets, worry, etc. It's quite remarkable considering where I used to be. Along the way, I chat with my Divine or use one of the tools I learned in the Super Trader program to do some self-reflection work if something wants to try to stick to me or I show some resistance to something. Otherwise, I just do what I do, minus all the old baggage.

To summarize, my life is now guided by my purpose and by my Divine. I let them lead the way, and I just focus on executing what I'm supposed to. It's a much more relaxed, stress-free, and happy way to live life!

Conclusions for You to Consider

There are many similarities among these purposes given as examples, and they revolve around common themes. To discover who I am, and in most cases that implies a connection with one's Higher Self and learning about that. A similar theme is to increase one's level of consciousness. It usually involves a state such as Peace, Joy, or Abundance, which is implied by increasing one's consciousness. And in most cases, it also involves sharing it with others.

In addition, you will notice that they are similar to my purpose, which is: **"Becoming one with my Inner Guidance and surrendering."** How much you "get that" depends upon where you are in your personal awareness. Many people could use these four points to easily find their purpose, but usually, you must somehow "get it" at an experiential level.

How to Connect to Your Purpose

The Why Are You Here Café Method: My friend John Strelecky has written several books to illustrate the importance of finding your purpose in life, and to help you connect to that purpose. The *Why Are You Here Cafe* book[2] book is a story to guide you through several steps to finding your purpose. Those steps can be summarized as follows:

- Do a life review, and as you do that, focus on why you are here.
- Discover your bliss and notice the relationship between what you love to do and why you might be here.
- Plan your day so that you spend some time in the day doing what you love to do.
- Perhaps there is more to your life than you even know about yet. As a result, expose yourself to different experiences and different ideas. What is that experience like?
- As you explore the first four items, decide what you want to do to fulfill that purpose.
- Your purpose may have many aspects to it. Explore them all.
- What gives you the most fulfillment? That is one of the best clues to your purpose.

In other words, what you love to do is a strong indicator of what you are meant to do. If you don't like what you spend your time doing, it probably has nothing to do with your purpose.

Durga's Method: My Inner Guidance is the Hindu Goddess, Durga.[3] She takes the "masculine" unlimited potential to create anything (this might be called the unmanifest universe or Shiva) and brings it to life. She always says to me: "You create it, and I bring it to life." To me, she is Divine Mother. She has helped me with my purpose and gave me the following steps to include in this book.

Here is a step everyone can do daily. If you follow your heart and not your head, you will be on purpose:

1. Take 15 minutes of watching your breath each day (or any other sort of meditation you are guided toward). When you finish, go into your heart and ask what to do. Surrender to that, and you will be on purpose.
2. The breathing should be prana breathing. When you inhale, feel the oxygen filling up the top third of your lungs, then the second third, and then the bottom third. As you are doing this, you should feel your abdomen push outward and downward. Most of the movement should be in your abdomen.
3. When you have inhaled fully, feel what is in the heart.
4. When you completed the inhale, then exhale. The exhale should be twice as long and you should move inward.
5. As you empty your lungs, feel as if all of your resistance is going away with the air.
6. The exhale should be twice as long as the inhale. If your inhale is a count of three, then the exhale should be a count of six.
7. As you are doing this breathing, pay attention to what your heart is telling you. If you do so, you are following your Inner Guidance and will be on purpose.

Other specific steps people could take might include:

- Your consciousness must evolve to a high enough level. You must transcend into the spiritual realm – say Hawkins 500 or VTI level 6. This either involves intensive self-work to increase your awareness or an intensive spiritual practice aimed at inner awareness or both. Remember, levels of consciousness might be called levels of awareness.

- But as you transcend, you will connect to your Divine (at least many people will). Some will just slip into silence and into a state of witnessing – both are fine.

- When you connect to your Divine and surrender, you will be on purpose. My Divine, from the very beginning, has said, "Who do you think you are?" And then She has shown me a light that fills the universe. That was all about purpose. If that's not clear, at the end of each meditation, I have a conversation with Her. She always concludes that with the statement: "Remember who you are really!" That statement describes my purpose, which really means become one with my Inner Guidance, have faith, and surrender. It's very powerful.

Notes

[1] This implies that God and I are separate, not one. On an intellectual level, I do know the Oneness teachings, and even had glimpses of experiences of Oneness with the whole creation. However, I'm not yet at a point of claiming I feel that Oneness regularly, or even often, so I accept I am where I am, for now.

[2] We have copies of this book at the Van Tharp Institute or you can get it from Amazon.

[3] The story of my connection to my Inner Guidance is given in Chapter 10 of *Trading Beyond the Matrix*.

CHAPTER 10

What's Left to Stop You? Focusing on Something Other than One's Purpose

Distractions are probably the biggest issue left for anyone who has gotten this far. You know what's important to you. You know your purpose. You know how you motivate yourself. But things just keep coming up that distract you. They come in many forms. We will deal with all of those, except one, in this chapter. The most important one, *Secrets and Hidden Agendas*, we will save for the next chapter.

Before people start the Super Trader Program, in their application form, I ask whether they have a problem with procrastination. Now, if they want to be in the program, they are not going to say, "Yes, I have a huge problem with procrastination." Instead, they tend to say something like, "When something is important to me, like the Super Trader Program, I'm good at getting things done. However, with some tasks that are boring, I do have a problem." In my view, procrastination has many causes. Find the cause (and remember you are a system with multiple dependencies), and you can accomplish miracles.

Why Can't You Get Things Done?

Let's talk about distractions and procrastination, and I'll use myself as an example:

- I have a clear purpose.

- I love what I do.
- I never want to retire.

At the same time, I'm not nearly as productive as I could be. Here are some examples. It's been seven years, as of February 2019, since *Trading Beyond the Matrix* came out, and this is the first book I've completed. Part of that is because financial books are not selling well. And when I go into bookstores now, I never see any of my books. I'm writing this book, however, and I have three other books planned. One of them has a huge potential, and that has a much wider audience than just traders and investors. I've also created three new workshops and greatly improved upon the Super Trader program in that time period.

If I look at myself and why I haven't produced more books, I have certain issues that are common to most people and explain why they have trouble getting things done. Other issues that are also common to most people don't really pertain to me, but I'll mention them as well.

Your experience in life depends upon your focus. Your focus will fall in one of twelve categories, and it will determine whether you are motivated and/or able to meet your goals.

Focus 1: What is Your Purpose

The first focus is your purpose and what you want in life (your "Big Why"). If you focus on your purpose, then your life will be fulfilling. However, if you focus on any of the other areas, then you will encounter something that will probably stop you cold.

Focus 2: What You Don't Want

I heard an amazing story about training to be a race car driver who can get out of dangerous situations easily. The key is focus when your car unexpectedly spins out of control. Where do you tend to focus? Most people focus on the wall that they hope not to crash into. What happens when they do that? They crash into the wall.

When you get training to be a top defensive driver, you will be with an instructor who can spin the car out of control when you least expect it. When your instructor does that, he is in danger as well. What does he do to prevent an accident? He turns your head to make sure that it is focused on where you want to go – rather than what you want to avoid. When your mind is focused on where you want to go, you automatically steer the car in that direction and out of trouble. The key is focus.

How does this apply to your life? First, for most people, fears tend to come up. People have a fear of success, fear of failure, fear of criticism, and many other fears. As a result, those stop them short of manifesting what's important to them. Why? Manifestation stops because people tend to focus on the fears rather than what they want.

I have certain issues that came up in the past that I've worked on in my life. They aren't really fears, but things I really wish to avoid. First, I don't want my company to get too big. I can't imagine doing something on the scale of Tony Robbins, but only because I want to spend my time relaxing and doing what I enjoy. I have no desire to be worth $400 million (Tony's estimated net worth). I get to meet all of my top values right now. As a result, there is no need to grow the Van Tharp Institute that much bigger.

Second, I'm what you might call famous anonymous. I've talked to people (at other people's workshops) when I was wearing a name tag. The other person probably had read at least one of my books, but they didn't know who I was – despite the name tag. I really like it that way. In Cary, NC, I'm probably much better known as Kala's husband than as Van Tharp. I can travel and don't have to worry about people recognizing me or asking for my autograph. I don't really want to be famous. I already get enough people who call us up wanting interviews, endorsements, etc. I don't need anymore. I actually really want to avoid becoming famous – that to me would be horrible.

Third, I don't wish to work for anyone else – in fact, I cannot imagine doing so, and I don't want the potential time obligations of having a big company where I might have to work and do management tasks that I've now delegated. You might say I move away from those things big time. Fortunately, I haven't manifested working for someone else. I actually never think about that unless I'm asking myself what I want to avoid.

I don't consider anything that I've mentioned to be fears, just preferences. I'd be happy living to be 100 just doing what I'm doing now. I have all the money I need. I could easily retire and not work, but I love what I do. Why would I want to make my company bigger or become famous and have lots of people wanting my time?

There is actually one reason which has to do with my purpose. That purpose is to become one with my Inner Guidance and just surrender. My Inner Guidance has told me that I must get over not wanting to be famous because I will be. I have surrendered to my Inner Guidance. She's already shown me how to deal with fame. She's told me that I'll write a book soon that will bring such fame. If it happens, then I'm ready. My preference, however, is still no fame – I like my anonymity.

While there are a lot of things I want to avoid, as mentioned, other people have definite fears that could cause procrastination:

- You could have a fear of success.
- You could have a fear of failure.
- You could have a fear of the unknown.
- You could have a fear of working on yourself because of how painful it might be or what you might discover.

Here is a general formula for getting rid of fears.

Do a feeling release exercise on the fear. I'd recommend the following simple method: Get in touch with the feeling you want to release. Welcome it. And then spend at least 30 minutes really feeling it – while maintaining a state of gratitude and welcoming. If at some point it goes away, notice the time. Then do the same thing the next day but only do it for how long you took for it to disappear the first time. Repeat the last two steps for at least a week or until you are sure it is gone.

Talk to the part with the fear and determine all its beliefs. Run a **Belief Examination Paradigm**[1] on all those beliefs and notice that most of them will not be useful. Get rid of the charges that exist on any non-useful charged beliefs, and then just drop them.

Find some beliefs that will be useful for you, and then run them through the Mind to Muscle Pattern. For a free video of how to do this, see www.abbyeagle.com. There are three excellent examples at the link.

Test the fear. Think about the success, the failure, the unknown or whatever that fear was about. How do you feel about it now? If it's done, then move on. If not, then repeat the process. More than one part might be involved and have stored fear to bring up to remind you what you don't want.

Focus 3: Lack of Energy

I don't know how much this impacts most people, but one reason that I'm at an Ayurvedic Clinic in India is that I want to increase my energy. I tend to sleep in spurts – perhaps four to five hours at night and then take a nap some time. However, I frequently find that a lack of energy will distract me when I'm trying to do a big project. When I do some major cleansing, where lots of toxins are coming out of me, that cleansing might be all I can do.

Not having enough energy is huge for me. When I'm tired, that's it. I don't want to be a self-help guru who personifies passion and can talk 12 hours a day at a rate faster than some people like to listen. I don't want that at all. I'd like enough passion to be able to complete important tasks and have some energy left over. I at least need enough to keep me going.

That brings up another issue. I believe that I can devote myself to doing one big thing at a time – writing a book, working on my health, spiritual growth. It's usually just one thing, and that's all I can do. However, my Internal Guidance just reminded me that I was doing all three here in India, so that belief was not at all accurate. In fact, I do spiritual work 90-95% of my days, and there is a good chance that I work on at least one of the others on the same day.

Focus 4: Compulsions and Distractions/Wanting to Feel Good Now

A huge reason for me to procrastinate is that when I don't have much energy, I get caught up in distracting things, sometimes compulsive things, that tend to energize me or at least make me feel energetic. This is also related to Focus 5: Creative Procrastination. What we tend to do is focus on what might make us feel good in the moment.

Here is an example: I'm a big Green Bay Packers fan. I watch most of their games. During Aaron Rodgers first year as a starter, I got a box seat at Lambeau Field and attended six home games. That took up 12 days of my time – 2 days for each game, and they only won 2 of the games I attended that year.[2] I'm always checking the news on several of Packer's websites. I've even attended one stockholder's meeting, which added an extra day on one of my driving trips. That's a huge waste of time, but I enjoy it.

I watch television most nights when I finish work and can get hooked on certain television shows – most seem to involve action and give me a feeling of energy. I enjoy it, but it's a huge waste of time.

When internet poker for money was legal in the US, I often spent as much as 5 hours a day playing poker. I already mentioned winning the one freeroll tournament in which I came in first out of 2,500 players. That one took about 8 hours. I was glad when internet poker became illegal – especially in my state of North Carolina. I enjoyed it, and I wanted to win the World Series of Poker. In addition, I learned a lot of things about odds and probability that apply to trading. I can also get hooked on internet games besides poker. I enjoy them, perhaps because of the adrenalin rush they give, but they are a huge waste of time.

Lastly, I try to take three to four vacations each year that take up one to two weeks of my time. That's one of my criteria for being retired and still working. That's six to eight weeks each year that is gone.

What do all these things have in common? First, I enjoy them. Second, they have nothing to do with any of my major values or my purpose in life. However, having fun is number six on my values list. Third, except for the enjoyment, they are a huge waste of time. We'll talk about how to manage these in the chapter on Moti-Maps (Chapter 12). Most of these things will be a part of my schedule just because I enjoy them, and I can do them. Two of my roles in life – Laid Back Dude (LBD) and World Class Adventurer (WCA) – are involved in these things, and they are actually planned. I want to spend time doing these things.

And there is a third aspect to these so-called "time wasters." When I do them, I frequently have huge insights that come out of nowhere and help me be more creative, and that's way up on my values list.

For some of you, distractions could be called addictions and compulsions. I've included an exercise to help you undo any addictions or unwanted compulsions you might have. Notice what they are and jot them down. When you finish the chapter, do the exercise on each of them.

My addictions and compulsions are:

_____

_____

_____

_____

Compulsion Pattern

1) Identify a clear-cut compulsion you have.
What is something you feel compelled toward (wildly excited about), such as eating your favorite food? Do you have a fetish? If you saw a bundle of €500 bills on the ground, would you feel compelled to pick it up? Immediately? Or would you think about it? If you are an American, you might not even know what a €500 bill looks like.

2) Get a picture of that compulsion (Picture 1).

Associate with the experience of being compelled. Hear it, feel it, see it, taste and smell it! Make it the most vivid and compelling picture possible. What are the feelings involved? What would happen if you doubled the intensity of those feelings? Then, what if you doubled it again?

3) Identify something you'd like to be more passionate about – a future compulsion (Picture 2).

What is something that you'd like to feel more passionate about? See it as a picture in your mind and be sure it has all the qualities you want and that it matches the submodalities of other things you might be compulsive about.

4) Do an ecology check (Is it congruent with your life? Does it work?) on your future compulsion.

Would having your new compulsion improve your life? Would it be useful? Is it possible that it could hinder you in some way? Does any part of you object to instilling that new compulsion? Reframe the objection by finding a context in which this compulsion might be useful to the objecting part.

Now do an NLP Swish Pattern on the pictures as described below.

5) Link the two pictures.

Put picture 1 (your compulsion) behind picture 2 (what you'd like more passion about). See the two pictures as being interconnected so that one is the front and one is the back …the way you have it set up.

- Now make a mental hole in picture 2 so that you can see picture 1 through the hole.
- Now make the hole big enough that you can bring picture 1 through it.
- Have it cover picture 2 and feel the excitement as you see it grow.
- Now reverse the process. Shrink the hole as rapidly as possible while keeping the positive feelings.

6) Repeat step five 3 times or more until thinking about the new activity has become associated with the desired feelings.

7) Break the state (i.e., get up and walk around) **and then test it**. Do you have more compulsion about that new activity?

Richard Bandler has always said there is nothing wrong with compulsion. The issue was always, "What are you compulsive about?" So, if you have some compulsions, why not use that to become compulsive about something that's much more useful. For example, you could become compulsive about working on yourself. Here is how you would do that.

Van's Example of the Compulsive Pattern:

1. **Identify a clear-cut compulsion you have.** What is something you feel compelled toward (wildly excited about), such as eating a candy bar? Do you have a fetish? If you saw a bundle of €500 bills on the ground, would you feel compelled to pick it up? Immediately? Or would you think about it?

2) Get a picture of that compulsion (picture 1).

Associate with the experience of being compelled. Hear it, feel it, see it, taste and smell it! Make it the most vivid and compelling picture possible. What would happen if you double the intensity? And then double it again?

Here is my picture. It's my favorite chocolate bar – Crunchie. As I turn it into a picture, I can taste it. I love the honeycomb inside. And the way it breaks up in my mouth. It's sweet. There is a sense of honey and crispiness. I see it in front of me and have a tightness in my chest (which means grab it). I see it as a picture. I take a bite; I taste the crispy sweetness, and I feel compelled to eat the next bite.

3) Identify a future compulsion (Picture 2).

What is something that you'd like to feel more passionate about? Now look at the picture in your mind and be sure it has all the qualities you want.

Outcome	Purpose	Action
To accomplish my dreams.	To transform myself to a higher level of consciousness and to help others do the same.	Use OPAs to develop a great time management system.

I would like to be passionate about doing a daily OPA procedure (see Chapter 10). I'm already excited about applying it to all my top values, but I want to make it a compulsion.

4) Ecology check (Is it congruent with your life? Does it work on your future compulsion?

Would having your new compulsion improve your life? Would it be useful? Is it possible that it could hinder you in some way? Does any part of you object to installing the new compulsion?

I can commit to 15 minutes a day doing this. It would be useful because I will probably get much more done. The only part that might object is the "I'm retired part, and I want my fun time."

Reframe or do a conflict resolution with any objections.

I don't have to do anything with that part because I have promised him that we'll schedule his satisfaction as a major outcome.

5) Link the pictures (this is a version of the Swish Pattern[3]).

Put picture 1 (your compulsion) behind Picture 2 (what you'd like more passion about).

See the two pictures as being interconnected so that one is the front, and one is the back … the way you have it set up.

- Now make a mental hole in picture 2 so that you can see picture 1 through the hole.
- Now make the hole big enough that you can bring picture 1 through it.
- Have it cover picture 2 and feel the excitement as you see it grow.
- Now reverse the process. Shrink the hole as rapidly as possible while keeping the positive feelings.

6) Repeat step 5 three times or more until thinking about the new activity has become associated with the desired feelings.

I did this about five times, and I wanted to eat the OPA diagram.

7) Break the state (i.e., get up and walk around) **and then test it**. Do you have more compulsion about that new activity?

Yes, I want to set it up now, but it will need to wait until I return home and get into my normal routine.

Focus 5: Immediate Accomplishments or Creative Procrastination

The fifth area of focus is on getting something accomplished. You have a busy day in front of you. You are swamped, and you're not looking forward to the day. Your first thought is, let me see if anything is important in my emails? You check the emails, get distracted answering unimportant ones, and the next thing you know, three hours have passed, and you've done nothing. Sound familiar?

You check the news on the internet. There is something that interests you, so you read the entire article. And that gets you thinking about it, and you look up some things on Google. And then you read another article. And the next thing you know, you've wasted two hours.

It might be worse. You are sleepy and decide to get a cup of coffee to start the morning. One of your co-workers is also there, and you start talking. The conversation is interesting and the next thing you know an hour has gone by, and you've done nothing productive.

Small tasks are creative procrastination. You feel and look busy. You think you are getting a lot accomplished, getting instant gratification and a dopamine rush, but really nothing important is getting done. This is much more likely to occur when you have something major to accomplish. It's the "present bias" – the tendency to prioritize more imminent payoffs over future ones. Most people will take $10 today over $11 tomorrow – yet the second amounts to 10% interest in a single day. It's called the present bias. If the choice is a year off – $10 in a year or $11 in 366 days – they will pick the $11. In the second case, there is little present bias.

In a procrastination study at Princeton University, 14 Princeton University students were given a brain scan as they were asked to consider delayed reward choices. One example of a choice that students were offered was if they would take a gift card to Amazon.com with values ranging from $5 to $40 at that moment, or an unknown larger amount if they waited a certain period, ranging from two to six weeks.

All the decisions made, both short-term and long-term, activated the abstract reasoning part of the brain. The immediate reward option tended to also activate their emotional centers. When the subjects chose the immediate reward, the activation in the emotional areas tended to dominate over the active reasoning areas. When subjects chose the long-term reward, then the abstract reasoning areas dominated in terms of brain activity. Our logical brain can see the future consequences of current actions, but apparently the emotional brain just wants immediate pleasure.

Focus 6: Less Significant Obligations and the Demands of Others

Suppose you have spent a busy day at work. You come home to accomplish some of your personal goals, and suddenly your spouse has a large to-do list and starts to dump it onto you. You could take it on, but if you did, it would be an example of the sixth focus – less significant obligations. Do you say "yes" when others ask you to do things for them? When I think about the most important values in my life and my purpose, the most important distractor is other life obligations. In my case, these are obligations that include some of my highest values, including having fun, but they are not necessarily part of my purpose.

The first of these are my family obligations. My wife, who is very important to me, requires some of my time, but she does not dump her to-do lists on me. Instead, she wants me to take her someplace because she doesn't like to drive long distances by herself. She wants to run an errand and would like me to come. She plans some social event and expects me to attend and be happy about it. Other things come up as well. Family is part of my top five values, so I do these things if I think they give me quality time with my wife.

The second of those is my work obligations. I'm the visionary for our company. I give workshops, which could take up more than a week of my time. I manage the staff on a macro level. I go to staff meetings. I write articles and monthly updates. I respond to my Super Trader Weekly reports and their lessons. My career/work is one of my top five values, and some of those things I do actually involve my purpose – helping others raise their consciousness. I just don't want a big company that could give me more things to do that are not aligned with my purpose.

Trading stocks (for my retirement fund) and investing in cryptocurrencies are also two things that take up time. However, both are part of my business. They give me a personal measuring stick for whether I'm following my own ideas of how to trade well, and I enjoy them.

I'm working with my Inner Guidance to triple my net worth in the next few years.[4] I'm pretty sure I can do it, and that aligns with my highest purpose. I'm doing this not because money is important, but because I want to see how easy it is to manifest a lot of money quickly. Right now, I'm asking my Divine to make it so easy for me to make money that I know I can give it all away and accumulate just as much very quickly. It's part of my number one transformation agenda. As I said, it really has nothing to do with money and everything to do with knowing what my Inner Guidance and I can do together – it becomes a sort of measuring stick for trusting my Inner Guidance. I find it exciting to do. Trading could be a distraction, especially for excitement, but for me, it's part of a proving ground of me figuring out who I really am.

Focus 7: This is More Urgent; I'll Do it Later

This common excuse is a reminder that you can work on the most important but big task later. You imagine that in just a few hours or a couple of days, you will have the perfect opportunity to accomplish your goal. You have something that you feel compelled to do now, so you put off your goal. However, this creates a strong disconnect between how you will ideally feel in the future and how you actually feel in the future.

Ideally, you will suddenly be gifted with boundless energy, eat a clean and healthy diet, exercise on a regular basis, and work well into the evenings in order to get everything finished. However, the realistic future could be that you are tired, unmotivated, worn-out, handling unruly children, and craving your favorite dessert.

This phenomenon relates to two concepts: the hot-cold empathy gap and dynamic inconsistency. What are those?

The Hot-Cold Empathy Gap (HCEG) is a mental state that causes people to underestimate the influences of their lower-level needs on Maslow's hierarchy on their attitudes, behaviors, and preferences. Human understanding greatly depends on one's mental state. If someone is angry, it is hard for them to picture themselves being calm. If you are hungry, it is hard to think of yourself as being full. If you are dealing with a primary drive, it's hard to change your state about those basic needs. For example, I was never able to like the food at the Ayurvedic clinic in India.

Subjective decisions, such as a doctor estimating the pain of a patient or an employer assessing the amount of paid leave someone grieving a lost family member should get, can easily be influenced by the HCEG. The doctor might use his own estimate of his pain at some time in the past. The employer might remember his grief after a family death. Their own memory of those experiences (which might not even be accurate) will influence their decisions.

What does this imply? The "future you" is unknown, and because of the HCEG, you can't predict what your feelings or moods will be like in the future. This could easily disrupt your plans to do something in the future. You might just not feel like it in the future, and that feeling will keep you from doing the task you had planned to do.

Dynamic Inconsistency refers to a situation where the decision maker's preferences vary over time and thus are not consistent. You have many parts. The part of you deciding to put off some task might not be the same as the part that's in charge at the time you want to do the task. Each of your parts represents the decision-maker at a certain point in time, and the inconsistency happens when their preferences, states, beliefs, and decision-making criteria are not aligned.

This also adds the unpredictability factor into your future self. Psychology researchers using typical college students as their subjects find that the night before an exam, most students wish they had one more day to study. If the students are asked that night, some may agree to pay $10 for the exam to be postponed just one more day. However, months before the exam, students generally don't feel the need to put the exam off and certainly are not willing to pay $10 to change the date of the exam. This is an example of time inconsistency because the choice is the same, but the decision is made at different time periods. While the choice is the same in both instances, it is made at different points in time, and they are exhibiting what's called dynamic inconsistency.

Another example of a dynamic inconsistency was shown in a 1999 experiment.[5] Here, subjects were offered a free movie rental, either lowbrow (such as *Austin Powers*) or highbrow (such as *Hamlet*). The results again showed dynamic inconsistency. When subjects were asked to pick a movie to watch immediately, they typically chose a lowbrow movie. However, when tasked with what movie to watch in four or more days, 70% of the subjects chose a highbrow movie.

People make different decisions for what will impact them in the immediate future than for what will impact them at a more distant time period. When you procrastinate now, thinking you'll do it later, then chances are you won't do it. In the Moti-Map chapter, we'll show you how to get around that problem.

Focus 8: Perfectionism

Perfectionism might be the major excuse for most people to procrastinate. Perfectionism is not a big deal for me. When I work on a creative project (workshop, book, article), I want it to be the best I can make it, I hate details, so when it's no longer creative for me, I'm done. I try to get others to proofread, etc. I'm also not going to worry about what people will think about me for producing the product because I have an internal standard (Internal versus External Referent Metaprogram) for making such decisions.[6] However, I do work hard to make sure it meets whatever my objectives were for creating the product.

Perhaps you are worried you might make a mistake in your work and expose a weakness. The fear of making mistakes is a real thing, and it can cause people to put off some of their important obligations for another day. Perhaps you are just concerned that other people might not like what you accomplish, and your effort will be wasted.

This is a type of mindset that is addressed by Carol Dweck[7] in her book, *Mindset: The New Psychology of Success*. Dweck explains that people either have a **"fixed"** or a **"growth" mindset."** Those with a fixed mindset believe that their abilities are set in stone, so they only focus on their current intelligence or talents, believing they cannot be developed. The classic fixed mindset that Dweck has researched extensively has to do with IQ. If a fixed-mindset person has an IQ of say 140 and believes they were born with it (and therefore cannot improve it), then they tend to find intellectual tasks to be easy. But if they run into a problem that isn't easy, they tend to go into helplessness.

I'm lucky because I never had this attitude. I think I was originally tested with an IQ of 135, around 3rd grade, but my best friend in 5th grade had an IQ of about 150. I wasn't getting good grades until he became my friend, probably because I was lazy. Once he became my best friend, I always felt that if he could do something, then so could I. Then interesting things started to happen with that idea. Later, when he was no longer in my life, I got a perfect score of 150 on the Army GT test. I have no idea how that happened and don't even remember taking the test. In addition, I got a perfect score of 800 on the GRE in math when applying to graduate school. Those things show that IQ[8] is a process, and it's not something fixed. I probably read 25 to 50 books a year, and I'm constantly trying to improve my models of the world and gain a new perspective.

If you believe your mindset is fixed, then it can be dangerous for you. **A fixed mindset hinders one's ability to grow, to learn, and to make positive changes. A growth mindset allows a person to believe their abilities can prosper and be developed through dedication and hard work.** What you are born with, in terms of talents and brainpower, is a mere starting point. People are born with their individual strengths, but there is no limit to what one can accomplish. The growth mindset creates a desire to learn and an ability to overcome problems in order to be successful. Great accomplishments are possible with the correct mindset. When you have it, you can motivate, lead, and teach in a way that can positively change your life and the lives of others.

According to author Hillary Rettig,[9] people who procrastinate due to perfectionism tend to have a fixed mindset. They procrastinate because they fear mistakes and looking less than perfect. Their work must be perfect. They believe that they will inevitably fail if the task is not in line with their given talents; they believe that it is best to set it aside for another time. Perfectionism is a trait that makes you non-productive, or low productive, at best. Nothing is ever perfect.

Focus 9: Overwhelm: It's Too Much Work.

People give up when they decide a project is too hard, too long, and seems overwhelming. These people are operating out of a high-level frame – it's a mind game. These excuses amount to putting a big metaframe around the project/task by saying it's just too big/too hard/too overwhelming. But that's all it is – a big metaframe. My metaframe for the project of working on this book is that it is exciting. It's making it easy for me to do the rest of the "somewhat unpleasant" things necessitated by being in the clinic. As I'm getting closer and closer to finishing the first draft of the book, all I want to do is work on the book.[10]

Think about it. What do you value more, money or your free time? What if you could give up all your free time and get paid double for working during that time. Would you do it? Most people would probably say, "No." They might give up some of it, but not all of it.

Dynamic inconsistency again is a major factor here. When a professor announces an exam, the students study. The professor can then cancel the exam (i.e., the students have already studied), not have to spend time scoring them and then devote the class time to a new topic. A Stanford University study found that people have a present bias when they are working on tasks on which they have full control. That means that they value their current time over future results because we value immediate rewards more than future rewards. You might say, "I don't have to work now; I think I'll take a nap or watch my favorite tv show." In other words, if you are not focusing on the "Big Why" behind what you are doing, you will probably just do something that makes you feel good, which we have already discussed.

This is one of the main reasons why many people procrastinate and is, in fact, one of the biggest predictors of future success. One project done by Walter Mischel[11] and his colleagues at Stanford University involved a series of studies that were done on delayed gratification. During these studies, a child was presented with a choice between receiving a small reward right away or two small rewards in 15 minutes. The researchers then followed up on what happened in the children's lives. Those who were willing to wait for the larger rewards tended to have more successful lives. Those who chose immediate gratification had more behavioral problems in school, less educational attainment, and higher BMIs (were fatter), in addition to being less successful.

Focus 10: Not Enough Juice to Do it

While some aspects of this excuse may fall under other categories, there are still enough individual reasons to include this as a separate category. Why have you been unable to do what you were supposed to do? It can come from any of the following:

- Lack of energy.
- Fatigue.
- Poor Health.
- Stress.
- An unexpected emergency.
- Trouble being creative.
- Lack of success in the past with similar tasks.
- Negative environment.
- Lack of confidence or other Metaprograms discussed earlier.
- Out of context environment.
- Unclear goals.

There are some clear components to motivation, already described in this volume but worth reviewing here.

- If you can see how your work relates to your purpose in life or your highest values, then you tend to be willing to invest energy into it.
- If you don't see the value, then the lack of motivation becomes high.
- In addition, you need useful metaprograms, such as self-confidence, that will see you through until the end.

- And finally, you need a high-level guiding frame that supports follow-through to the end of the task. For example, one metaframe might be – this is important and exciting to me. It will really help me achieve my highest values.

My lack of energy tended to get worse and worse. I could say, "Oh, it's just a function of my age, but I won't accept that." As a result, I'm constantly looking for things to try. Finally, I bought a machine called the AMI 750, which puts vibrations into your body. It has various settings with different functions, and one of the settings has to do with vitality. I've been doing it for about 30 days and I feel much better. I don't feel any particular changes from working with the machine, but the effects seem to be cumulative. Thus, if you lack energy, this might be one solution.

Focus 11: Lack of Know-How

When you focus on just working on a project, rather than the "Big Why" behind the project, you might give up because 1) it seems too hard; or 2) you have no idea how to accomplish certain parts of the project. But, when you focus on the "Big Why" behind the project, and you don't know how to do something, then you'll learn how to do it, one way or another.

I'm writing a book, but I've written many books in the past. I know how to do it. Typically, I might go through the following steps:

Have a conversation with my Inner Guidance[12] about the book. I might ask for ideas about the content. My Inner Guidance will then ask me what I think. Suddenly, ideas will flow out at a rate that never would have happened had I not asked the questions, and then She might make some clarifications.

I will also read or review some of the books and material that I have on the topics that I'm covering in the book to see if there are some points that I might not have thought about before. Usually, I read them, and then they remind me of something else that I want to include.

I then divide the book into sections that appear logical and important. At this point, I need to become very clear about my objectives in writing the book and the objectives for each chapter. And several times, I've developed a marketing plan for the book prior to writing it. Whether or not I do that depends upon my objectives for the book.

I repeat the same process for each section. As I'm doing it, I frequently think of resources I might have for this section. For example, the section on purpose was largely taken from materials my Super Traders have submitted to me on their purposes.

When I'm ready, I start writing with the goal of doing a rough draft of a chapter per day. I will frequently read, edit, and rewrite what I have down on paper. Often, sections will be deleted or changed or moved to a different part of the book.

There might be as many as five such reviews. At that point, the hard part comes, and that's getting all the typos out and letting others read it (and to some extent) accepting most of their changes. I don't like doing such details, so I try to do as little as possible during this phase. This part is hard for me because I already feel like it's done, and all the little corrections and details seem like "busy" work to me.[13]

This book, for example, will be reviewed by at least three to four staff members at the Van Tharp Institute and probably by at least ten of our Super Trader students, depending upon how many are willing to read it and make comments. Probably because I don't like to do this part of the task, and because I can't devote full time to it, it has taken about 20 months to get the book ready for publication. Contrast that with the six weeks that it took for me to get through the first draft and then the first edit of that draft.

What if you haven't written a book? What would you do? Such a task is complex, with a lot of moving parts, you might not have a clue where to begin. If you don't know the first step, you may never know where to begin. For example, at the Super Trader Professional level – the third phase of the current Super Trader program – our Super Trader candidates are supposed to write a business handbook. Some of the students we have who do not have a college degree seem to have a lot of trouble with this, and I suspect that it is because they have little training in writing reports, theses, etc. They just lack the writing skills and don't realize those skills can be developed.

Perhaps you know the first step, but as you delve into the project, you believe you have underestimated the size and scope of the task. For example, I might be able to write the first draft of a major book in a few months. Subsequent drafts might take a month each, but I can usually finish in six months or less. All of that, however, never prepared me for the fact that when I submitted a book to a publisher, it might take as long as a year for them to publish it and that they would want me to continually reread the book for mistakes and changes.

- I'd have to look at an editor's suggestions to see if I would accept them.
- Then they'd typeset the book (before it was automated), and whole new errors would come from the typeset process.
- Then there might be at least one more process in which new errors could enter.
- After a year of making such corrections, some of the material in the book might seem outdated to me, and I'd want to change it.

What if the task at hand is too complex, unique, or difficult? What if it has a lot of moving parts, making it unclear where to begin? This uncertainty may keep you from starting some project because you don't know your first step.

Even if you can figure out the first step, once you are considering the whole process, you realize that you have underestimated the level of time and commitment that is needed to complete this task. What's the best way to overcome this? A very effective method is to use a simple "get things done" approach. Focus on the "Big Why" behind the project. This will help break down your complex task into a series of smaller tasks.

There are several steps to doing this, so if you don't know how to do something that's important, then consider doing the following:

- Find a course or book that describes how to do the task. You can find something for almost anything these days. Study that course and then determine what needs to be done. As you are doing this, focus on the why behind doing it.

- Learn as much as you can about the topic. I had one of our instructors give a course on systems thinking because I thought it was important for me to understand his thinking as a systems thinker and for others to understand it. The first presentation of the course was not what I wanted, so I said that he and I would present it together to make it more organized. Now I was committed to learning the topic well enough to present on it. Not only that, but about three months prior to the course, he had to cancel, and it was up to me to deliver the entire course on my own. I've given the course about five times now, and very little of the original course content remains. In fact, I've evolved it to something else that will be the basis for my new book (when I get around to writing it) entitled: *The Holy Grail of Trading: Understanding Systems Thinking and that You Can Only Trade Your Beliefs.*[14]

- Based upon the first two steps, write what tasks you think are important to complete your projects. Then list specific actions for each project. While you are doing this, focus on why you are doing it. Knowing the why behind it might also allow you to simplify the actual task. You might not need to do all those things to achieve the purpose behind the outcome.

- Organize the rest of the task.

- Constantly review this process, doing each task, until they are all complete.

- Make this process one part of your Moti-Map as described in Chapter 12.

Focus 12: Secrets and Hidden Agendas

Secrets and Hidden Agendas are topics that one doesn't see in books about motivation and procrastination. Typically, secrets have to do with things about your past that you don't want to reveal or beliefs you have about other people that you don't want to share, or what you think about others (usually negative) that you don't want them to know. It could be something as banal as the password on a very sensitive account.

Secrets imply that you have some sort of belief that you want to keep from the world, and if something you are motivated to do runs into a secret buried in your mind, it will stop you cold. They are one of the biggest killers of motivation as well as a huge cause of procrastination. I consider this section so significant that I have decided to cover it in an additional chapter.

Three Exercises to Overcome What Stops You

Exercise 1: Getting Rid of Addictions

Addiction occurs when you get too much enjoyment from the things that you consider to be inappropriate or wrong. And it might be someone else's judgment that your behavior is wrong or inappropriate.

Step 1: Determine the "unwanted" addiction.

What enjoyment do you have in your life that you wish was not so addictive? This might include smoking, over-eating, drinking, taking the path of least resistance, social media, online games, watching too much TV, too much sex, etc.

_____
_____
_____
_____

Step 2: Identify the primary level elements behind this pleasure.

Describe it fully. What is the activity or experience like? Describe it in sensory-based terms. What do you see, hear, feel, taste, or smell?

_____
_____
_____
_____

Step 3: Discover the meanings you have given to the addition.

Take the item you picked out and answer the following questions:

- What does this behavior mean to you?
- What is important to you? Why is it important? How is it important?
- What other positive meanings do you give it?
- What else do you give to it that you really like? Fill out at least four higher-level meaning bubbles in the diagram. In other words, list four different higher-level meanings that you give to the primary meaning.

Step 4: Continue repeating the questions in Step 3 to get a deeper understanding of the structure of your addiction.

- What does this behavior mean to you?
- How/why is it important to you? What is important about it?
- What other positive meanings do you give it?
- What else do you give to it that you really like?

Create a diagram of meta-level meanings by drawing a circle, designating the primary pleasure level and then adding higher-level meaning bubbles above that with the answer to each question of meaning.

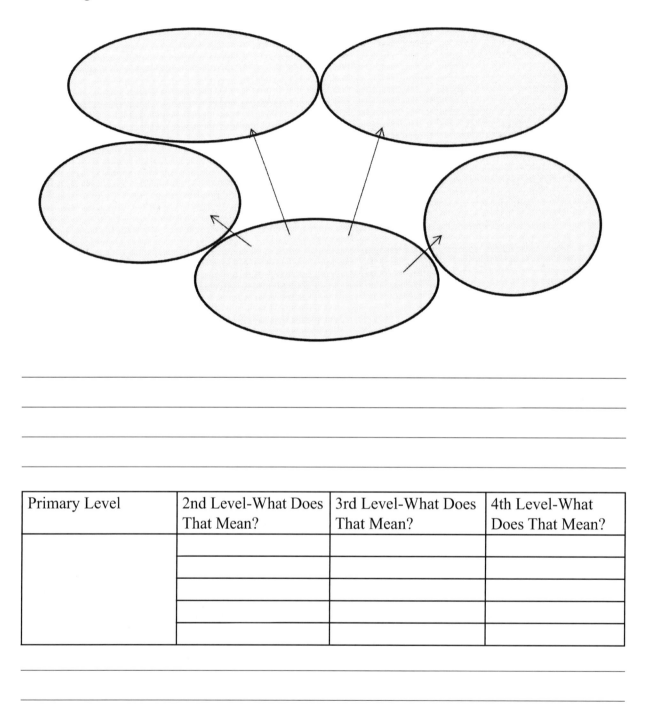

Primary Level	2nd Level-What Does That Mean?	3rd Level-What Does That Mean?	4th Level-What Does That Mean?

Step 5: Appreciate the total picture of your addiction as you've laid it out.

- Read over what you wrote in this exercise. What do you think?
- Do you know why this activity holds so much pleasure for you?
- Do you also understand how you have given it so much meaning, energy, and motivation?

_____
_____
_____
_____
_____

Step 6: Take the meanings away, which will reduce the addiction.

Take away one set of higher-level meanings and ask, "If we take away this avenue of meanings about the pleasure, how much would it reduce that enjoyment?"

Continue this process for all the different higher-level meanings about the pleasures, notice the impact of each.

How many levels do I have to take away before it just exists at the primary level of whatever it is?

Once you know which meanings drive the addiction, step into deciding to refuse to allow these higher-level meanings for the pleasures to set the frame for the primary pleasure:

"These higher-level meanings have not served me well at all. They have undermined my resourcefulness, health, and sanity. At this moment, I choose to no longer give it that much power. I will tolerate this no longer. I will only allow this kind of intense motivation for things that enhance my life."

Step 7: Take the de-powering of the addiction (your new perspective) into the future.

Imagine yourself fully engaged in the primary pleasure. Now hear yourself say: "This is just a primary pleasure _____ it has the purpose only to _____ I refuse to overload it with meaning."

Then attach whatever displeasure you like to the overuse of it.

Step 8: Access your highest meta-pleasure states fully.

Step into that highest level of meaning and experience it fully. As you do, realize that you can do so at any time without needing to engage in that other behavior any more.

Note: All you need to do is withdraw the psychic energies. When you frame the meta-pleasure as not important, it loses its semantic hold on us.

Van's Example:

Step 1: Determine the "unwanted" addiction.
What pleasure do you have in your life that you wish was not so addictive?

I'm not sure I want to get rid of anything, but the biggest waste of time is probably playing addictive games, so I'll pick that one.

Step 2: Identify the primary level elements of this pleasure.
Describe it fully. What is the activity or experience like? Describe it in sensory-based terms? What do you see, hear, feel, taste, or smell?

There is a sense of getting lost in it. I'm fully present in the game to the exclusions of all else. The game seems to test me. There is a tingling in my head and chest. I feel a charge around the center of my chest. It's like a shot of adrenaline. I'm not really in my body. I'm in the game.

Step 3: Discover the Meanings You Have Given to Drive the Addiction.
Take the item you picked out and answer the following questions:

- What does this mean to you?
- How/why is it important to you?
- What other positive meanings do you give it?
- What else do you give to it that you really like? Again, fill out at least four metastate bubbles in the diagram with four different meanings that you give to the primary meaning.

These are shown in the next diagram.

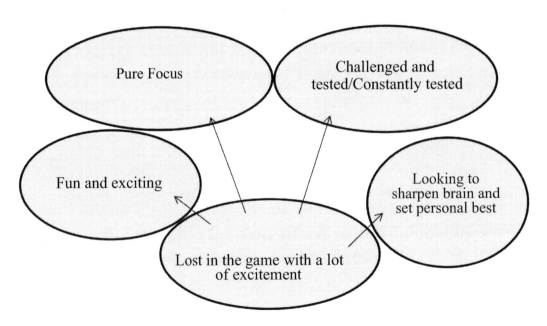

Step 4: Keep Repeating the questions in Step 3 to get a deeper understanding of the structure of your addiction.

- What does this mean to you?
- How/why is it important to you? What is important about it?
- What other positive meanings do you give it?
- What else do you give to it that you really like?

Create a diagram of meta-level meanings by drawing a circle, designating the primary pleasure level and then adding meta-state bubbles above that with the answer to each question of meaning.

Primary Level	2nd Level-What Does That Mean?	3rd Level-What Does That Mean?	4th Level-What Does That Mean?
Lost in the game with excitement	Fun and exciting	Adrenaline state	Feel energized
	Pure focus	In the now	Spiritual domain
	Challenged & tested	Test myself	Moving forward
	Sharpen brain & personal best	Constant improvement	I am at my best

Step 5: Appreciate the new big picture of it all.

Read over what you wrote in this exercise. What do you think?

Do you understand why this activity holds so much pleasure for you?

Do you also understand how you have given it so much meaning, energy, and motivation?

Yes, it's spiritual (that's a meaning I give to the Gestalt); it's energizing, it's me evolving constantly; it gives me a feeling I'm at my best.

Step 6: Take the meanings away and reduce the addiction.

Take away one set of higher-level meanings and ask, "If we take away this avenue of higher-level meanings about the pleasure, how much would it reduce that enjoyment?

Continue this process for all of the different avenues of higher-level meanings about the pleasure? Notice the impact of each.

How many levels do I have to take away before it just exists at the primary level of whatever it is?

Once you know which meanings drive the addiction, step into the higher-level meaning of making a decision to refuse to allow those other higher-level pleasures to set the frame for the primary pleasure.

I have to take away all of them. And there would still be some adrenaline rush that I could not remove. It could become me wasting time to get an adrenaline rush.

When I looked at it a second time, taking away "focused" will do it. The problem is that's the meaning I give to a state, and you'd have to take away the state.

Step 7: Take the de-powering of the addiction into the future.

Imagine yourself fully engaged in the primary pleasure. Now hear yourself say: "this is just a primary pleasure _____ it has the purpose only to _____ I refuse to overload it with meaning. And then attach whatever displeasure you like to the overuse of it.

This is an adrenaline rush, and its purpose is for when I have nothing else to do. Its only purpose is to kill time. I refuse to overload it with meaning. It's not spiritual. Playing it a lot means I'm non-productive and wasting my time.

Step 8: Access your highest meta-pleasure states fully.

Step into that highest level of meaning and experience it fully. As you do so, realize that you can do so at any time without needing to engage in that other behavior any more.

Note: all you need to do is withdraw the psychic energies. When you frame the meta-pleasure as not important, it loses its semantic hold on us.

I can step into "I'm working on myself and changing my level of consciousness. My Beloved Durga is with me strongly, protecting me, helping me move to a higher state of awareness. I can do this any time and it doesn't require me to play a game."

Postscript: When I feel run down, the adrenalin run is actually quite useful. It makes me feel energized.

Exercise 2: Exploring the Higher-Level Meanings of Procrastination

Step 1: Access a Trigger for Procrastination

When/where/under what conditions do you procrastinate?

Are you putting something off that you ought to do/that would change your life? (i.e., like doing an exercise in this book).

How do you know to procrastinate? What starts the process?

Is the trigger one of the following:

- An unpleasant feeling, something that feels emotionally painful?
- The idea of doing a lot of work?
- The notion that it seems boring, trivial, tedious, a chore?
- Something else?

_____

_____

_____

Step 2: Acceptance as a new higher-level meaning:
Notice that you tend to procrastinate. Acknowledge it, accept it, and then welcome it. Notice what happens when you welcome negative feelings?

_____
_____
_____
_____

Step 3: Determine how you organize your mental map in order to create those feelings you don't want.

- How have you mapped reality to experience this feeling?
- What are the criteria you are using to evaluate the activity you are procrastinating?
- What are your expectations of what might happen if you do what you are putting off?
- What does procrastination mean to you?
- Do you tend to have some perfectionism in your expectations? If so, how does that impact you?

_____
_____
_____
_____
_____

Step 4: Permission

- Do you have permission to have the feelings that seem to cause you to procrastinate?
- How about the activity you are procrastinating? Do you have permission to engage in that activity?
- Do you have permission to make mistakes and be fallible?
- What happens when you give yourself permission? What happens to the sense of putting something off?

_____
_____
_____
_____

Step 5: Identify the importance of the procrastinated task.

- What value do you place on it?
- How is this activity important? In what way does it benefit/improve your life?
- Determine the value involved in this activity and step into that? What does that give you? And when you have that, step into it? What does that give you? And when you have that, step into it? What does that give you? Continue this process until you find your highest intention!

_____
_____
_____
_____

Step 6: Find additional resources.

- What other resources could you bring to the state of procrastination to blow it away?
- What if you procrastinated the putting off?
- What if you became a person who refused to put off anything that was for your betterment?
- What if you became super passionate about the procrastinated activity?

_____
_____
_____
_____

Step 7: Now step into the future with this new perspective.

- What is your future like with this new perspective?
- What would happen if I decided to take it back?

_____
_____
_____
_____

Van's Example:

Step 1: Access a Trigger for Procrastination

- When/where/under what conditions do you procrastinate?
- Are you putting something off that you ought to do/that would change your life (i.e., like doing an exercise)?
- How do you know to procrastinate? What starts the process?

Is the trigger one of the following:

- An unpleasant feeling, something that feels emotionally painful
- The idea of doing a lot of work
- The notion that it seems boring, trivial, tedious, a chore?
- Something else?

What starts the process for me is a feeling of being tired, and when I'm tired, I'm not motivated to do anything, or I will want to play a game that gets my energy up or watch an action show on television that gets my adrenaline up. It also comes if I haven't planned what I'm doing, or I am not in the middle of some exciting task that I haven't finished. For example, I'm a little tired now, but I am doing something exciting, so I'm doing it – finishing this book.

*Also, determining the trigger was very useful because I was not aware of what triggered it. It's definitely **the feeling of being tired and not having enough energy.***

Step 2: Acceptance as a higher-level meaning:

Just notice that you tend to procrastinate. Acknowledge it, accept it, and then welcome it. Notice what happens when you welcome negative feelings?

This is not hard for me. I consider myself retired. If I want to play a game or watch television, it is fine. I don't beat myself up over it. I get tired, and I procrastinate. I'm working on improving my health, so I have more energy.

Step 3: Determine how you organize your mental map in order to create those feelings you don't want.

- How have you mapped reality to experience this feeling?
- What are the criteria you are using to evaluate the activity you are procrastinating?
- What are your expectations of what might happen if you do what you are putting off?
- What does procrastination mean to you?
- Do you tend to have some perfectionism in your expectations? If so, how does that impact you?

My frame tends to be that I'm getting older. I'm showing signs of getting older, and that includes me being tired.

I also have a frame that I'm surrendering to my Inner Guidance and that if She really wants me to do something, it will happen. Being in India is an example of this.

I have a frame of the perfection of the "what is." If I'm procrastinating doing an important task, it's okay, and it must not be time to do it. I don't have any experience of not getting things done (on time if I decide to do it and set a deadline). For the newer book that I plan to publish next – The Holy Grail of Trading: Systems Thinking and Knowing that You Can Only Trade Your Beliefs, I have totally organized it in OneNote. I believe that when I'm supposed to write it that it will just happen like this book is happening.

I also think there may be some high-level spiritual experience that I might need prior to starting to write it. I don't know, and I surrender.

What I haven't done is develop a Moti-Map as I recommend in Chapter 12 to organize my time better, and I'm willing to commit to that.

Step 4: Permission

- Do you have permission to have the feelings that seem to cause you to procrastinate?
- How about the activity you are procrastinating? Do you have permission to engage in that activity?
- Do you have permission to make mistakes and be fallible?
- What happens when you give yourself permission? What happens to the sense of putting something off?

Yes, I have permission to have all the feelings listed above. If the activity is writing my next book, then I have permission to write it from me, but I'm looking for impetus from my Inner Guidance that it is the time. I believe it should just flow out. I absolutely have permission to make mistakes. I always do. Perfectionism is not an issue.

Step 5: Identify the importance of the procrastinated task. What value do you place on it?

How is this activity important? In what way does it benefit/improve your life?

Determine the value involved in this activity and step into that? What does that give you? When you have that, step into it. What does that give you? When you have that, step into it. What does that give you? Continue this process until you find your highest intention!

Writing my next book is very important to me. I think it will be my best book and it will make me famous. I'm ready for that. This book serves my purpose in life even more than Trading Beyond the Matrix.

I don't need to go any higher than my purpose and my two highest values.

In fact, I'm so juiced that I managed to finish the first draft of this book in less than a month that I'm now eager to start another one.

Step 6: Find additional resources.
What other resources could you bring to the state of procrastination to blow it away?

What if you procrastinated the putting off?

What if you became a person who refused to put off anything that was for your betterment?

What if you became super passionate about the procrastinated activity?

I'm already super passionate about writing this book. Why not? I'll commit to having a first draft of the book before I leave this clinic and to optimal health by the end of the year, and if that causes me to want to change the content of the book, so be it.

Step 7: Now step into the future with this new perspective?
What is your future like with this new perspective?

What would happen if I decided to take it back?

When I return to the US, I will commit to spending two hours per day writing this book.

When I return to the US, I will also commit to getting rid of the toxic metals in my body by doing chelation therapy. When those heavy metals are gone, I will commit to doing Bruce's ketogenic diet for a period of three months.

At the end of the three months, or if I find out I cannot do the diet plus spend two hours per day writing the book, then I will re-assess. Then I will decide what to do going forward.

I understand that I can stop either commitment when I'm preparing for a workshop or VTI event.

Exercise 3: Demolish Excuses.
What activity do you want to do, but you always seem to have excuses not to do it? Are your excuses over something you really value? If so, then is what you procrastinate about is something important to you?

_____

_____

_____

_____

_____

Step 1: What is your desired outcome?
What do you want that's important to you?

Is it well-formed and ecological (i.e., it doesn't change other important factors)?

Positively stated	Self-initiated and maintained	When, where, how, and with whom? Contextualized
Evidence of getting it	Resources identified	Ecological
First step determined		

Will it improve the quality of your life?

OUTCOME: _____

_____

Positive? _____
Self- initiated and maintained? _____
Contextualized? _____
Evidence of getting it? _____
Resources identified? _____
Ecological? _____
Self-determined? _____
How do you feel about it? _____

_____

_____

_____

Step 2: Let your excuses emerge.

Take a moment to think about engaging in this activity. What excuses start to emerge? Let them flow.

Notice what each one is like and feel it in your body. Listen to the voice.

How do you know it is an excuse?

_____

_____

_____

_____

Step 3: Look at each excuse and do a quality control on it. What value does that excuse have for you? Does it serve you? Is there some aspect of this excuse you want to preserve?

Excuse 1: _____

_____

Excuse 2: _____

Excuse 3: _____

Excuse 4: _____

_____

Step 4: Preserve any values.

Get all the value out of each excuse so that the rest of it is just hollow and empty.

Keep the value in a separate place, different from the excuse, if there is any.

_____
_____
_____
_____

Step 5: Reject what's left of the old excuse using a meta (higher level) no.

Think about how you would react to eating a bowl of live slugs or drowning a small puppy. Hopefully, your reaction to this is something like "Hell, no." Get that sense of "Hell, no" and then anchor it in a spot on the floor. That's your "Hell, no." spot. When you've anchored that spot sufficiently, then take each excuse there and give it a strong "Hell, No." You should be able to convince anyone around you by your expressions that you no longer want that excuse.

Will that excuse stop you anymore?

1. _____
2. _____
3. _____
4. _____
5. _____

Step 6: Test the future activity.

Imagine this desired activity, being sure that it's ecological for you, and notice how you feel about moving toward it? Are you propelled? How do you feel? What comes to mind when you think about it? Can anything stop you from doing it now?

___

Step 7: Now, access your executive (captain) part and ask if you will do this.

Go to the part of your mind that makes decisions and commission it to go ahead and engage in the desired activity. What happens? Will you keep your word and do it?

___

Van's Example:

What activity do you want to do, but you always seem to have excuses not to do it? Are your excuses over something you really value? If so, is what you procrastinate about something important to you?

The one I've been working on in these examples that I'm most worried about not completing is having more choice over food and being willing to order at least one new thing when I go to a restaurant. I will work on that one. Right now, I think that eating what I know I like is more important than eating healthy and more important than having more choices.

Step 1: What is your desired outcome?

What do you want that's important to you?

Is it well-formed and ecological?

Positively stated	Self-initiated and maintained	When, where, how, and with whom? Contextualized
Evidence of getting it	Resources identified	Ecological
First step determined		

Will it improve the quality of your life?

I want more choice in my food when I go to a restaurant. I will order at least one new thing.

Positive – yes

Self – initiated and maintained? Yes, I will keep a list of what I like. I will order what I like and one new thing. I can afford to order one new thing, and if I don't like it, I won't eat it. I will maintain a list I like with the goal of doubling it every six months.

Contextualized? Yes, when I go out to eat.

Evidence of getting it? Yes, I will keep a journal of what I order new and a list of what I like by date.

Then I can measure the growth of the list. Goal, make the list four times as big.

Resources Identified? Yes, my journal and my lists.

Ecological. Yes, my wife, Kala will be happier that I'm trying. I still get to order what I like (just one more thing.). The restaurants will be happy because I will be spending more money.

First step determined: Make a list of what I like at each meal.

I'm actually quite excited about this.

Step 2: Let your excuses emerge.

Take a moment to think about engaging in this activity. What excuses start to emerge? Let them flow.

Notice what each one is like and feel it in your body. Listen to the voice?

How do you know it is an excuse?

> *Why should I spend the extra money?*
> *What if I don't like what I get?*
> *It's extra work to keep a journal of what I order and a list of what I like.*
> *I already know what I like? What does this task even add to my life?*

Step 3: Look at each excuse and do a quality control on it. This means, "What value does that excuse have for you?" Does it serve you? Is there some aspect of this excuse you want to preserve?

Excuse 1: *Why should I spend the extra money? It serves nothing. I'm working on being super abundant, and I can easily afford to do this, and it helps the restaurants we go to.*

Excuse 2: *What if I don't like what I get? Not a useful excuse because I just won't eat it. Perhaps if the restaurants see I'm not eating it, they might give me something else to try?* That means *I get something else new. Otherwise, no big deal if I don't eat it.*

Excuse 3: *It's extra work to keep a journal and a list of what I like. It is extra work, and I want to honor that, but I could keep the notes on my phone so it could be done while I'm at the restaurant. Okay, excuse blown.*

Excuse 4: *I already know what I like. What does doing this even add? Response: That's a legitimate question and deserves an answer. I'm working on myself. I'm giving myself more choices and more options. I could find that there are many other healthy foods that I really like.*

Step 4: Preserve any values.

Get all the value out of each excuse so that the rest of it is just hollow and empty.
Keep the value in a separate place, different from the excuse, if there is any.

The values include having a feeling of abundance by ordering more; keeping the lists on my phone; I don't even have to start the list until I get to a restaurant. I could have more choices, be healthier, and make my wife happier in that I'm giving her more options.

Step 5: Reject what's left of the old excuse using a higher-level no.

Think about something for which your reaction would be "Hell, no." Examples might include eating a bowl of live cockroaches. You should be able to convince anyone around you by your expressions that you no longer want that excuse.

Will that excuse stop you anymore?

Extra money: Hell, no.
What if I don't like it: Hell, no.
It's extra work: Hell, no.
What does doing this even add? Hell, no.

Step 6: Test the future activity.

Imagine this desired activity, being sure that it's ecological for you, and notice how you feel about moving toward it? Are you propelled? How do you feel? What comes to mind when you think about it? Can anything stop you from doing it now?

I can test it in India after I leave the clinic, assuming I can find things I like to eat. I have more choices and I get to have more awareness about food. What comes to mind when I think about it? It's excuse 5.

Excuse 5: What if I go to a new restaurant where I can't figure out if there is even something I would like – like an Indian restaurant in India or a Vietnamese restaurant?

Then I get to order something new. I get to try it, and if I can be aware of what it is about it that I don't like, I don't have to eat it. That really works.

Step 7: Now, access your executive (captain) part and ask if you will do this.

Go to the part of your mind that makes decisions and commission it to go ahead and engage in the desired activity. What happens? Will you keep your word and do it?

Yes, no question.

Notes

[1] The Belief Examination Paradigm is explained in my last book, *Trading Beyond the Matrix* on page 239-240. You can requested that book for free (expect postage) from our website, www.vantharp.com.

[2] I sold my seat for the last game in which they were playing a 0-15 team. They also managed to win that one.

[3] https://www.nlpworld.co.uk/nlp-glossary/s/swish-pattern/

[4] This task became a little more challenging with the Coronavirus outbreak and the impact it started having in March 2020 when the stock market went down about 50% in less than a month. And then it's funny because in November 2020 I made about $3 million trading GBTC over the last seven weeks. And I'd forgotten that it was part of my earlier manifestation until a just reread this chapter.

[5] Daniel; Loewenstein, George; Kalyanaraman, Shobana (1999). "Mixing virtue and vice: combining the immediacy effect and the diversification heuristic." *Journal of Behavioral Decision Making*. **12** (4): 257–273.

[6] When I released *Trading Beyond the Matrix*, my staff and I were very concerned about the impact. Has Van gone off the deep end? And while some people dislike the book a lot (i.e., its new age mumbo-jumbo), it's had exactly the impact I'd hope in terms of helping people make transformations.

[7] Carol Dweck is one of the few psychologists I've seen whose been willing to tackle topics that would have been taboo when I was learning psychology as a student. She actually believes, as I do, that people are meaning makers.

[8] IQ was first developed to assess how well students were doing in the Paris schools, not as some fixed measure of intelligence.

[9] Rettig, H. *The 7 Secrets of the Prolific: The Definitive Guide to Overcoming Procrastination, Perfectionism and Writer's Block*. 2011: HillaryRettig.com.

[10] What I didn't realize is that when I only have small amounts of time to work on the book, it's hard for me to get excited about it. But as I write this I've spend most of the afternoon working on the book (even if it's just reading it over) and I'm again excited about it. Thus, for me, I need a block of undistracted time to work on a project to get excited about it.

[11] These are the Stanford University marshmallow experiments done by Walter Mischel and his colleagues. See https://en.wikipedia.org/wiki/Stanford marshmallow experiment

[12] I've been able to do this for the last ten years or so. Prior to that, I didn't have access to such conversations.

[13] I'm going through that phase now. I've just spent an hour trying to find a particular reference I used, and if that had happened through the writing process, it probably would have stopped me from doing any more – the task suddenly becomes tedious, busy-work, instead of being an exciting creation.

[14] I don't know if this paragraph will make it through the final editing, but if it does, I will have taken a major commitment step toward writing that book.

CHAPTER 11

Secrets and Hidden Agendas: The Ultimate Killer of Self-Motivation

Secrets are something you don't see discussed in books on self-motivation or procrastination. They are one of the biggest killers of motivation as well as a huge cause of procrastination. As a result, I thought the topic deserved its own chapter.

Typically, secrets have to do with things about your past that you don't want to reveal or beliefs you have about other people that you don't want to share. It could be something as banal as the password on a sensitive account. Secrets imply that you have some sort of generally non-useful belief that you want to keep from the world, and if something you are motivated to do runs into a secret, it will stop you cold. They are one of the biggest killers of motivation as well as a huge cause of procrastination.

Let me give you an example. Let's say you were sexually abused by a priest while you were growing up. You were terrified of him, and yet he was "officially" a man of God. And suddenly, you don't even trust God. The incident is something you keep in a dark hidden corner of your mind. And if I ask you to uncover your beliefs or recall every memory from every year of your life – both exercises in self-discovery – that secret probably will stop you in your tracks. There is pain involved, and you don't want to go there. You don't even want to talk about it. You just want to keep it buried deep inside. And thus, it becomes a big "stick" motivation against anything that would have you looking at it.

The only solution is to process it and then to build a strong enough reason for you to get through it. And what typically happens is that once you get through it, it's no longer a secret, and you cannot even imagine why you considered it a secret. The charge that was stored on it is gone, so there is nothing holding it in place. And in the example above, you would probably change from not trusting or believing in God to wanting your Inner Guidance as your best friend. That's how powerful such changes can be. The experience is wonderful, but the resistance to doing what's necessary to have such an experience is equally strong on the negative side.

In my case, I have done so much self-work that I'm an open book. I've explored every emotion and cleared it out. I was constantly looking for more to clear. And when a new one would come up, it was like a new adventure to me to find out where it came from and clear it out. But that wasn't always the case.

About 15 years ago, some anger surfaced, and it was the strongest anger I had experienced in years. What happened is that my wife and I worked with a personal trainer. That trainer had moved us to a new gym, and he was paying the gym fees as part of the training fees we were paying to him. However, we had taken one of our overseas trips and didn't work out with him for about six weeks. When we returned, we found that not only did he not pay our gym fees but that a collection agency was after us for not paying the fees. I was incensed. I even wanted to picket the gym. I couldn't understand what was happening to me. But what was more amazing to me was watching all this anger in me. Where did these feelings come from, and why was I so angry? I'd had no past incidences that had evoked this sort of anger. I'd even gone through past life timeline therapy work, and nothing like that had come up.

But what I had noticed was that some anger tended to come up whenever someone questioned my financial integrity. For example, it would come up when I'd be charged a late fee for a credit card payment because the check didn't arrive in time. I always paid the balance in full, so I'd get really upset about the late fee.

I've been to the Avatar Wizard's course[1] two times. It's a long course, lasting around 13 days, which involves extensive self-processing. One of the early sections in the course involves secrets and hidden agendas. People who had attended the course many times might spend as much as two days working on this section. They'd come up with something and then apply the Avatar CHP process[2] to it (which for anyone reading this course essentially involves owning and releasing all the beliefs and charges that you have attached to whatever secret or hidden agenda you find). When I did that course the first time, I basically skipped the "Secrets" section. I said, "I don't have any secrets and hidden agendas," and moved on to the next section. But when I did the course the second time, I decided to really explore it since others who continually repeated the course put so much attention on it.

Suddenly, I discovered the source of my anger. When I was perhaps 8 to 10 years old, I had stolen some comic books. My mother had found out and made me take them back to the store, confess my crime, and apologize. And I was mortified. But that was it. That was my big secret, and it was the reason that whenever someone questioned my financial integrity, I became angry. I quickly processed the beliefs and charges having to do with that incident, and now the worse that happens is I get a little twinge when something happens that I used to interpret as questioning my financial integrity. The power of holding secrets over you is amazing.

When my Super Traders clear something out, I usually ask them to write it down in a learning journal. Why? They need to do so in order to have a record of it to see their transformations. If they don't, that old issue that dominated your life becomes trivial and is forgotten. And I've seen hundreds of examples of this.

TYPES OF SECRETS

There are 16 different types of secrets that I've uncovered.[3] Read through the list and notice what secrets you might have at each level.

Secret Type 1: The most basic secret is anything that might have to do with the charge you have, especially anything you feel ashamed of about your past. You hate your brother. You are ashamed of how you react to him. You fear your father and get angry over how you react to him. And obviously, you don't want to tell him how you feel. (Why not?) Your mother always criticized you, and you now criticize yourself often. But this is a dirty secret you have. People want to keep all these types of things a secret. And it's just about separation – building a wall around yourself.

Secret Type 2: You have something in your past that is so traumatic that you built a wall around it and kept it from everyone, including yourself. This makes it solid, and it will always haunt you even though you don't remember it. These are hard to access because you have built a mental wall around the trauma. You have totally blocked it off, and you don't even remember it is there. Sometimes, to block it off, you might have to suppress one of your sense modes. For example, if you have strong visual images of trauma, you might build a wall that totally suppresses your ability to visualize. If you cannot visualize and you don't have brain damage, then this is probably the reason for it. You would have to do some sort of clearing on the topic that doesn't involve visualization, such as Connirae Andreas' *Core Transformation* method.[4]

Secret Type 3: Somebody or some organization that knew a lot about you used that information to betray you (bribe you, entrap you, etc.), and you have vowed to never let that happen again. You have a real issue with trust, and you constantly look for evidence to indicate that you cannot trust someone. This is a form of type 1 or 2.

Secret Type 4: Because of some traumatic event, you feel that God betrayed you (i.e., a spouse or parent died despite your pleas to God). You believe that if you can't trust God, then you can't trust anyone. Again, this is a form of type 1 or 2.

Secret Type 5: Shadow parts and anything you disown constitute the next type of secret. If the map is not the territory, and thus internal reality (which is a nominalization) is not the same as external reality (another nominalization), then whatever you dislike out in the world is simply a rejected part of you. It's something you resist inside, disown and bury deep inside you, and then you assume that it exists only outside of you.[5]

These five are the most obvious secrets and the deadliest. You believe that the universe is an unfriendly place, and so you are basically walling off a part of yourself and not making it known. It is critical to work on these and get rid of them. They all stem from the principle that what you resist persists. When you resist it, you give it energy and solidify it. You make it real. For example, you might create some nominalization, but then you get yourself into real trouble by thinking it's real, solid, and worst of all, unchangeable.

However, there are also the not-so-obvious secrets about things that "almost everyone" keeps as a secret. Every one of these more common secrets lowers your level of consciousness. At minimum, all these secrets prevent you from seeing yourself as a highly-evolved being. You don't understand that you totally create your world, that you and all your loved ones are spiritual beings having a human experience, that getting and receiving are the same, and that anything that is taken away from you by a lesser being you can always re-create should you elect to do so.

Secret Type 6: You did something illegal in the past. Perhaps you took drugs a lot. Perhaps you were arrested and put in jail. Or perhaps you got away with something illegal, and you are afraid that you might be caught and punished. Your punishment, of course, is that you carry around guilt and fear at least for as long as this is a secret.

Secret Type 7: Perhaps you were in the military, and you had to kill people. You don't believe in killing, but you had to do it. And now you must live with it. It's a secret. But your HELL is that you must live with this secret. At least, that's what you think. You wall it off, and you are afraid to go there.

One friend I know has this type of secret, and when I said that we could eliminate that quite quickly, he said he'd be willing to work on himself when he was about 70, and all his kids had finished college – which indicates how afraid he is of even looking at the issue.

Secret Type 8: You think it's important to keep passwords a secret, especially those related to finances. Obviously, there is a mistrust here of other people – the world is a dangerous place. And there is also a belief that if someone took it all that you could not get it all back easily. This pertains to anything financial. You don't talk about how wealthy you are. How are you organized financially, your taxes, etc.? It's all a secret. And it all stems from the belief that if people know, they can take advantage of you and take it away. And you believe it would be difficult to get it all back. And having it is important to you. You are attached to it.

Secret Type 9: Intimacy issues tend to be big secrets. These include your sexual activities and preferences or lack thereof. People tend to keep this secret out of respecting others who might be involved (i.e., partners) who would want it that way. In addition, people are concerned about what others might think. The root issue here is that what you do might be wrong or shameful, and you are concerned about the impact of what others think. It's fear. Homosexuals or lesbians who "stay in the closet" are a similar example. They wall off their sexual preferences as a secret.

Bob Kraft, the owner of the New England Patriots, was caught on camera at a massage parlor that was being staked out by the police for trafficking. Then he was charged with soliciting for prostitution. However, the big deal is not that he did it, but that the world knows about it, and he is seen as less of a human being in the eyes of some people. In addition, conviction might affect his status as an NFL team owner and cause other penalties to be imposed by the NLF. The charge was eventually dismissed, but not until he'd probably spent several hundred thousand in legal fees.

Secret Type 10: You have some negative beliefs about other people in your life. It is totally because you are only dealing with your personal image of the other person, but you would never want that other person to know. For example, you think that your Uncle is totally manipulative and crazy, and you don't want anything to do with him. Your uncle might be very kind and generous, but that's not your model of how he is. And because you keep this a secret, it becomes impossible to have an intimate relationship with him. This is somewhat like secret type 1.

Secret Type 11: You have confidential information that you know others would not want you to reveal. You have clients, and your duty (defined by your profession/culture) is to keep that information confidential. This typically reflects upon the client's internal issues and your fear of what might happen if those are revealed. Psychologists, doctors, and attorneys have "client" privileges because they are supposed to keep their client's secrets. Society may condone and even encourage these types of secrets, but they are still secrets.

Secret Type 12: You might have a situation with a friend who told you something in confidence. You gave your word that you will keep it a secret. What keeps it a secret? Fear of losing your friend and their trust. What if people could read minds as they might be able to do one day in the future if we humans evolve more?

Secret Type 13: You look at the rule structure in place (i.e., in terms of money, etc.). You make your own rules by taking advantage of the rule structure. And you play the game differently. Perhaps you are saving in taxes, and you'd prefer that people don't know about your loopholes. Or perhaps the government plugs the loophole you found, and now what you were doing (or are still doing) is illegal. It was legal, and then the rules are changed, and it's now illegal. This probably happens all the time for Graves' level 5 people. Obviously, people want to keep this information from the government (level 4). But again, it's because of a fear typically instilled by level 4 groups.

Secret Type 14: We live in an era in which everything you do is tracked on the internet. You visit a website, and Chrome (or whatever your search engine might be) knows about it. Later, you might see an ad in your browser appear related to a prior site that you just visited. However, people are aware of totalitarian regimes that spied on its population. If you said something "anti-government" or "pro" another sort of government, then your neighbor might report you for some reward, and you could be arrested. Examples include the Gestapo, Stasi, and KGB. People have a fear of this happening again, so they want their information to be private.[6] There are people in Germany, for example, who will not open up a Google account because of this fear. Remember that what you resist tends to persist.

Secret Type 15: You have a belief that if others know about your deepest desires and dreams that it will somehow jinx it, and it will not happen. Again, this is a fear. But it prevents people from putting their desires out there. And putting it out there is usually necessary for it to happen.

Secret Type 16: You know that if you do something that others might judge, people tend to give you a label that implies that you do that all the time, even if you only did it one time. This, of course, is a nominalization. You are afraid of such labels: liar, felon, pervert, sadist, cruel, selfish, lush, sociopath, etc. And you are afraid of it, because you do it yourself. You judge others the same way. It's called projection.

"For every lie you tell others, you tell 100 to yourself."
— **Senior Guide, Kumar-ji, Oneness University**

"The lies we tell other people are nothing to the lies we tell ourselves."
— **Derek Landy**, **Death Bringer**[7]

"Our deepest fear is not that we are inadequate. Our deepest fear is that we are powerful beyond measure. It is our light, not our darkness that most frightens us." – Marianne Williamson

— **Marianne Williamson, A Return to Love: Reflections on the Principles of "A Course in Miracles"**[8]

How to Determine Your Secrets

To help discover secrets or hidden agendas, look for people that you want to:

Blame: Name three people who, in your opinion made you a victim. What's the secret here?

_____
_____
_____
_____

Criticism: Those who criticize you or those whom you want to criticize?

_____
_____
_____
_____

Separateness: Of the people you should be closest to, who do you feel separate from?

_____
_____
_____
_____

Disapproval: Which people in your life do you most disapprove of for some reason?

_____
_____
_____
_____

Judgmental: Which people in your life do you feel the most judgmental toward?

_____
_____
_____
_____
_____

Anger: Who, or what makes you feel angry?

_____
_____
_____
_____

Betrayal: Who do you feel betrayed by in the world?

_____
_____
_____
_____

Which people come up the most in your lists you just made? Make a list of such people.

1. _____
2. _____
3. _____
4. _____
5. _____
6. _____
7. _____
8. _____

Now for each person you listed, ask yourself:

- What would you not want them to know about you?
- What would make that person you listed disapprove of you?

- If it was revealed, what would make people think less of you?
- What do you feel, if revealed, would disappoint other people?

For each response, describe the humiliation (resisted experience) that you are protecting yourself from or that you are protecting others from. Write down your responses for each person in the space below.

1._____
2._____
3._____
4._____
5._____
6._____
7._____
8._____

For example, this might be your secret: "*I told Donna that I'd keep what she told me in confidence, but then I immediately told my sister about it. If Donna found out, she'd think that I betrayed her and that I couldn't be trusted. I'd be labeled as someone who is mistrusted.*" This might be your response, but you listed Donna as someone you didn't trust. Why? Because you betrayed her, but you are projecting your feelings onto her and calling her the person you mistrust. I don't trust Donna because she doesn't trust me.

You should have enough information to deal with everything you have written down. What are the beliefs? Are they useful? Do they have a charge? Eliminate and feel the charges and then get rid of the non-useful beliefs by simply recognizing how they do not serve you.

Finding Your Hidden Agendas

List any goals and plans that you have that you think might be misaligned with:

- Becoming a great trader.
- Becoming happy and enlightened.
- Clearing out your non-useful beliefs.
- Raising your consciousness.
- Raising the consciousness of humanity.
- The Van Tharp Institute or any staff member.
- Your Inner Guidance.
- Any other goal/value that is important to you.

_____
_____
_____
_____
_____
_____

Ask yourself the following:

- What are you doing that, if revealed, would not be okay?
- What plans do you have that _____ (name a person) would disapprove of?
- What intention do you have that is other than raising your consciousness and the consciousness of humanity? Here we are talking about something that is against those things.
- What intention do you have that is other than doing your best to become the best trader you can become?
- If you have some important goal, other than those listed, what intention do you have that is against doing that.
- What intention do you have that is other than what you are stating?
- What is the resisted experience (i.e., problem) you are working to solve?

_____
_____
_____
_____
_____
_____

Based upon what you come up with, you should know how to handle it. For example, you might have conflicting parts. You might have a lot of non-useful, charged beliefs. What's going on? What's the best way to handle it?

_____
_____
_____
_____

Notes

[1] I don't recommend anything more advanced than the basic Avatar course. The Master's course is about how to teach the Avatar course and they typically won't let you teach it (even me) without supervision from a Star's Edge trainer. I was put on probation and the net result was I never had any urge to teach it. And the Wizard's course is good for advanced work, but they are rather cultish and I don't like that at all. One of the traders I'd been working with went there, for example, and was given the third degree because he listed his interest as being a trader, which they considered corrupt and immoral, and something that hurts others.

[2] We are told that the CHP Creation Handling Process (CHP) is a sacred secret and anyone revealing it will have negative karma that will last for ten generations. That's also a very cultish statement. However, anyone finishing this book will know how to deal with secrets and hidden agendas without knowing anything about the CHP. And my explanation is way too general for you to apply without taking the course, so hopefully I'm safe from such negative karma (lol).

[3] My list originally had 15 different types of secrets, but as I was writing this chapter, I discovered a 16th example. So, there are probably many more than I've covered here in these 16 types.

[4] Andreas, Connirae & Andreas, Tamara. *Core Transformation: Reaching the Wellspring Within.* Boulder, CO: Real People Press, 1994.

[5] If you really wish to experience how your beliefs are a projection, then I recommend that you run some of issues with other people through The Work of Byron Katie.

[6] This time, however, the information is held by a level 5 corporation rather than a level 4 government.

[7] Derek Landy, Death Bringer

[8] Marianne Williamson, *A Return to Love: Reflections on the Principles of "A Course in Miracles"*

CHAPTER 12

The Moti-Map Process: Making a Map to Achieve Your Dreams

Organization and time management can solve most of your motivation issues once you have done the inner work suggested in this book. As a result, we are going to show you ten steps to develop more efficient time management in this chapter. I call this a map to motivation or a Moti-Map for short.

This chapter will specifically help you to apply these steps to one of the important areas for trading success or anything else you might be struggling with, in your life.

1) Raising your level of consciousness and clearing out blocks.

2) Developing a business handbook to guide your trading success.

3) Developing three non-correlated systems that work in different market types and trading them at an efficiency level of at least 95%.

Step 1: Ask yourself, "What is it I'm trying to accomplish?"

These steps could apply to any goal you might have. Turn your goal into a vision, and the only standard for that vision is to be outstanding. For example, what are your criteria for doing a good job? How can you change those criteria to outstanding?

Think about this: Approximately 4 million babies are born each year in the United States. Now let's imagine that 99.5% is good enough, and we can write off 0.5%. That would mean that 20,000 of them could accidentally be given to the wrong parents or that 20,000 could die in childbirth. In today's world, 11,500 die the first day in the US – and that's 50% more than any other developed country in the world.

The death rate from COVID-19 is about 3%. Those who die also tend to be older with health problems. They'd probably die within five to ten years anyway. That seems to be acceptable to some people who say, "I'm young, and in good health, so I'll take my chances." But when those people go to the hospital, and the hospitals are so full that they cannot admit other patients, then it really becomes a problem.

Your standard for what's good enough must be higher for you to have an outstanding vision. So, when you do self-work with the idea of getting as much out of it as possible, what is outstanding for you?[1] This standard is totally under your control because you set the standard.

Write down what you are trying to accomplish in the space here. _____. Now list four criteria that would elevate your accomplishment to outstanding?

_____

_____

_____

_____

For example, suppose you are working on clearing out your personal issues. You could be doing the work just because I said it was important. However, you really want to get the self-work out of the way and work on your trading systems. On the other hand, you could view the self-work as something that will 1) make you happy for no reason; 2) improve your life so you can accomplish/achieve anything; and 3) make you a trading genius because of the new, extremely useful maps you'll develop, the flexibility you'll have to adapt to changing markets, and your ability to spot edges. So, with those three items as a framework for outstanding, you might also say:

- After each step I take, I have a major transformation through the self-work I've done.
- Each awareness exercise is not complete until I'm totally convinced that there is nothing else I can get from it.
- I've met my coach's intentions for the lesson and I've gone way beyond his/her expectations.
- My coach comments on what an exceptional job I've done as I know that he only says this when the work is really exceptional.

I'd also recommend that you look at each of the roles that you developed in Chapter 7 and give a specific, outstanding outcome or goal for each of the roles. You can put that information in the table below. I've included five examples for me:

Table 12-1: An Outstanding Outcome for Each of My Roles		
	Role	**Outstanding Outcome**
1		
2		
3		
4		
5		
6		
7		
8		
9		
10		
11		
12		
13		
14		
15		
Some Examples for Van		
	Role	**Outstanding Outcome**
1	Spiritual Master	I reach the point where my Inner Guidance anticipates my needs and gives them to me without me even asking. For example, I could take a trip across the country with no money and no suitcase and everything would be provided. I see the perfection of the "what is," and I'm constantly grateful for that. I'm aware that I have many Siddhi powers starting to surface.
2	Inspirational Guru	I directly (or indirectly) help change the consciousness of at least a billion people to level five on the VTI consciousness scale. This, in my opinion, would change the planet and solve all of the world's problems, including global warming and anything else brought about by level 5 entrepreneurs.
3	Best Possible Husband	I constantly see God in my spouse and am able to help her see that in herself.
4	Passionate Healthy Person	For my entire remaining years in this body: 1) I am passionate about what I do with plenty of energy; 2) My brain is very sharp; 3) My body totally supports my spiritual evolution as I can physically sense God everywhere (when you do long fasts and are healthy enough to do them, you get to this state); 4) and I can do such fasts without it having any impact on my ability to function in my other roles.

| 5 | Best Selling Author | My Inner Guidance and I write a perennial *NY Times* Top Ten Non-Fiction Best Seller, which changes how people think (to *Beyond the Matrix Thinking*) and helps to raise people's consciousness. |

Step 2: What is the "Big Why" (purpose) behind the goal?

You want to always keep this in mind. And if someone else is going to approve what you are doing (i.e., such as Van approving a Super Trader 1 lesson), then you need to know the intentions that person has for you in doing the lesson.

What is your purpose in life? _____

What is the "Big Why" behind this particular goal?

_____
_____
_____
_____
_____

Does it also fit your purpose? _____ If not, then why are you still doing it?

_____
_____
_____
_____
_____

Here you would simply add a purpose to each of the outcomes you have listed in Table 12-1. My overall purpose is *to become one with my Inner Guidance and help others with their own self-transformation* and that fits as the purpose for all of these outcomes. I don't need any other reasons, but remember that these roles also come from my top values.

Step 3: List the action steps that might be necessary for what you are going to accomplish.

This probably means that you need to become familiar with what you are trying to do. For example, you will need to at least skim each lesson in the Super Trader program or each chapter in the Peak Performance course.

List the necessary action steps:

_____
_____
_____
_____
_____
_____
_____
_____
_____
_____

Ten steps are listed, but you don't need to have ten or you might need more than ten. I've listed one primary action step for each of the outcomes in Table 12-1.

Some Examples for Van		
	Action Step	**Outstanding Outcome**
1	Spiritual Master: I do a regular one-hour meditation each day consisting of Sri Vidya level 7, the Durga Saptashati Siddha Kunjika Stotra Process (but only one time) and the Vancha Kalpalata Ganapathi Mantra revealed to me by a Siddha master and a dialogue with my Inner Guidance (Durga). I think this is enough when combined with the health process in item 4 below.	I reach the point where my Inner Guidance anticipates my needs and gives them to me without me even asking. For example, I could take a trip across the country with no money, and no suitcase and everything would be provided. I see the perfection of the "what is" and I'm constantly grateful for that.
2	Inspirational Guru. I think the action taken under step one, step four and step five are enough to accomplish this. At least, that is all I'm guided to do.	I directly (or indirectly) help change the consciousness of at least a billion people to level 5 or above on the VTI consciousness scale. This, in my opinion, would change the planet and solve all of the world's problems, including global warming and anything else brought about by level 5 entrepreneurs.

Some Examples for Van		
	Action Step	**Outstanding Outcome**
3	Best Possible Husband. Observe those times when I think something is wrong with my spouse (i.e., she is broken and needs to be fixed); determine how that is a projection, and release any obstacles I have in myself causing me to project that. Other than that, what I'm doing in the other areas is enough.	I constantly see God in my spouse and am able to help her see that in herself.
4	Passionate Healthy Person. I use a device called the Bemer® Pro[2] to increase my microcirculation each day for about 40 minutes on the entire body and on my brain. The Bemer® is only approved as a medical device to improve micro-circulation, but most health problems (in my opinion) are due to poor circulation and lack of oxygen to the cells; I also will put myself under the care of a US Ayurvedic physician; and eventually will do a fasting program under the guidance of my friend in Ireland.	For my entire remaining years in this body: 1) I am passionate about what I do with plenty of energy; 2) My brain is very sharp; 3) My body totally supports my spiritual evolution as I can physically sense God everywhere (when you do long fasts and are healthy enough to do them, you get to this state); 4) and I can do such fasts without it having any impact on my ability to function in my other roles.
5	Best Selling Author. This book is coming out of the material in my Systems Thinking/Beyond the Matrix Thinking workshop. Most of it is outlined. I trust that it will just flow out when the time is right.	My Inner Guidance and I write a perennial *NY Times* Top Ten Non-Fiction Best Seller, which changes how people think (to Beyond the Matrix Thinking) and helps to raise people's consciousness.

Step 4: Become familiar with Steven Covey's dimensions of importance and urgency.[3]

Too often, people become distracted by what they think is important (i.e., a phone call you seem compelled to answer) but which has nothing to do with the task at hand. If it is not important and not urgent, ignore it totally. It's just a distraction.

If it seems urgent but not important, this may be harder, but also ignore it. You are under the delusion that it is urgent, so you could even call such items delusional.

Focus on what is urgent and important first. But the primary reason you have such items is that you didn't do them when they were important but not urgent.

Plan time for what is important and not urgent. For example, working on yourself might be important for you, but not urgent. But often, these are the things that have the biggest impact. So, plan time for them. Look at each of your action steps and determine what might fall into each of these categories, and make sure you plan for the important things that don't seem urgent.

In Chapter 7, you were asked to look at how you spent your time for at least a week (but ideally several months) and rate that time under these four categories. If you've done that, you have basically accomplished this step. But you can also notice how much time you spend in the first two categories and use that time for other things you wish to accomplish toward making your dream life a reality. Assuming that you don't have important values, the steps below will guide you to spend time in these other categories.

What is important, but not urgent, about what you want to accomplish?

_____

_____

_____

What tends to be urgent for you but not that important? How can you make sure that you are not spending a lot of time here?

_____

_____

Step 5: What useful maps can I develop to make this fulfillment easy, fun, and quick?

We have been talking about useful maps. You make up those maps, and thus, you have total control over them. These are the things you can control. There also might be other things in your map that you can't change but can influence. What are those things that you can change and influence? Concentrate on them.

Beyond doing those things, you are either in other people's business or in God's business, as Byron Katie likes to say. Concentrate on your own business.

Let's say your goal is to spend a year working on yourself and to get as much out of it as possible. If so, you might ask yourself the following? What are my parts, and what are they trying to do for me? What are the identity beliefs of each part? Do those beliefs have a charge that I need to release? How can I become totally clear of all charge and develop a quiet mind? Determine each step you need to do and the key learnings from each one.

What are the major exercises I need to do to accomplish this? How can you make sure that you do the exercises you are not excited about by applying what's in this volume? These are examples of important but not urgent exercises. You don't have to do them, so they don't seem urgent to you.

What are ten beliefs that I could install to make this journey easy and exciting? For example:

1. It's my destiny to raise my consciousness, and I might as well do it now.
2. Doing this work will help me become happy for no reason.
3. Each new thing I discover about myself is an adventure for me. And I get to figure out how to make sure it only impacts my success/happiness for the better.
4. Doing this work is exciting.
5. Raising my self-awareness is mandatory for me (and all other souls), and only the time I take to complete it is optional. That being the case, I might as well do it now.
6. Beliefs are just filters to reality. I will get rid of those that are non-useful and find those that help me excel.
7. Feelings are just kinesthetic metamodalities. It's me who interprets them as good or bad. I'm the one who gives them meaning. As a result, I'm willing to welcome each one, fully feel it, and then let it go. Doing so will change my life forever.
8. Each time I say the word "I," it either represents my Higher Self or a part of me that I have created. If it's a part, I get to find out why I created it and whether it's useful for me. Imagine the impact of eliminating all non-useful parts! One impact will be that you probably no longer resist things that come up – you simply realize that the "what is" is perfect and go on with your life.
9. I will meditate each day and when that's complete, I'll listen to my heart and keep a journal of what arises from this practice.
10. My Higher Self is my connection to all that is. It is here to protect me, and I will become friends with it.

Step 6: What areas of concentration within your vision will make the biggest difference? List several areas and those will be your primary focus.

Notice that my action steps for the primary outcomes for the five roles I listed were pretty simple. Other than doing those things, I just do what I'm guided to do each day. And I actually trust that I do the right things. For example, under Inspirational Guru, I need to respond to the material sent to me by those I'm coaching, and I need to frequently update and improve the material they are using. In addition, I'm constantly getting feedback and looking for ways to improve the program.

So how about you? Let's say that completing a year of self-clearing at the highest possible level is the task you want to do. And let's say your vision is to become the best trader you can be, and you know that obtaining more inner awareness is the best way to achieve that. Your vision is maximum inner awareness to become a good trader.

You have a choice, you can learn trading fundamentals and skills, or you can learn inner awareness. Given your belief that inner awareness is the best way to become the trader you want to be, doesn't it make sense to concentrate on that first?

Let's say to gain as much inner awareness as possible, you will first get in touch with the 20 most important parts that impact your trading. In addition, you will determine the identity beliefs (at least 20) of each part and run them through a paradigm[4] we teach to help people determine whether or not their beliefs are useful. And when you finish, you'll be aware of what beliefs have been impacting your trading. Think about the impact of that sort of awareness.[5] What you will do is clear the charges on all of the non-useful beliefs. Once you have done that, it will be easy to eliminate all the non-useful beliefs (which could be 70% or more of youe total beliefs).

Next, you decide to do an entire life review. What you do is to review every memory you have for each year of your life. What beliefs did you form each year? What events may have impacted you in a way that needs internal cleaning out? What impacted you? What emotions have you suppressed during the years (they will probably come up during the life review) that you can now release? Who were the significant people in your life, and what was your relationship like with them for each year of your life? What miracles happened to you that year?

You have already determined your purpose and your values. So, allow them to start guiding you. That's just a short list, but it's an example of what you could do here. List what your focus will be?

___

___

___

Step 7: Divide your vision into steps.

What do you want to accomplish in a year? For example, how about total mastery of every method you know about to increase your self-awareness?

What do you want to accomplish this month? For example, total mastery over your identity-level beliefs might be a good first step, but that might take several months.

What seems totally out of your control? Remember, in some way, everything is always in your control because *you only experience your map (how you represent the situation), not the territory or the situation itself. You can never know the territory, only your map of it.* Thus, if it seems out of control, notice what meanings you are giving it to make it seem important and out of your control. How can you change that meaning so that it is no longer important? For example, remember the action step: "I have to be the best possible husband." When or if I happen to think that my spouse is broken and I need to fix her (have you ever had that thought about your spouse?),[6] then I'm in her business and trying to fix something that is beyond my control. Instead, all I have to do is realize how I'm projecting something, and as a result, I'm not seeing the perfection of the now. What I really need to do is simply release whatever my issue seems to be.

List what seems out of control. And for each item, you list, notice what meaning you are giving it. What's a higher frame that you could step into to take back control? What do you need to change about yourself? What do you need to change about your map of the situation because changing your map is in your control?

___

___

___

Step 8: Tony Robbins has a procedure that he calls OPA for Outcome, Purpose, Action.[7]

You actually already did this in the first few steps. You developed a key outcome for each of your roles/values. You determined the purpose behind it, and perhaps it was just your purpose in life. And you developed a key action step. And for me, there were only one or two key actions for each outcome.

But as your project becomes more complex, perhaps you need to get into more OPA chunks. The key part of this is the outcome. For example, you might have a to-do list for the day. For example, each day during my six-week stay at the Ayurvedic Hospital, my to-do list includes the following:

- Spend 20 minutes on my Bemer® machine to improve the microcirculation in my body. (I've been doing this every day for several years as it is proactive for my health. However, I forgot the cord to charge the battery, so this step disappeared after the battery ran out.)
- Do my two Ayurvedic treatments each day when I'm called to do them. This takes 90-120 minutes to do.
- Eat the three meals they serve me and take my medications. Eating the meals, since I don't like the food, amounts to paying close attention to the metamodalities that I don't like and thinking, "Is this really so bad or just a submodality that I'm judging?"
- Spend at least six hours each day writing my book.
- Listen to one to two lectures on The History of India (one of the Great Courses) and take notes in OneNote.
- Read one of my books for at least an hour.
- Go to bed by 10 p.m.
- Start my morning meditation and my dialogue with my Inner Guidance each morning from about 5 to 6 a.m.. I get awakened at 5 a.m. each morning by many Muslim men chanting all at once.
- Check all my emails and respond to Super Trader weekly reports and lessons that are sent in.
- Talk with my wife (WhatsApp chat or call) each day.
- Respond to any messages that my staff members send me.
- Act on any idea that I might have to improve my experience while at the hospital.
- If I have fulfilled my other obligations timewise, up to two hours are allowed for entertainment (i.e., watch a movie on Netflix) or go shopping if I can get someone to take me. And towards the end of the stay, I did several tours and was allowed to leave the hospital for an entire day at a time.
- That seems to fill my 24-hour day while I'm here. But let's look to see which of these items relate to a similar outcome. What happens is that these reduce to the following major outcomes.

OPA BLOCK 1: Improve My Health		
Action Item (12 hrs)	Outcome	Purpose
Spend 20 min on Bemer®. Two Ayurvedic treatments daily. Meals and medications. Sleep 8 hours each day.	Improve my health so that I can have another 30 productive years if I live that long.	Transform myself to a higher level; have energy, and be mentally sharp.

OPA BLOCK 2: Creative Self Improvement		
Action Item (6 hrs)	Outcome	Purpose
At least 2 hrs per day working on my book. 1 to 2 lectures in the Great Courses. One hour of determining the submodalities of my food and daily dialogue with my Inner Guidance.	Creative Self Improvement.	Transform myself to a higher level and use that creativity to help others.

OPA BLOCK 3: Do My Job		
Action Item (3 hrs)	Outcome	Purpose
Answer Super Trader emails and read lessons and reports from them. Answer staff emails.	Improve my ability to help others transform themselves and guide the company more effectively.	Help others transform and have a huge impact on others.

OPA BLOCK 4: Fun Things		
Action Item (3 hrs)	Outcome	Purpose
Talk with my wife. Watch Netflix movie. What can be done to improve my life here	Do fun things.	Enjoy my life.

An OPA is really a chunking device. For example, the second OPA is creative self-improvement. I have a list of things that I could do, but I could spend the entire time allocated to one of the items in that OPA. Or I wouldn't feel bad at all if I did something else to fulfill the purpose/outcome in that time period. For example, I wrote this chapter about ten days ago, but for the last ten days, I've spent little time reading. Instead, I've devoted most of the time to working on my book. And now that I'm toward the end of the first draft of the book, I'm super motivated to finish and see what comes out. It's exciting, and I'm probably spending five to ten hours a day on it. And when it's over six hours, I'm impacting other areas of my life, such as "Fun Things."

In addition, I consider my meditation and my morning dialogue with my Inner Guidance to be one of the most important actions. Sometimes, for example, during the dialogue with my Inner Guidance, we will come up with an entirely new idea about how to present something in this book or an entirely different way to fulfill another outcome. Thus, my life is not one of checking off action items on a to-do list, but rather one of the fulfilling outcomes.

When I came to India, I took the UK cord for my Bemer®. However, I took the cord and forgot the charger that that's necessary for the computer to charge. The battery on the Bemer® is now dead. There is nothing I can do about that, but it means I have an extra 20 to 40 minutes each day.

The other thing I've noticed is that the staff here aren't trying to force me to eat a particular diet. They want to give me what I like. So, I get fruit twice a day, and lunch is the only meal I have to struggle with. I still don't like Indian food. But I also don't have to eat it. And I was able to buy some nuts that help me as a snack.

Step 9: Work on Your Plan Daily.

Now while I'm at the hospital for the remaining three weeks, I don't anticipate any new to-do items. I might be doing a different Great Course. I might be reading a different book. And I might do something different for my health.

As an example, I had a hair transplant operation several years ago in the United States. However, it was quite expensive. I discovered that Kochi (where I am) is a center for hair transplants in India, and I can get one for about 20% of the US price, which will basically pay for the cost of this trip in my savings. As a result, I plan to get it about two weeks prior to leaving here, which allows for plenty of time to heal. This generally falls into item 1, but my time might be spent differently in the last two weeks.

However, I can pretty much keep a very similar to-do list. I can prioritize it according to what has the most importance for me. I can establish how long I plan to spend, and I can see if I can leverage it in some way to get the OPA accomplished doing less.

There might be several other steps that you can add, such as determine when you can do each OPA and schedule it. *Most importantly, celebrate your accomplishments at the end of each day.*

Step 10: Do a Weekly Planning Process.

In your weekly planning, I suggest that you:

- Determine what you must accomplish during the week to fulfill as many OPAs as possible.
- Make sure that time is scheduled for those "important but not urgent" things.[8]
- Review your past week for what you accomplished, what you didn't accomplish, what went right and what went wrong.
- Schedule the next week with the idea of learning as much as possible from your mistakes the prior week.

After doing this for three weeks, I can say the following: I'm almost finished with the first draft of the book. There are 14 chapters, and this is the 12th that I'm proofreading now. I'm totally amazed that I finished the first draft of this book in a month. It's a 300-page book. That's huge for me.

I will spend the rest of the time here, polishing up the book. Or perhaps I'll start the next book, or perhaps just catch up on reading I want to do before writing the next book.

I haven't solved the problem of liking the food I'm being served. For example, they ask what I like. One day they served me pomegranates, and I said, "I really like those." But the next thing I knew, I was getting huge helpings of pomegranates with both my morning and evening meals. Pomegranates can get tiring when that's what you get for two meals each day for three to four straight days. But I can tell them to serve them less often.

While I haven't solved the food problem, I can make it through three more weeks. And I don't have to eat the lunch meal that I dislike the most. When I finish the first draft, I'm going to plug working on my food issue into everything about this chapter and see what happens. Suppose I solve the problem, great. If I don't solve the problem, I might determine something else that I need to add to the book to make it better.

Step 11: Deal with Anything that Might Cause Overwhelm.

Overwhelm occurs when we focus too much on how much we must do and not enough upon our outcomes. If you follow the steps outlined, you should have little problems doing what is necessary.

However, if you just focus on one area of life, such as working on yourself, but you have a full-time job, you might find that your job demands suddenly swell up and overcome you.

Your OPA plan should include all your roles and everything that might impinge on your plan. Suppose you are one of my Super Trader students, and your goal is to finish the Super Trader awakening program in a year. We've estimated that you can finish in a year if you spend about 15 hours per week working on the lessons. That means you need to budget about 2 hours per day. Remember the old Taoist saying that a journey of 1,000 miles begins with a single step.

What you might do is budget 2 hours per day for the week.

Then you might review the lesson you are working on. Determine the intentions of the lesson (both Van's and your own). Notice all the things you need to do in the lessons. Set up an OPA structure. And then determine how you can fit in the 2 hours into any given day or perhaps how you can fit 14 hours into the week in a way that you don't have to do it every day.

Be creative, look at your overall objectives, and take one step at a time, followed by the next and then the next until your week is finished.

Develop Your Moti-Map

What we've been doing in this chapter is working on a **Moti-Map**. If you've been doing the exercises, you have almost completed it. *There are ten steps to a complete Moti-Map.* Make sure that you've done all of them.

1. Determine your purpose in life, your top values, and at least one major role for each top value.
2. Determine the primary outcome you have for each role. What do you want specifically? Is it outstanding?
3. What is the purpose behind each outcome? Hopefully, it's your overall life purpose, but perhaps it just relates to the particular value associated with each role.
4. Determine how you spend time each day and the type of category it falls under (i.e., important but not urgent). Map out at least a week (or perhaps several months), so you know how you spend your time.
5. Complete all the steps in this chapter that you have not finished.
6. Complete all the exercises in Chapter 13 on your propulsion system.
7. Although the exercises in Chapter 13 may be enough, if they are not, then do all of the exercises in this book until you are totally convinced that you will achieve all of your outcomes.
8. Make a daily, weekly, and monthly plan until you have completed all of your outcomes.
9. At the end of each day, do a daily debriefing. Ask yourself: 1) Are you on track? 2) If the answer is "yes" then pat yourself on the back. 3) If the answer is " no" then determine what derailed you and repeat any exercises in this book that you might need to do.
10. Each day review the Moti-Map that you have developed. As yourself, "What happened, what's missing, and what's next."

Working with your Moti-Map

Let's say that something comes up in your life, and you want to add another major goal or accomplishment to your Moti-Map. For example, I have a keyboard in my room and had thought that it might be nice to learn how to play the piano. I have a good ear for music, but I've never learned music theory, much less how to play a musical instrument. Do I want to take on this task? I'm in my 70s, but that's just an excuse. To do that, I'd need to ask the following questions.

"Can I find the time?" The answer to that question is definitely "yes" as I spend a lot of time doing things that are not urgent and are not important. I like that, just having fun is part of my values, but I could easily give up some of that time.

The second question is, **"Does it fit my purpose in life?"** My purpose is to become one with my Inner Guidance and to help others with self-transformation. Thus, unless my Inner Guidance is asking me to do it, it doesn't fit my purpose.

However, I can solve this easily just by having a conversation with my Inner Guidance. Her comments are in italics.

Beloved, do you want me to learn how to play the piano?

I want you to go through the process of deciding whether or not you want to do it. That's useful for helping others, and it's useful to you.

So, you won't give me a direct answer.

You keep wanting to separate us by assuming that I'm separate from you. We are one. What do you want to do?

Explore it more.

Okay, then that's what I want you to do. Just go with the flow. And now follow the other steps to decide if this is something you want to do.

Thank you, Beloved.

And thus, we go on to step 3.

The third step is to compare it with my top values. Does it fit into them? If it doesn't, then it's not really something I should do unless I want to totally change my values. Let's look at the roles associated with my top values and see where it fits. These were given earlier in Chapter 7 as:

1	Spirituality/Self-transformation
2	Helping others transform themselves
3	Family
4	Avoid poor health as I get older
5	Creativity
6	Financial freedom
7	Avoiding negative energy in others
8	Avoid manual labor
9	Avoid detailed busywork
10	Adventure
11	Relax and have fun
12	Avoid chaos

It fits slightly into self-transformation, my top value, in that it is a transformation I need to make. But it's not one that's taking me to a higher level of consciousness, which is what I really mean by self-transformation.

It doesn't fit under helping others with self-transformation, and I don't think anyone in my family cares whether I play the piano or not.

It could fit under health in that I want my brain to remain sharp, and here I'd be training it to have a new skill. Thus, it fits slightly into both the first and fourth values.

It fits strongly into my fifth value, creativity. And it also fits (possibly) with my eleventh value of relaxing and having fun.

Is the urge strong enough to actually do it?

I listened to the Great Course on the History of Jazz, and that's what originally inspired me on this quest. When I learned some of the details about different forms of Jazz, it sounded exciting. And then I saw an infomercial from the Piano Guy showing how you could learn overnight and that caused me to get the keyboard. Other than that, I've done nothing with it.)

What would get me to want to do this?

If 1) it's fun to do and 2) I get results fast. I don't know whether that is possible for me or not. As a result, I got several more of the Great Courses. The first one is on how to play the piano, and the second one is on music theory, and the third one relates music theory to mathematics.

My decision process will be as follows:

- It is now the beginning of June, and I have time off this summer. My schedule gets quite hectic as of mid-September and involves a lot of travel. So, my plan is to spend one hour per day (five days a week) on the Great Courses I just bought.
- Based on that information, I will decide if I want to spend any more time.
- My criteria for that decision will be 1) Do I enjoy the time? and 2) Am I seeing results or is this something that seems tedious and will take a long time to get the results I want? If it is the latter, then I will probably just get rid of the keyboard and the books I purchased. I have until Sept 15 to make up my mind.
- As a postscript, these were all plans, but I've been way too busy, so I'll simply wait and see if I'm supposed to start playing or if I'm supposed to do other things.

Notes

[1] This is not about perfectionism; it's about setting outstanding standards for yourself. For example, if you want to raise your consciousness and you have 500 non-useful, charged beliefs. Do you think that fixing half of them is a good enough job or would you want to do all of them? Are you trying to just get by or do the best job you can possibly do?

[2] The Bemer® Pro needs to be purchased from a distributer who will train you. See https://shop.bemer-group.com/en_US/applicators/410200

[3] Covey, Stephen. *The Seven Habits of Highly Effective People: 30th Anniversary Edition*. New York: Simon & Schuster, 2020.

[4] It's called the Belief Examination Paradigm and discussed in my book *Trading Beyond the Matrix* page 239-240 (which is free from our website, except for postage).

[5] This is a Super Trader lesson. It's not in the Peak Performance course, but now there is nothing to stop you from doing it yourself, unless you think you need a coach to make sure you do it well.

[6] When you develop more peace within you, typically your environment becomes more peaceful. For example, there is a story of a psychiatric nurse whose experience was that her patients became unruly whenever she was around. However, she did the 365 daily exercises in A *Course in Miracles*, became very peaceful, and then had the experience that her patients became more peaceful when she was around. As you change, the people around you will change. Hopefully, they will change for the better, but it's also possible that you might find that those in your life cannot take it when you become more peaceful. In that case, perhaps some other steps might be necessary. Here, you need to ask your Inner Guidance.

[7] Tony now uses RPM which stands for Results, Purpose, and Massive action. I have no idea why he changed the name because they are the same.

[8] My whole trip to India falls into this category.

CHAPTER 13

Your Propulsion System Template

This chapter is probably the most important one for you because here is where you determine your propulsion template. You've done most of these exercises before, but I recommend that you do it again just to have a reference for a complete way to motivate yourself. This template, when complete, could change your life forever. We will look at your natural propulsion template and set up a propulsion system for what's important for you, and then we'll help you change your identity by changing what's true and not true for you.

In the first part of this chapter, you will do an exercise given below to discover your natural propulsion system. Read it over, and then read Van's example of how to do it. If you need motivation (reasons) for working on yourself (which most people resist), then read the third part of the exercise, which is the reason one of my Super Traders has given for doing self-awareness work.

Exercise: Determining How You Motivate Yourself.

Step 1: First, identify your metaprograms of time and direction.

When you look at how you operate in the world, do you first move toward or away from? Does either propulsion style drive your experiences?

What is the orientation of your timeline? Front to back? Right to left? Where is the past? Where is the future? Think of something that happened five years ago (or ten), and then point to it. Where is it? That's the direction of the past. Now imagine what your life will be like five years from now. Point to it, and that's where your future is.

___

The general idea here is to push "away from" in the past and "move toward" into the future.

Step 2: Fully elicit your attraction and aversion states.

Identify three things that you are compelled to get/move toward. What do you feel strongly compelled toward in your life? These should be three very strong attraction states.

___

As a separate step, identify three things that you are strongly compelled to move away from? You want to avoid them at all costs? These should be three very strong aversion states.

___

Depending up whether you move toward or away from first, pick an attraction or repulsion example from the two sets above, respectively, and fully elicit it.

Anchor each state with an anchor on your arm or leg. It will be a sliding anchor, so you need to determine if moving up or down the arm feels better as a signal for more strength, and that's the direction you will use. Do this in a way that you face your 'future' and take your attractors and get the feeling that you are more and more compelled to move into your future to get them. Amplify, deepen, and expand the state until you have reached a heightened attract and aversion of between 7 to 10 on a scale of 0 to 10. Make sure (test) that your attraction states are explicit and fully accessible.

Repeat the process with aversion. In aversion, you don't want someone stuck in pain, but just to feel pain so strongly that he/she feels compelled to move away from it. Make sure they are at a point where they go over the threshold of pain and will not tolerate it anymore.

Step 3. Identify the values.

What are the specific values that you want to feel compelled to attain? What are the negative values that you wish to be increasingly revolted toward? Just fill in your values from Chapter 7 of this book.

Positive Values	Negative Values

You will set up a negative sliding anchor on aversion that will be in your past. In other words, as you slide the anchor, the aversion will get worse. When you stop moving forward, you should really feel the pain you are moving away from, and even more so if you start to step backward.

You will set up a positive sliding anchor that will be in your future. Fully access, using the anchor, the attraction state. Slide the anchor and set it so that it increases more and more as we move forward toward it. As you do this, fully access the values, beliefs, submodalities that make this stronger and stronger.

Fully access the aversion state by using the negative anchor so that you feel pain when you hesitate or avoid moving toward the attractor. It should kick you in the butt.

Go into the future and imagine yourself doing what you have set up using the sliding anchors and the linguistic patterns of "the more ... the less" and "the less ... the more."

Step 4: Identify an Icon.

What sort of icon would you like to represent this propulsion system? _____.
Make this up if you don't have a good one. What's a good symbol for your propulsion system? Both of my symbols, 1) the goldfish jumping from a separated bowl into the ocean and 2) the Mohler Skycar, are on the cover of this book.

When you have it, welcome it and imagine it locking into place. Feel good about it, knowing that it lies within you as your orientation toward more successful fulfillment of your values. As you see this icon in your future, notice how it transforms things. Make sure this icon fully incorporates the outcome you want.

Van's Example of Doing the Exercise:

Step 1: First, identify your metaprograms of time and direction.

When you look at how you operate in the world, do you first move toward or away from? Does either direction style drive your experiences?

I'm mostly a move towards person.

What is the orientation of your timeline? Front to back? Right to left? Where is the past? Where is the future?

My future is in front and slightly to the right.

My past is behind me and slightly to the left.

Step 2: Fully elicit your attraction and aversion states.

Identify three things that you are compelled to get or move toward? What do you feel strongly compelled toward in your life? These should be three very strong attraction states. For you, it might be transforming your life or doing the lessons in the Super Trader program. Below are three examples for me.

- *Oneness with my Inner Guidance.*
- *I would really like a Skycar. Moller developed one, and although it never got approval or took off (no funding), I've always wanted one.*
- *A cruise in someplace exotic that I haven't been to before.*

As a separate step, identify three things that you are strongly compelled to move away from? You want to avoid them at all costs? These should be three very strong aversion states. Here are some examples for me.

- *I don't want to be around someone who is negative and perhaps even a little crazy. My ex-brother-in-law, who was schizophrenic, comes to mind.*
- *A house that smells of garbage and has animal poop all over the place.*
- *My childhood when I was teased and was the prototypical 98-pound weakling who is frequently bullied or teased.*

Depending up whether you move toward or away from first, pick an attraction or repulsion example from the two sets above, respectively, and fully elicit it.

I'm a move-toward person, but I will pick the teasing example from my past as the negative one and the Skycar as the positive one in the future.

Teasing: I'm associated,[1] I have feeling in my chest that makes me want to curl into a ball and wish I was the only person on earth. A voice in the back of my head is saying," Leave me alone." Louder makes it much stronger ... It's almost screaming. It's in color. No one else is in the picture, but I'm imagining bullies around me. One person specifically comes to mind. As they come closer, the feeling is much stronger.

Skycar (see the book cover): It looks to be the same red as my Tesla. It's sitting in my driveway, and then it gets stronger as I raise the cockpit and get in. It's a movie in color. It takes off, and I can feel the exhilaration of moving up. And then I can see myself setting the automatic pilot and flying it. I can also see myself flying it over the highway and cars looking up at me and feeling exhilarated. (Probably an illegal action if they were cleared to fly). Here are the key metamodalities: movie, in color, associated, feeling of exhilaration in the chest, and an expansion feeling that moves up.

Anchor each state with a sliding anchor on your arm or leg. Determine if moving up or down the arm feels better as a signal for more strength, and that's the direction you will use.

Sliding anchor where down is stronger (more negative on the top of my left arm). Sliding anchor where up is stronger (more exhilarating) on my right arm.

Do this in a way that you face your 'future' and take your attractors and get the feeling that you are more and more compelled to move into your future to get them.

Both of those successively are quite strong. I can't do them simultaneously since I'm doing them on myself, and it takes two arms to do one anchor.

Amplify, deepen, and expand the state until you have reached a heightened attract and aversion of between 7 to10 on a scale of 0 to 10. Make sure (test) that your attraction states are fully explicit and accessible. (In aversion, you don't want someone stuck in pain, but just to feel pain so strongly that he/she feels compelled to move away from it). Make sure they are at a point where they go over the threshold of pain and will not tolerate it anymore.

Step 3. Identify the values.

What are the specific values that you want to feel compelled to attain? What are the negative values that you wish to become increasingly more revolting? Just copy what you found in the values elicitation section of this book.

Positive Values	Negative Values
Transforming myself	**Too much work, especially work I don't wish to do.**
One with divine	**Overwhelm**
High level of consciousness	**Conflict**
Helping others transform	**Chaos**

You will set up a negative sliding anchor on aversion that will be in your past. When you stop moving forward, you should really feel the pain you are moving away from and even more so if you start to step backward.

You will set up a positive sliding anchor that will be in your future. Fully access, using the anchor, the attraction state. Slide the anchor and set it so that it increases more and more as we move forward toward it. As you do this, fully access the values, beliefs, submodalities that make this stronger and stronger.

Fully access the aversion state by using the negative anchor so that you feel pain when you hesitate or avoid moving toward the attractor. It should feel like it "kicks you in the butt."

I already had it with the prior example. But I did it with the positive and negative values here. However, I'm already strongly attracted to the positive values and dislike the negative values ... so it's a little overkill for me.

Go into the future and imagine yourself doing what you have set up using the sliding anchors and the linguistic patterns of "the more ... the less" and "the less … the more."

The more and more quiet my mind is, and the more I'm one with my Inner Guidance, the less chaos, and conflict I'll experience. Everything will be going with the flow.

Step 4: Identify an Icon.
What would you like to stand for this propulsion system – what sort of icon?

Make this up if you don't have a good one. What's a good symbol for your propulsion system?

When you have it, welcome it and imagine it locking into place. Feel good about it, knowing that it lies within you as your orientation toward a more successful fulfillment of your values.

As you see this icon in your future, notice how it transforms things.

I love the Skycar image. It really makes me want one. The only thing stopping me is that it was never cleared for consumer use, so they never mass-produced it. Basically, they went public with their stock at a terrible time (during 2001), and it decreased in value, and then they lost their primary way of raising money (i.e., private stock sales). Paul Moller says it costs about $20 million to get it approved for flight, and because of the decrease in the value of the stock, they have no way to raise the money.

Motivational Reasons to Do Massive Self-Work

This section was written by one of my Super Trader clients, and hopefully, it might inspire you to do self-work.

Why Do I do Massive Self-Work: When I was a child, around five or six years old, I became conscious of a very strong emotional pain to a "normal" life situation, so it was surprising for me. Later, when my parents divorced, I started to feel it again very often in situations with my father and his new wife. And it was tremendously painful for me. As a result, I promised myself that I would find a way to never again allow anyone to cause me to feel such strong emotional pain – pain that was so bad that I was willing to do anything (literally anything) to stop it. That included suicide, which I attempted once as a teenager. After that, I began to learn how to sedate myself with good feelings from trivial things such as thinking, learning, working, eating, movies, spending money, and so on. In fact, I suppressed those emotions so much that I became like the typical male action movie hero (i.e., John Wayne) who doesn't ever bother with feeling feelings. I actually entered the Super Trader program in a mild depression. That state was so normal for me that I just got used to it and didn't pay attention to it.

In the Supertrader program, I learned that besides suppressing and running away from negative feelings, one can embrace them, experience them, and then just let them go. Such a life-changing concept. Thus, my goal changed from making sure no one could ever make me feel that way to embracing any emotion of which I become aware. My intention, as a result, was very strong, although it is not that easy to go through the process.

So, what kept me going through this process is that I remembered the promise I'd made to my child part as I'd feel that pain, which was like someone sticking a knife in me. It would hurt like that for days, and as a result, I'd made a promise to the child to no longer feel that. Suppressing it was a good strategy until I started to trade. And then it guaranteed that I'd lose money. But thanks to the Super Trader program, I've been on a journey to release all of that emotional pain.

I understood that if I couldn't help myself with that emotional pain when I was a child or teenager, then I would not be able to do anything in the world at all, really nothing at all. Because if I couldn't help even myself, then I would be a liar. So, I could have avoided looking at these feelings and dropped out of the Super Trader program, but I'd be a fake person. And I'd be living the rest of my life with a strong charge stored in my body, and so giving up was not the easiest solution. As a result, I keep going. That was the basic motivation behind working on a lot of painful feelings.

But there were nine more reasons that I could think of why I didn't give up and kept going. Perhaps these will help others through the process as well.

First, I understand that I have an "outdated type of mind" if I am not able to easily release some emotion in me (it is like a muscle which I needed to train). If I am not able to release particular emotion within an hour, then it means I am not up to date in this century – it is my belief.

Second, I understand that feelings are another source of information in the world, and if I am stuck with a particular emotion, then I am not receiving additional information which I could obtain through this source and hence I am not having a full scope picture of the situation or reality. Besides, my life review helped me to remember situations in life in which emotions helped me understand that emotions are a very useful tool that I am not totally using because of the charge in myself.

Third, I understand that even if I procrastinate in some way – it doesn't mean that I should totally give up in some lesson – it is like three steps forward and then one step back, and again, three steps forward and one step back, and that it is fine. I should accept that I am moving in such a way.

Fourth, I was really curious about what it would be like after I transform enough and get rid of all of this stored charge.

In addition, I had the support of my husband, and I told him everything that happened with me in the Super Trader program. He is totally open-minded and is willing to accept it all. He even went with me to Oneness University India and has been supporting everything I do to grow spiritually and as a trader.

Sixth, as Oneness suggests, I've been doing Japa yoga[2] with the phrases:

- **"Mind is not mine."**
- **"Thoughts are not mine."**

I did this for several months for 49 minutes each day. When I had a lot of useless thoughts about the Super Trader program or about myself or anything similar, it really helped to distinguish between myself and thoughts which were coming, which were a very negative type, including revenge/destruction and negative life experiences.

As I progressed through this process, I had several night dreams in which I had finally accomplished transformation, which I believed was possible. I believed in my dreams, and I knew that it would happen. And that would bring me closer to my true identity, that of my Higher Self. Thus, the only question was when.

I did lots of Deeksha and Oneness Meditation sessions online because I believed it would help me transform my brain. I was encouraged by the fact that people like Van Tharp, Sri Bhagavan, Byron Katie, Libby Adams, and Lester Levenson have all given me the ability to deal with emotions in another way. I knew that would make me happy and successful, so I could not give up. These teachings are such a huge gift for humanity, and they are coming from the spiritual realm.

Another reason was that I thought I might be stuck in this emotional pain for many, many lifetimes. This lifetime was my opportunity to change all of that, and I have been given everything necessary to make the changes. Thus, as I progressed through the releases, I was suddenly more interested in living a happy, successful, and peaceful life than I was in trading success. But I also realized that I would never be financially successful unless I made these changes in myself in the Super Trader program.

And the final reason was the state I'd be in (more often than not) when I completed all the releasing work: love of freedom and independence. I so much love my freedom that the thought that some part or emotion uses me for their conflicts and so on was a big motivator for me to never stop. I had to be in charge of my internal board of meeting and no one else because I am the captain.

As I was writing these reasons out, I got a big insight from doing so. Although I was thinking about not facing this, giving up on the Super Trader program, and how doing that really wouldn't make my life easier, I never really felt that I could give up. NEVER. It was like, although thoughts about giving up came to me, I never really believed in them because I never really **felt** that I could give up.

I spent months and months and months on that part of the Super Trader program because I am very kinesthetic, so I danced around that emotional pain from my childhood for so long. My belief is that all people who procrastinate have some feelings that they can't release/live through from the beginning. Others just live through it or don't give it much meaning, so it doesn't become a big charge. There is a huge difference between being stuck in emotions because you resist them and the freedom of just feeling things as they come up and letting them go. And some people just give up because they think they can totally resist and escape all of that. For me, the core issue was to start feeling emotional pain and become able to stay with it and embrace it.

Desired/New Propulsion System, Part II

Now that you have completed all of that, let's give you a template for a new propulsion system that you can make a part of your life. This should become part of your business plan, and using it should become automatic for you. If you do that, you will experience tremendous power over your life. Read through both the exercise and Van's example of filling it out before you actually do it.

Your Propulsion System Template

I absolutely/must/live for/am passionate about/have to:

_____

_____

_____

This has forced me to move-away (i.e., if you are passionate about losing weight, you might be forced to move away from night binging) _____

_____

What will you no longer tolerate?

_____

What is the aversion behind your desired outcome? What would happen if you continue (so that you don't get it)?

_____

_____

_____

_____

How will you feel about moving away from this?

_____

_____

_____

_____

How does this impact you?

Personally

_____

_____

_____

_____

Spiritually

_____
_____
_____
_____
_____

Why will you refuse to allow this anymore?

_____
_____
_____
_____
_____

This has forced me to move-toward:

_____

Why must you become ferociously and highly motivated to move toward this?

_____
_____
_____

How will you feel when you have this just the way you want it?

_____
_____

How will this enrich your life?

Emotionally:

_____
_____

Personally:

_____

Spiritually:

What Beliefs, Ideas, Values support this highly desirable motivational state?

What meta-states/meta-frames support and govern this?

How do you go about stepping into this way of:

Thinking:

Feeling:

Speaking:

Acting:

What (if anything) could stop you from achieving this highly motivated state? Could anything? How will you respond? What resources do you need to become unstoppable?

___

___

What steps fully describe the process? Identify the visual-auditory-kinesthetic (VAK) strategy (i.e., your motivation strategy)?

___

___

What perceptual filters (metaprograms) will you use to look at yourself/life/others/work/play/faith, etc.?

___

___

___

___

Could anything STOP you? How will you respond? What resources will you need to become un-stoppable?

___

___

___

___

What one thing will you do today to set out in this direction? What symbol will you use for this?

___

___

___

Van's Example: Desired/New Propulsion System Part II

I absolutely/must/live for/am passionate about/have to:

Have a strong, healthy body that will allow me to live to be over 100 with a sharp mind and the energy to continually be passionate about my future accomplishments to help people transform.

This has forced me to Move-Away: (i.e., if you are passionate about losing weight, you might be forced to move away from night binging) What will you no longer tolerate?

I will no longer tolerate eating junk food and eating anything after 7 p.m.

What is the aversion behind your desired outcome? What would happen if you continue (so that you don't get it)?

My aversion is not having energy, feeling sluggish, and unable to get anything accomplished, and feeling my brain get less and less sharp.

How will you feel about moving away from this?

Right now, I feel good about the states, and I'm concerned about the food.

How does this impact you?

Personally

I love my life, and I get to continue that love affair.

Spiritually

A healthy body is a spiritual body. When my body weight is normal, my liver is rebuilt, and my metabolism is normal, and I have no more than 5% body fat, I will feel spiritually alive and feel God in everything.

Why will you refuse to allow this anymore?

I want the spiritual body, and I don't want the lack of energy and the sluggish brain.

This has forced me to Move-Toward: Why must you become ferociously and highly motivated to move toward this?

This is the rest of my life that I'm talking about. It can be great, or it could be 20 years as a vegetable. I'll take great any day.

How will you feel when you have this just the way you want it?

Exhilarated and one with God

How will this enrich your life?

Emotionally

Exhilarated

Personally

I will be as sharp as I was when I was 20, but much, much happier. I will also have the passion to really impact others. And the knowledge that I have done it myself.

Spiritually

My senses will be finely tuned, and I will sense God everywhere.

What beliefs, ideas, and values support this highly desirable motivational state?

These are my top four values – self-transformation, helping others transform, family and overcoming health issues as I age.

What higher-level state or frame will support and govern this?

A sense of wonder about doing it. A sense of physical clearing, just like I've done emotional clearing. And, I won't be afraid to take it step by step and ask for help. For example, before I do Bruce's diet to lose 40 lbs., I will do chelation to get the toxic heavy metals out of my system.

How do you go about stepping into this way of:

Thinking

I'm already there. But right now, I'm not eating much. The key is to resist what I desire. Not eating what I don't like (even if there are no alternatives) is not that bad or difficult.

Feeling

I will feel proud of my accomplishments. I will feel resilient. I'm doing what I'm doing right now in India to make this happen. I could give up and go to a hotel, but I can do this.

Speaking

I'm resilient. I can do it. I'm confident.

Acting

With time, the tempting foods I used to like will no longer attract me.

What (if anything) could stop you from achieving this highly motivated state? Could anything? How will you respond? What resources do you need to become unstoppable?

The biggest two risks are 1) healing crises and 2) tempting foods around me.

Healing crises: I will eliminate what could derail me first, for example, by doing what I'm doing and by getting chelation treatment to get rid of the toxic metals in my system.

Temptation: I'm good for 30 minutes. I will attempt to remove temptation before that amount of time has passed.

If I happen to give in, I will restart the next day.

What steps fully describe the process? Identify the visual-auditory-kinesthetic (VAK) strategy (i.e., your motivation strategy)?

This is referring to my motivation strategy. I'm already motivated to do this. I'm moving away from (closed ball, get away from me, I wish I was the only person in the world, no more) I'm moving toward exhilaration (expansion in the chest). YES sound. Sense of running forward to get it.,

What perceptual filters (metaprograms) will you use to look at yourself/life/others /work/ play/faith, etc.?

Internal control, and I will make sure this applies to food. This is big because I think food controlled me.

I have responsibility for myself.

Could anything STOP you? How will you respond? What resources will you need to become Unstop-able?

What could stop me are four things: 1) healing crisis; 2) I feel so weak that I can't function; 3) I have other commitments; and 4) tempting food.

First, I'm going to use the material in Chapter 10 to prepare for this.

I will set up rules I can follow.

My other priorities will be part of the schedule, and I'll work around them to be sure critical things are not sabotaged by the program.

I will also use 1) self-analysis, 2) mental rehearsal, and 3) daily debriefing to prevent mistakes and keep myself on track.

I also won't beat myself up getting off track, but will simply keep the end goal in mind.

What one thing will you do today to set out in this direction? What symbol will you use for this?

I have already done it by filling out this form.

For the next three weeks (remaining time in the clinic), I will stick this out and get the most I can out of it.

When I return home, I will set up the OPAs to make sure this is accomplished.

Fun will also be a part of that as well as occasional "food treats" that won't throw me off too much.

Exercise: Pattern to Clean Your Mind

And our last exercise is the mind cleaning pattern developed by Dr. Michael Hall. This exercise will make automatic updates in your self-definition. It will build up an internal system that will keep cleaning things up as you move through life. You've done the exercise earlier, so you can just copy your answers here.

Step 1: Make an extensive list of your desired and undesired traits.

What qualities, behaviors, and traits do you have that you no longer want (ways of talking, emotion, thinking that no longer serve you)? What qualities and highly-desired traits do you want to include?

	Non-desired Qualities	Desired Qualities
1		
2		
3		
4		
5		
6		
7		
8		
9		
10		

Step 2: Elicit a self-image representation of "True of Me."

Think of something that is true about yourself that you absolutely love, appreciate, and value. Pick something that you feel great about? What quality do you really adore about yourself?

_____
_____
_____
_____
_____

How do you represent it (visually, auditorily, kinesthetically, and the key submodalities)?

_____
_____
_____
_____
_____

What thoughts and feelings do you have about it? Get all the meta-detail you can find. These are the different Matrices of the Matrix Model of Neurosemantics.[3]

Meaning	
State	
Intention	
Self	
Other	
Power	
Time	
World	

What makes these representations stable?

_____
_____
_____
_____

Step 3: Elicit a self-image representation of "Not True of Me" or a "No Longer Me" representation.

Think of something that was true of you once but is no longer true of you. What fits this category for you? For example, was something true of you as a teenager that is no longer true? Is there something that fit you as a child but is no longer fits you? Or was there something that fit you when you were younger that no longer fits you now that you are older? Did you once hold a limiting belief that you now think is stupid?

_____
_____

How do you represent "Not True of Me" and/or "No Longer True of Me?

_____
_____

Meaning	
State	
Intention	
Self	
Other	
Power	
Time	
World	

Step 4: Contrast the two representations from Step 2 and Step 3.

	True of Me	Not True of Me
Visual		
Associated/dissociated		
Location of picture		
Color/black and white		
Movie or still		
Framed or panoramic		
Contrast (1-10)		
Color intensity		
Brightness (1-10)		
Focus (fuzzy/clear)		
Horizontal or vertical		
Number of pictures		
How far away?		

Your Propulsion System Template

	True of Me	**Not True of Me**
Distance to central object		
Other visual differences		
Auditory		
Voice? Whose?		
Other sounds?		
Location of voice		
Pitch		
Volume		
Intensity		
Speed		
Tonality		
Inflection		
Rhythm		
Clarity		
Duration		
Music? What music?		
Kinesthetic		
Location		
Intensity		
Size		
Sharpness		
Pressure		
Duration		
Rhythm		
Vibration		
Movement		
Warm/cold		
Heavy/light		
Other kinesthetic		

Step 5: Identify the meta-levels in the structures of the two self-representations of "True of Me" or a "No Longer Me."

Identify the meta-levels/meta-states within these experiences.

Matrix	True of Me	No Longer Me
Meaning		
State		
Intention		
God		
Self		
Other		
Power		
Time		
World		

How do you represent them?

_____
_____
_____
_____
_____

How do they differ?

_____
_____
_____
_____
_____

What do you say "Yes" versus "No" to?

_____
_____
_____
_____
_____

What historical representations do you use that "makes sense" of them?

Step 6: Look at your lists from the prior step. Determine the differences and then become fully aware of them by stepping into them.

What is the difference between "true of me" and "not true of me?" Sort them out.

Step into the differences. Do this for each one until you are fully aware of the two formats. Comments:

Step 7: Set up a machine to delete what hinders you and install what serves you.

a. (Picture 1) Get a picture of "not me" and put what you don't want in that format.

b. (Picture 2) Set up a "true of me" image for each "not me" that you wish to change. For example, if the "not me" is one of being an employee, then the "true of me" image would be being self-employed (or a self-employed trader).

Associate with the experience of "true of me." Hear it, feel it, see it, taste and smell it! Make it the most vivid and compelling movie possible. What would happen if you double the intensity? And then double it again?

c. Do an ecology check of your "true of me" image.

Would having that improve your life? Would it be useful? Is it possible that it could hinder you in some way? Does any part of you object to installing that new "true of me" image? For example, part of you might object if you were not financially able to leave your job and also not yet ready to be a good trader.

Reframe or do a conflict resolution with any objections. For example, in the case of the above objections, the "true of me" image might change to being a Super Trader student who is working to become a great trader.

d. Link the pictures.

Put picture 2 ("true of me") on picture 1 ("not true of me)" but just in the corner.

Instantly make picture 2 swish so that it fills up and takes over picture 1.

Break the state.

Repeat the process about 5 to 7 times.

e. Break the state by getting up and walking around and then test it by asking: "Do you have more compulsion about that new activity?"

Van's Example:

Step 1: Make an extensive list of your desired and undesired traits.

What qualities, behaviors, and traits do you have that you no longer want? (ways of talking, emotion, thinking that no longer serve you.) What qualities and highly-desired traits do you want to include?

	Non-desired Qualities	Desired Qualities
1	Tired	Passionate
2	Feeling old/thinking I'm old	Feeling young
3	Won't experiment with food	Willing to try new foods

Step 2: Elicit a self-image representation of "True of Me."

Think of something that is true about yourself that you absolutely love, appreciate, and value. Pick something that you feel great about? What quality do you really adore about yourself?

I'm a big picture person. *I can listen to a lot of details and then come up with the essence of something. It's one of my greatest strengths.*

How do you represent it (visually, auditorily, kinesthetically, and the key submodalities)?

I see myself moving from limitation (empty gold fish bowl) into unlimited potential (represented by the whole ocean). That's shown by the figure on page 268.

What thoughts and feelings do you have about it? Get all the meta-detail you can find. These are the different Matrices of the Matrix Model of Neurosemantics.

Meaning	It's my greatest skill. It allows me to model
State	Confidence
Intention	I must get the essence of this.
Self	It's who I am.
Other	I can get the essence of their skill even if they do not know consciously. Find a number of people who do it well.
Power	It's what I do best
Time	I've done it many times in the past. I can do it any time in the future.
World	The world needs my skill.

What makes these representations stable?

It's connected to who I am. There might be some structure to that, but I'm not yet aware of what it is.

Step 3: Elicit a self-image representation of "Not True of Me" or a "No Longer Me" representation.

Think of something that was true of you once but is no longer true of you. What fits this category for you? For example, was something true of you as a teenager that is no longer true? Is there something that fit you as a child but is no longer fits you? Or was there something that fit you when you were younger that no longer fits you now that you are older? Did you once hold a limiting belief that you now think is stupid?

- *I'm an employee who works (directly or indirectly through contracts) for the government.*

How do you represent "not true of me" and/or "no longer true of me?"

- *I see an image, and it's very small, dark, and it's down and to the right. I feel the urge to step on it.*

Meaning	I hated everything about that. I needed to pay attention to the criteria of others. It's hard to get published if you are creative or outside the box. It's also a game of politics, and there is a clear hierarchy to the science game.
State	Revulsion … a META "NO" response.
Intention	Never again.
Self	It's not who I am … that's it.
Other	It's stifling bureaucrats. Ignorant. Graves Level 4 people
Power	They have the power (in this context), and I have none
Time	Past only.
World	It goes on still, but that's not my world

Step 4: Contrast the two representations from step 2 and step 3.

	True of Me	Not True of Me
Visual		
Associated/dissociated	Associated	Dissociated
Location of picture	Up and centered	Down right
Color/black and white	Color	Black and white
Movie or still	Movie	Still
Framed or panoramic	Framed	Framed
Contrast (1-10)	5	1
Color intensity	5	0
Brightness (1-10)	6	2
Focus (fuzzy/clear)	8	Fuzzy
Horizontal or vertical	NA	NA
Number of pictures	1	1
How far away?	2 feet	5 feet
Distance to central object	2 feet	NA
Other visual differences		
Auditory		
Voice? Whose?		YUK
Other sounds?		

	True of Me	Not True of Me
Location of voice		
Pitch		
Volume		
Intensity		
Speed		
Tonality		
Inflection		
Rhythm		
Clarity		
Duration		
Music? What music?		
Kinesthetic	Tingling "that's it"	Urge to step on it
Location	Chest	Throat
Intensity	Strong	
Size	Fills chest	Lump
Sharpness		
Pressure		
Duration		
Rhythm		
Vibration		
Movement		
Warm/Cold		
Heavy/light		
Other kinesthetic		

Step 5: Identify the meta-levels in the structures of the two self-representation of "True of Me" or a "No Longer Me."

Identify the meta-levels/meta-states within these experiences.

Matrix	True of Me	No Longer-Me
Meaning	Greatest skill	Up to others; politics
State	Confidence	Revulsion
Intention	Get the essence of it	Never again
Self	Its who I am	It's not me
Other	Can get it; can help them	They control me; bureaucrats
Power	All mine	All theirs
Time	Now. Can do it in the future	Past
World	World needs my skills	Goes on still, but not my world

How do you represent them?

Visually … diagram versus meaningless picture in corner.

Me/confidence versus not me/revulsion.

How do they differ?

Big differences visually and semantically.

What do you say "Yes" versus "No" to?

"Yes," to freedom to use my skills and talents as I see fit.

"No," to being told what to do out of models I don't believe in. "Yes", to level Graves level 7 people and "No," to Graves level 4 people.

What historical representations do you use that "makes sense" of them?

GOVERNMENT WORKER DOING BUSY WORK – DEFINITELY NOT ME

TRUE OF ME: Jumping into Oneness with no limitations.

Step 6: Look at your lists from the prior step . Determine the differences and then become fully aware of them by stepping into them.

What is the difference between "true of me" and "not true of me "? Sort them out.

Associated diagram that is movie with confidence versus dissociated and dark picture down and to right with feeling (desire) to "step on it".

Strong sense of me versus not me.

Step into the differences. Do this for each one until you are fully aware of the two formats. Comments:

Differences are clear.

Step 7: Set up a machine to delete what hinders you and install what serves you.

7a. (Picture 1) Get a picture of "not me" and put what you don't want in that format.

7b. (Picture 2) Set up a "true of me" image for each "not me" that you wish to change.

Associate with the experience of "true of me." Hear it, feel it, see it, taste and smell it! Make it the most vivid and compelling movie possible. What would happen if you double the intensity? And then double it again?

I did this, and it was very strong. I'm the jumping fish, and I'm definitely not the guy surrounded by paperwork to keep him busy and satisfy some bureaucrats.

7c. Check your "true of me" image.

Would having that improve your life? Would it be useful? Is it possible that it could hinder you in some way? Does any part of you object to installing that new "true of me" image? For example, part of you might object if you were not financially able to leave your job and also not yet ready to be a good trader.

The only concern I had was a part that believes those are facts. It says, "You are over 70, you are going to have issues. And you haven't done the health work so, how can you expect to be passionate?"

Reframe or do a conflict resolution with any objections. For example, in the case of the above objections, the "true of me" image might change to being a Super Trader student who is working to become a great trader

It's okay to have a frame for passion before I do the health work – part said okay.

7d Link the pictures.

Put picture 2 (true of me) on picture 1 ("not true of me)" but just in the corner...

Instantly make picture 2 swish so that it fills up and takes over picture 1.

Break the state. Open your eyes and shake your body.

Repeat the process about 5 to 7 times.

7e Break the state (i.e., get up and walk around) **and then test it**. Do you have more compulsion about that new activity?

Yes, I want to work on my health and passion and eat different foods.

Notes

[1] Associated is a submodality, meaning that you are experiencing something from the perspective of being in your body rather than from the perspective of watching yourself (dissociated).

[2] Japa yoga is where you repeat a phrase for 7 or 49 minutes over and over in order to instill it deeply inside.

[3] Dr. L. Michael Hall. *The Matrix Model: The Premier Systems Model of Neuro-Semantics, 3rd Edition.* Clifton, CO: Neurosemantic Publications, 2016.

CHAPTER 14

Postscript: How Did India Turn Out?

How did India turn out? Would I do it again? Did I do what I'd set out to do? Did my Moti-Map for India do its job? This chapter is not necessary for any sort of self-transformation. You don't need to read it unless you are curious. But I've been telling my story in this book, and if you are interested in how things turned out, then this chapter is your chance to find out how my life went after I returned home from India. This chapter was written 18 months later, so know it has taken over a year to actually publish the book.

Did I meet my goals? In order to answer this question, let's look at my goals for India.

First, I wanted to improve my health through Ayurvedic treatments and an Ayurvedic diet. What did improve my health mean?

My biggest issue was the lack of proper sleep and always being tired. If I could sleep better and have more energy, I'd feel much better, and I'd be totally happy with the results of the clinic.

How did that one work out? First, it's important to know that I've been tested for sleep apnea, and that is not an issue, so it's something else. And these were the results: While I was in India, I got plenty of rest even though my bed was basically a wooden board with a two-inch mattress on top of it – so the hardest bed I've ever slept on in my entire life.

The Ayurvedic clinic was located in an area with a lot of Muslims. Each morning I'd hear what sounded like at least 50 men chanting at about 5 a.m. So, I was pretty much guaranteed a wake up at 5 a.m. Sometimes I didn't go to sleep until midnight, so that was only five hours of sleep. But remember, I was pretty much confined to a 10-foot by 14-foot room, so it was no big deal to take a nap. If I only got five hours sleep, I'd probably nap another three hours, and I never had any problems sleeping when I wanted to nap. Thus, while I was in India, I was well-rested.

When I returned home, I didn't feel that well, and I found myself sleeping 12 to 14 hours a day at minimum and still felt tired. I don't know what was happening here. My sleep wasn't that good for the first week but was better during the second week.

When my wife was in Australia, she visited her old nursing roommate from 30 years ago. This woman had moved to Australia. She subsequently developed some back problems and had to have surgery. But after the surgery, she was in such pain that she couldn't sleep. She had averaged just a few hours of sleep each night and had also become quite depressed. My wife had brought some CBD oil, which had cured her chronic leg pain, after about a month of use. My wife gave her former roommate some of it. And after one dose, she went to bed at 9 p.m. (instead of 3 a.m.), slept at least eight hours, and awoke pain-free. My wife left the CBD oil with her.

After that recommendation, I also tried the CBD oil, and I had a great night of sleep. I've been taking it ever since, and my sleep is better. So, while the Ayurvedic treatment didn't fix my sleep, the CBD oil did – when I remember to take it. Thus, problem solved but not by anything done in India.

Also, I went to Las Vegas in July 2018. I spent a lot of time walking, perhaps as much as eight hours a day. That, plus the CBD oil made for some of the best sleep I've had.

My second complaint was a cyst on my back.

My understanding is that the cyst is actually the result of undigested food and that the Ayurvedic diet should be able to fix it. I'd had surgery on it but was told that if it came back, I'd have to go to the hospital and have deeper surgery under general anesthesia. I was hoping to avoid that possibility in India. But I don't think I was ever on an Ayurvedic diet – just healthy food that I didn't like. I got two treatments with leeches while I was there, but I think at best, they have just postponed the surgery. Four months later, there is a small bump on my back that is itchy. Also, a different dermatologist told me I should could take care of it in a 15-minute surgery, which wouldn't hurt. I haven't done that, but it's not growing, and it doesn't bother me that much. It's now 20 months post-India, and the cyst just itches occasionally.

My third complaint was chronic neck pain.

I get neck pain[1] when I don't use a contour pillow for sleep, and I'd gone a week without one in November 2018. I had lots of massages and chiropractic work. When X-rays were taken, it turns out that two vertebrae in my neck were fused, so there was probably only so much that could be done. I got lots of treatments for head pain, including putting Ghee in my nostrils. Many of the treatments I got during the six weeks were for that, and when I returned home, I didn't have any neck pain. However, one night without the contour pillow (on a recent trip) brought the pain back. But the pain is not serious and doesn't impact my sleep or anything like that. Overall, I'd say the chronic neck pain is gone, but I do have fused vertebrae and need to be careful.

Joint pain when I run.

This wasn't a high priority goal because I don't run anymore. But it would be nice to be able to do it again. I was given pills for joint pain throughout the six weeks in India and also had oil treatments for such pain. At this point, I have no idea how effective those treatments might have been because I still have not tried to run since I returned home.

The clinic I was at specialized in skin problems. And I had 1) several skin tags, 2) a rash, 3) fungus under the nails of two toes, and 4) an issue with itchiness.

Here the clinic failed miserably in most of these areas.

First, they didn't treat the skin tags. At the end, I asked about it again and got an ointment for it, which I was told might produce a burning sensation. A dermatologist in the US just froze them off.

The rash got worse, and the itchiness never went away. It turns out it was my hand showers in India that had a lot to do with it. I was getting soaped up with a sponge bath by one of the attendants, and it was the soap. In the US, I was told by a dermatologist to shower and to only use soap in critical areas – not all over my body. That suggestion solved the problem. Subsequently, we have gotten a water softener for the house and that has solved the itchiness problems.

However, one of the oils in my treatments (I probably got about five treatments) penetrated under my toenails and the fungus totally disappeared after that. But it came back, and I'm still treating it 18 months later. But it doesn't seem that serious, and it doesn't want to go away, and so far, nothing seems to work.

Toxic heavy metals. When I went to the Whittaker clinic in May of 2016, I was given chelation treatment. The mercury in my system was gone (from a prior diagnosis), but I had toxic levels of tin, aluminum[2], and lead. And when I had chelation treatments, I felt miserable for about 36 hours. When I did the ketogenic diet my friend from Ireland recommended, I got the same symptoms. As a result, I need to do more chelation (which I can do locally) before I can do that diet again.

I don't know if they did anything for toxic metals or not. I would have to restart the ketogenic diet or do a chelation treatment to find out.

Kidney stones. About three weeks before I was due to go to India, I had a kidney stone. I passed it in about a week, but the nephrologist told me that I had two more stones in my right kidney, and these two could drop any time and give me massive pain.

I mentioned this to my doctor and I was given medicine for kidney stones throughout my stay at the clinic. The doctor said it would dissolve the stones before they dropped. One night, about three days before I was due to leave, I had intense pain that felt like a kidney stone. I had kidney stone pain medication with me and took one. I was really worried about the travel I was going to be doing in a few days. But once the pain left after taking the pain medication, it never returned. Big success here. I may have actually passed the stone in a few hours.

I'm used to a comfortable bed and chairs with great back support. My two chairs in my room had absolutely no back support. I considered going out to buy a chair and just donating it to the clinic because my back hurt constantly.

The pain in my lower back, after about three weeks, was so bad that I actually considered checking out of the clinic and going to a hotel.[3] However, when I mentioned the pain to the doctor, they did treatments for it. The pain totally disappeared within three days. I did buy a back-support cushion, which is typically used in cars, to put on the chairs I sat on every day, but I did not leave the clinic or buy a chair, and my back was fine for the rest of the time at the clinic. Another big success with this one, but it was in an issue created by being at the clinic.

Those were my major health goals for the clinic, and I think the results are somewhat mixed.

But there were a lot more things.

I hated the food there. Thus, a major goal was to 1) make sure I stayed at the clinic the entire time despite hating the food, and 2) see if I could learn to like the food.

If you remember prior chapters in this book, taste submodalities do not have the impact of visual submodalities. For example, taste submodalities are just thought to be the taste buds – salty, bitter, sour, etc. But in the visual submodality, you have things like clarity, framed or panoramic, big or small, close or far away, that have to do with how you represent it to yourself. I determined that I like sweet and crispy, for example, but there is no way that I can change the actual taste of bitter and spicy to sweet and crispy. Thus, that part failed miserably.

However, I did determine that I could start trying new foods when I go out to eat. I've gone out to eat about once a week since my wife returned from Australia, and I've ordered something different quite often. And I've enjoyed some of those new dishes. That change was a big success. However, when the COVID-19 pandemic started in early 2020, we stopped going out to eat.

In addition, I stayed at the clinic for the entire six weeks. I didn't leave. Yes, I sometimes threw some of the food I got down the toilet, but I was not tempted to eat a lot of unhealthy food while I was there. As a result, I was pretty successful in staying there and eating healthy food. I just ate a lot less than I would normally have. One of my goals was to lose weight, and I lost about 12 lbs. during the six weeks at the clinic. I think some of their treatments (besides the food) actually helped with weight loss.

I wanted to write a book on propulsion systems while I was at the clinic.

This was a huge success. It would have taken me about six months (minimum!!!) to write the first draft of such a book here in the US, but I completed the first draft of the book in about a month in India. But I haven't had time to get into the busywork/details of getting it ready for publication, and it's now 20 months later.

Get a hair transplant at a price that would pay for the trip.

I got the hair transplant. They did about 1,500 hairs (out of 3,000 planned), and it cost me about $1,200 US dollars. That same treatment would have cost $5.99 per hair in the US plus another $1,000 for the blood platelet procedure. As a result, I saved about $8,485. That savings pretty much paid for the trip.

Was it a success, though? Well, I equate the hair transplant in India to flying around the world economy class. In the end, I'm happy about the savings, but I'd never do it again. I always fly, at minimum, business class. The hair transplant was like third class. Here are some of the reasons:

Every time I visited the hospital to do something, I'd spend about three hours there. This included the first appointment to determine the cost and when they could do the procedure. It would have taken about 15 minutes in the US to do the same thing.

The doctor didn't do everything himself, he had other people helping him with the procedure, and it was brutal. For example, I got a pain block injected into my right eyelid. That really hurt, and I could feel something wrong with my eye. And the next day, my eye was all red and almost swollen shut. I never had any issues like that in the US.

In the US, I was seated in a comfortable chair and on a local anesthetic and Valium with another Valium in front of me in case I wanted it. The time went by very rapidly, and except for the injection of the anesthetic, I didn't feel anything. It was just me and the doctor. All those who were assisting were generally in another room.

In India, I was in a room that looked like a large kitchen on a flat table that was very uncomfortable, and being on the table hurt my neck. All the technicians were around me (about ten people), and the doctor wasn't the only one working on my head. During the last hour, I felt every hair injection, and it was very painful, but I preferred that to having a needle inserted in my eyelid again.

In India, I was supposed to be getting the latest procedure – the FUU method. They basically shave my head, take out individual follicles from the back of my head, and transplant them on the top. Thus, no cuts and no stitches. However, after about five hours of surgery, the doctor told me that they were having trouble getting my follicles to take and that they would have to cut a strip of hair from the back of my scalp. Remember, I was partially knocked out, and, under those conditions, I said okay.

In the US, a second cut would have been along the same cut line as the first, so no additional scar, and there was hardly a scar anyway. But in India, it was a very jagged cut starting at my ear and then going down. I had a lot of problems with that cut for the next two weeks. And for a strip that was the same size as the prior cut, I'd had in the US from which they got 3,000 follicles; they only got about 500 follicles.

The goal was 3,000 follicles transplanted, but from two procedures, they only managed 1,500. And the front of my head, where more follicles were needed, was where the fewest were transplanted. The only consolation was that I paid for 3,000 follicles upfront, and they refunded half of that money.

After about two months, I looked like I had less hair in the front than I had before the surgery. After 18 months, it's a little thin, but it still pretty good.

Three days before I was due to leave the clinic to go to Delhi, I had the stitches removed. I had to wait in a very crowded hospital for about an hour to see the doctor. I complained that the stitches still hurt, but he said, "It's fine to remove them, now." He then shook my hand and left. He told me that his Intern/Resident (I'm not sure who he was, but he helped with the surgery and was particularly brutal) would remove the stitches. It was ten minutes of pain. They were also supposed to shampoo my head, but they told me I had to pay for the stitch removal and then come back. I stood in line for 30 minutes to pay a bill that amounted to $US2.85. When I came back, they were gone. I waited about 15 minutes more and then decided that I could either wait some more and risk them coming back and giving me more pain, or I could leave. I elected to leave.

The bottom line about this is that I might have saved a lot of money, but I would never do that sort of thing again in India. And right now, it's over, and I'm happy with the final result.

The way I look at my experience in India is through the frame that the "what is" is perfect. I'm fine and certainly not worse off than before, although I will have a second scar (covered by hair) to show for it. In addition, I'm fairly happy with the results. And perhaps some new doctors got some experience that they might have needed, and I was simply their volunteer to get that experience. And, I did pay for the trip to India with my savings. And I'm actually laughing to myself as I'm writing this. It really is sort of funny that I actually did that.

Notes

[1] When I was doing the index on motivational references, I realized how many times I used the word pain in this chapter (referring to me and my health). Noticing that was a big ah-ha as I didn't realize how much I do move away from pain. But perhaps that's just getting older.

[2] When you get something like a flu shot, it is loaded with a toxic metal such as aluminum. This is to stimulate the immune system, but the net result is that you now have toxic levels of aluminum in your system. It probably also occurs if you drink too many drinks out of aluminum cans – which is probably the case for me – as I avoid flu shots like the plague.

[3] The thought of leaving didn't last that long because I thought buying a chair and donating it to the clinic was a better solution.

Reference Notes

Chapter 2

Dweck, Carol. *Self-Theories: Their Role in Motivation, Personality, and Development.* New York: Psychology Press (Taylor & Francis Group), 2000.

Dweck, Carol. *Mindset: The New Psychology of Success.* New York: Random House, 2006, 2016.

Hall, Michael L. *Figuring Out People: Reading People Using Meta-Programs.* Clifton, CO: Neuro-Semantic Publications, 2006.

Chapter 4

Hall, Michael L. *Persuasion Engineering – Simplified.* Clifton, CO: Neuro-Semantic Publications, 1998.

Chapter 5

Hall, Michael L. *Persuasion Engineering – Simplified.* Clifton, CO: Neuro-Semantic Publications, 1998.

Chapter 6

Hall, Michael L, and Bobby G. Bodenhamer. *Figuring Out People: Reading People Using Metaprograms.* Clifton, CO: Neurosemantic Publications, 2006.

Chapter 8

Maslow, Abraham. *A Theory of Human Motivation.* Sublime Books: Floyd, VA, 2014.

Beck, Don E and Cowan, Christopher. *Spiral Dynamics: Mastering Values, Leadership and Change.* Blackwell Publishing (a division of Wiley), New York, 1996.

Goodheart, George J. *You'll be Better: The Story of Applied Kinesiology.* Geneva, Ohio: AK Printing, 1980.

James, Adriana. *Values and the Evolution of Consciousness.* Sidonia Press: Henderson, NV, 2016.

Hawkins, David. *Power Versus Force.* Sedona, AZ: Veritas Publishing, 2002.

Hawkins, David. *Truth Versus Falsehood*. Sedona, AZ, Veritas Publishing, 2005 In this book, he ranks the level of consciousness/true of many individuals, animals, incidences in history etc. I was a so-so believer of what Hawkins was doing (muscle testing until I read this book, and then became much more skeptical. However, I love the idea of levels of consciousness.

Chapter 9

Strelecky, John P. *The Why are you Here Café: A New Way of Finding Meaning in your Life and your Work.* London: Piatkus, 2006.

Strelecky, John P. (2012). *The Big Five for Life*. Windermere, FL: Aspen Light Publishing.

Carroll Quigley, Tragedy and Hope: The History of the World in Our Time. 1966, p. 53.

Tharp, Van. *Trading Beyond the Matrix.* New York: Wiley, 2013.

Chapter 10

Mischel, Walter. *The Marshmallow Test: Mastering Self-control.* New York, NY, US: Little, Brown and Co, 2014.

Rettig, Hillary, & Deutsch, Barry. *The Seven Secrets of the Prolific: The Definitive Guide to Overcoming Procrastination, Perfectionism, and Writers Block.* Place of publication not identified: Hillary Rettig, 2011.

Read, Daniel, George Loewenstein, and Shobana Kalyanaraman. (1999). Mixing Virtue and Vice: Combining the Immediacy Effect and the Diversification Heuristic. Journal of Behavioral Decision Making. 12 (4): 257–273.

Chapter 11

Andreas, Connirae, and Tamara Connirae. *Core Transformation: Reaching the Wellspring Within.* Moab, Utah: Real People Press, 1994.

Chapter 12

Covey, Stephen R. *The 7 Habits of Highly Effective People Powerful Lessons in Personal Change.* London: Simon & Schuster, 2013.

Index of Propulsion Related Topics

A

Addictions Ix, 21,33, 64-68, 185, 196, 185-196-202
Asking the right questions. 10-12, 24-25, 29-33, 76-84

B

Basic Needs, Maslow 145-147
Become bold and ferocious 7-84
Beliefs, useful and non-useful xii-xiv, xvi-xx, 23,26-28, 51, 69, 77, 99, 100, 102, 104, 145, 160, 183-4, 196, 215, 218, 231-3, 247, 256
Belief Examination Pattern 183, 241
Belief, installation (Mind to Muscle) 184
Big Whys Chapter 1 (p. 1-13), 16, 34-35, 93
Blowing out Excuses 207-213

C

Compulsions xx, 15-16, 33, 184-8
Context, for beliefs and finding the context xii-xiv, xvii-xviii, 7, 22, 39, 43, 49, 64, 77-78, 88, 90, 100, 163, 186, 193, 266
Creative procrastination 33, 188-189

D

Decisions, poor or inadequate 16. Chapter 9 (p 169-177), 191
Details of your representation (submodalities or metamodalities) 17, Chapter 3 (p 39-61)
Distractions 16, 33.Chapter 10 (p 181-211), 230-181, 184-5
Dynamic Inconsistency 191

E

Excuse Demolition 207-213

F

Fear (See stick motivation, move away from motivation) 16, 23, 29, 33, 92, 117, 159, 162, 165, 172, 182-184, 191-192, 218-220
Fear release 183
Focus on what you do not want 182-184

G

Give Yourself Super-Power Pleasure 84-90, 199, 202

H

Hot-Cold Empathy Gap 190-191

I

Inappropriate Focus Chapter 10 (p 181-214)
Internal Guidance, Higher-Self 5, 10-11, 32-33, 51, 104, 108, 156, 163, 184, Chapter 9 (p. 169-181)

L

Less significant obligations 33, 189-190
Levels of Consciousness, Clare Graves 29, 147-157
Levels of Consciousness, David Hawkins 157-160
Levels of Consciousness, Van Tharp Institute 160-165

M

Meaning you give things, You are meaning maker 19-20, 26, 78, 205
Mental State Not Appropriate 21-25
Metaframes, Metastates 25-28, Chapter 5 (p 75-94)
Metaprograms (Specific ones have M in front) xxi, 15-19-21, 37, Chapter 6 (p. 75-94), 193, 279
M1 Black & White thinking 20, 31, 99-100
M2 Durability, Impermeable 20, 100-101
M3 Others referent thinking 20, 16, 101-103
M4 Pessimism 20, 103-105
M5 Modal operators of necessity and impossibility 20, 105-106
M6 Perfectionism in achieving goals 21, 106-107
M7 low self-esteem 21, 108
M8 Self-Monitoring Low and External 21, 109, 189-190
M9 What We Deem to be Important (Values) 21, 110
Mind Clearing Exercise 257-270
Motivation strategy 17-8, Chapter 4 (p 3-74), 91, 254, 257
Motivation,-Move toward, Carrot Motivation 1, 18-20, 95-99. 114-117
Motivation, getting into carrot states 39-41
Motivation, Move Away From, Stick Motivation 2,15-18. 93 96-98, 117-119, 215
Moving away from Stick States 23

N

Not enough "know-how" to do it 34, 194-196

O

Others control your propulsion 16, 101-103
Organization and Time Management 35-36, 136-142
Overwhelm 36, 192-193, 237
Intolerance of pain (See Stick Motivation)

P

Perfectionism, See M6 above 21, 33, 191-192
Procrastination xx, xxii, 16, 33-4, 181, 188-9, 196, 202-207, 280
Propulsion, too little 15
Propulsion, too much 15
Purpose/mission xx, xxii, 16, 24, 30-33, Chapter 9 (169-179), 181-183,

R

Reality, How you see it xx, 26, 28-32, 100, 217

S

Secrets and Hidden Agendas xxi, 34, 181, 196, Chapter 11 (p 215-224)
Self-Image, how you see yourself 29-32, 49-59
Swish Pattern from NLP 59-60

T

Taboos against motivation 16
Time Management 34-36, 137-142

W

Work, seems like too much (See overwhelm) 34

U

Urgent, not important, tasks 34-35, 190-191
Using the Moti-Map Process to Achieve Your Dreams Chapter 12 (p 225-241)

V

Values (see M9), also see purpose xiv-xx, 2-7. 29, 110, Chapter 7 (p 113-144), Chapter 8 (p 145-168), 245, 247, 253

Y

Your Propulsion System Chapter 13 (p 243-270)

Made in the USA
Columbia, SC
29 April 2021